African Philosophical and Literary Possibilities

African Philosophy

Critical Perspectives and Global Dialogue

Series Editors: Uchenna B. Okeja, Rhodes University; and Bruce B. Janz, University of Central Florida

Editorial Board
Anthony Appiah, Valentine Mudimbe, Gail Presbey, Achille Mbembe, Robert Bernasconi, Samuel Imbo, Tsenay Serequeberhan, Thaddeus Metz, Katrin Flikschuh, Niels Weidtmann, Christine Wanjiru Gichure, Kai Kresse, Joseph Agbakoba, Souleymane Bachir Diagne, Dismas. A. Masolo, Pedro Tabensky

The *African Philosophy: Critical Perspectives and Global Dialogue* book series aims to promote emerging critical perspectives in different branches of African philosophy. It serves as an avenue for philosophers within and between many African cultures to present new arguments, ask new questions, and begin new dialogues within both specialized communities and with the general public. By merging the critical and global dimensions of thoughts pertaining to important topics in African philosophy, this series beams the lights and rigour of philosophical analysis on topical as well as classical questions reflective of the African and African diaspora search for meaning in existence. Focused on the best of African philosophy, the series will introduce new concepts and new approaches in philosophy both to intellectual communities across Africa, as well as the rest of the world.

Titles in the series:
African Philosophical and Literary Possibilities: Re-reading the Canon, Edited by Aretha Phiri
Derrida and Africa: Jacques Derrida as a Figure for African Thought, Edited by Grant Farred
Afro-Communitarian Democracy, By Bernard Matolino
A Discourse on African Philosophy: A New Perspective on Ubuntu and Transitional Justice in South Africa, By Christian B. N. Gade
Disentangling Consciencism: Essays on Kwame Nkrumah's Philosophy, Edited by Martin Odei Ajei
The Rule of Law and Governance in Indigenous Yoruba Society: A Study in African Philosophy of Law, By John Ayotunde Isola Bewaji

African Philosophical and Literary Possibilities

Re-reading the Canon

Edited by Aretha Phiri

LEXINGTON BOOKS
Lanham • Boulder • New York • London

Published by Lexington Books
An imprint of The Rowman & Littlefield Publishing Group, Inc.
4501 Forbes Boulevard, Suite 200, Lanham, Maryland 20706
www.rowman.com

6 Tinworth Street, London SE11 5AL, United Kingdom

Copyright © 2020 by The Rowman & Littlefield Publishing Group, Inc.

All rights reserved. No part of this book may be reproduced in any form or by any electronic or mechanical means, including information storage and retrieval systems, without written permission from the publisher, except by a reviewer who may quote passages in a review.

British Library Cataloguing in Publication Information Available

Library of Congress Cataloging-in-Publication Data

Library of Congress Control Number: 2020939172

ISBN 9781498571241 (cloth) | ISBN 9781498571258 (epub)
ISBN 9781498571265 (pbk)

"In Memory of Harry Garuba" (1958–2020).

Contents

Acknowledgments ix

Introduction: Re-reading the Canon, Re-reading Africa xi
Aretha Phiri

1 Philosophy and an African Conscience 1
 Oritsegbubemi Anthony Oyowe

2 African Literature as a Handmaid of African Philosophy 17
 Chielozona Eze

3 Conflict and Compromise in Three Novels of the Eastern Cape 33
 George Hull

4 Blind Sisyphus: Two Perspectives on Meursault 59
 Pedro Tabensky

5 Digital Media, Literacies, Literature, and the African Humanities 75
 Pier Paolo Frassinelli and Lisa Treffry-Goatley

6 African Gaze: Hollywood/Nollywood and the Postcolonial
 Science Fiction Imagery in Nnedi Okorafor's *Lagoon* 93
 Rocío Cobo-Piñero

7 Transgressing Borders: (Re)imag(in)ing Africa(ns) in the World 113
 Aretha Phiri

8 "The Whims of the White Masters": Miriam Tlali's *Between Two Worlds* and the Totality of White Power   131
Marzia Milazzo

Index   149

About the Contributors   157

Acknowledgments

This collection emerges from a continued and shared interest in the current decolonizing imperatives of (South) African higher education curricula in particular and global (South) transformation exigencies in general. Probing the intersectional and interdisciplinary possibilities afforded by two canonical and institutionalized disciplines, Philosophy and Literature, *African Philosophical and Literary Possibilities* advances the continued creative and intellectual resources residing in and *for* the African continent. Conceived in 2016, this book has been a laborious but fundamentally rewarding process in which many were involved.

I would like to acknowledge the support of Rhodes University. In particular, my colleagues and students in the Department of Literary Studies in English who afforded me the space and time necessary to see this project to fruition. My residencies at the Stellenbosch Institute for Advanced Study (STIAS) were characterized by warmth of spirit and intellectual generosity that contributed to the refining of this book.

I am grateful to the anonymous reviewers of the individual chapters whose astute observations as well as judicious comments and recommendations were much appreciated. To the editing staff at Lexington books, thank you for your professionalism and guidance throughout the process.

I am indebted to the contributors to this volume namely Tony, Chielo, George, Ped, Pier Paolo and Lisa, Rocío, and Marzia for your incisive and provocative scholarship and for your commitment to this project. It was a sincere pleasure and honor working with you all. I am thankful also to my colleague, and friend, in the Philosophy Department at Rhodes University, Uchenna Okeja, for the many invigorating discussions and for pushing me, gently, to make this project happen.

Finally, I cannot express enough my immense gratitude to my extended and immediate family including Tom Martin, Olive, Pippa, and Oscar for their singular display of patience which did not, finally, wear (too) thin. And my sincere thanks to you, dear reader, for the time taken to read these words and this book.

Introduction

Re-reading the Canon, Re-reading Africa

Aretha Phiri

Between 2015 and 2017, universities across South Africa witnessed student unrest unparalleled since the Soweto "uprising" of June 16, 1976. Following the initial RhodesMustFall movement and its subsequent derivative, FeesMustFall, discussions regarding the lingering sociopolitical and socioeconomic effects of colonial apartheid in post-apartheid South Africa persist. Recognizing this ideological continuum and underwriting what Kirk B. Sides argues as the transgenerational "terrain of a racialized global modernity" (2017, 224), central to these movements was the demand for the decolonization of institutional knowledges in the interest of realigning global South epistemologies and in line with national and global transformation imperatives.

Of particular insistence in the call for the decolonization of higher education curricula was the need for a deWesternized, specifically "Africanized," curriculum. Echoing the volatile FeesMustFall movement, various critics weighed in on what was and continues to be a fractious and divisive debate. Some have called for a curriculum that can reflect and transmit indigenous knowledge systems and ways of being (Le Grange 2014) arguing for a "reconfigured Pan-Africanism" (Zeleza 2005, 1) that acknowledges and repositions African epistemologies and ontologies as central to the global knowledge economy. Still others have called for a revisionary, "post-African" (Ekpo 1995, 2010) approach that, in rejecting continued pan-African, essentialist perceptions of the continent, attempts to reposition Africa within and as part of an increasingly transnational and diasporic, globalized landscape.

The urgent tonality of some of these discussions suggested, ostensibly, an exceptional, critical moment in African history. But as with the June 16, 1976 "uprising," all history, to borrow from George Orwell's dystopian novel, *Nineteen Eighty-Four*, is a palimpsest (1949, 42). The place and role of Africa in an evolving milieu have certainly been debated before. In June 1962, the inaugural African Writers Conference was convened at Makerere University in Uganda in order to deliberate, at the onset of growing independence movements and at the imminent demise of colonial regimes, the efficacy of African literature written in English. The divergent positions between Ngũgĩ wa Thiong'o and Chinua Achebe were evinced in their respective texts, *Morning Yet on Creation Day* (1975) and *Decolonizing the Mind: The Politics of Language in African Literature* (1986). In addition, Obiajunwa Wali's essay, "The Dead End of African Literature?" pronounced, rather cynically, that "Perhaps the most important achievement of the last Conference of African Writers of English Expression . . . is that African literature as now defined and understood leads nowhere" (1997 [1963], 330). The primary and necessary questions posed here included: What constitutes African literature; does African literature need necessarily to be written by Africans and depict "authentically" the African experience; and does African literature need to be written in indigenous African languages?

Similarly, the accusations of racism that shook the Philosophical Society of South(ern) Africa (PSSA) in 2017 initiated the ensuing debate about the place of (Western, Eurocentric) philosophy in a changing political, social, and ideological, African landscape. Unveiling the historically racialized and gendered, prejudiced character of philosophy studies, Mabogo P. More (2017) identified in South African philosophical circles:

> the exclusive emphasis on Anglo-American and continental philosophy, the systematic disregard of Eastern traditions, the exclusion of feminist theory or women philosophers, the *a priori* denial of the existence of African Philosophy in mainly white universities in a country which is a part of Africa is an idealisation of the world by philosophers, and thus justification for and perpetuation of the established ideological, political and social order.

Underwriting the discipline's perceived institutional and structural marginalizations and exclusions (Manzini and Mncube 2018), the "Transforming Philosophy in South Africa" draft report edited by Sharli Anne Paphitis and Martin H. Villet maintains that, while the undergraduate-level Philosophy in South Africa has shown "dramatic improvement in demographic diversity in terms of student enrolment," the paucity of "demographic changes at the postgraduate and staffing level" reveal the "lack of deeper transformation at the level of curriculum, pedagogy and epistemic norms governing [South African] academe" (2017, 1).

In accordance with the 1997 Education White Paper 3's recognition of the challenge post-1994 "to transform the higher education system to serve a new social order, to meet pressing national needs, and development of a learning society . . . towards meeting the challenge of reconstruction and development" (3) it is evident, then, the continued need for South African higher education to be made "relevant to the material, historical and social realities of the communities in which universities operate" (Letsekha 2013, 14). Yet the terms and processes of epistemological decolonization continue to be disputed. What precisely constitutes pedagogical, curriculum Africanization remains unclear. Despite consensus on the "failure of transformation as conventionally understood to challenge old value systems, notions of what counts as excellence, or the validity of the old hegemonic cultural norms," decolonization and Africanization are not "self-explanatory, nor unproblematic conceptually" (Price and Ally 2016).

More specifically, where matters of conceptual decolonization are concerned, we would do well to consider, as Kwasi Wiredu has done, "in what sense we may call any philosophies [and literatures] emerging from such an intellectual milieu *African* and to what extent such philosophies [and literatures] can be useful to a post-colonial Africa sensitive to questions of her own identity" (2002, 57–58). Rather than simply and fixatedly condemning (colonial) or romanticizing ("traditional") history, and in order to guard against globally emerging cultures of populism and concomitant neo-imperialist ideologies, we also need to be responsive to (contextual) changing realities. That is, we should be in the habit critically "of responding directly to the questions that reality asks of us, for it may be that it is reality that interrogates us rather than we who interrogate reality" (Wiredu 2002, 57–58).

In this regard and as part of a series on "Critical Issues on Higher Education" facilitated by the Centre for Higher Education, Research, Teaching, and Learning (CHERTL, Rhodes), the Department of Philosophy at Rhodes University in May 2016 hosted the "Transformation of Higher Education and the Formation of the Canon in African Philosophy and African Literature" roundtable. Recognizing the significance and capacity of these cross-referential, intersecting disciplines in influencing, informing, and shifting not just sociopolitical but higher learning agendas, the colloquium sought to examine the role, relevance, and efficacy of African literatures and African philosophies in problematizing and critically enhancing contemporary decolonizing transformation imperatives. Where African philosophy continues to evolve an established philosophical search for and assertion of a uniquely cultural interpretation of the human condition, African literature has enjoyed great appeal in its ability creatively to speak to and illuminate the lived realities of its subjects. Acknowledging the enduring status of these established disciplines, then, implicit in this enquiry was the interrogation of the constructions of canons of African philosophy and African literature and which included two central concerns:

a) With the resurgence of pan-Africanist ideology and within transformation discourses, how can we reimagine/reinterpret the canon of African philosophy?
b) Notwithstanding the centrality of language in the epistemological decolonization debate, can African literature serve as a source of normative thinking in African philosophy, especially in the area of political and/or ethical philosophy?

Where the first question presents a methodological inquiry into the distinctive conceptual contribution of African philosophy to sociopolitical and epistemological transformation imperatives, the second question interrogates the ways in which African literature(s) can be utilized to re-read, inform, and, thus, revitalize African political and moral philosophies.

* * *

African Philosophical and Literary Possibilities: Re-reading the Canon continues the queries posed and discussions generated at the colloquium. Recognizing philosophy's traditional influence on, and literature's typically creative stimulus for, sociopolitical discourses, imaginations and structures, the volume probes the cross-referential, interdisciplinary relationships between African literature and African philosophy within the broader context of renewed interest in and concerns around epistemological decolonization and as part of an African scholarly transformation project in particular. It suggests that, in their convergent ideological and imaginative attempts to articulate an African conditionality, African philosophy and literature present similar provenances of overlapping concerns and aspirations. In engaging and examining the intersectional canons of African philosophy and literature in order to determine, specifically, their epistemic transformational possibilities, this book extends the link between the disciplines to examining the appeal and potential of African philosophy and literature as meaningful and effective resources within broader societal explorations of the current moment of decolonization.

At the same time, however, the volume also acknowledges the contrapuntal character (Garuba 2015) of two disciplines that exhibit comparable challenges regarding canonical formations and the contestation for space in academia. Interrogating and reflecting the tensions inherent herein, then, affords a critically dialogic and imaginative approach to re-interpreting both disciplines. Within this framework, *African Philosophical and Literary Possibilities* evaluates the agential efficacy of philosophy to both engage and enhance normative societal ideologies and practices represented in African literature. Conversely, it interrogates the ways in which African literature re-reads canonical, particularly existential, moral, and political, African philosophy. This demonstrates not just the limits of approaching African literature with a "philosophical intent," but also works to unsettle epistemological assumptions of Africa and African subjectivity.

Indeed, although the focus of this book is on African philosophy and African literature, implicit in the examination of both disciplines is an interrogation of a universally putative (idea of) Africa. With the resurgence of pan-Africanist ideology and rhetoric on the continent and in order to avoid perpetuating the "very narrow and particular way in which Africa is used, signified" (Wright, 2013, 6) in the global imagination, this interrogation attempts to reflect and advance the diverse, multidimensional and dynamic understandings and visions of Africa within broader discourses of transformation. In this way, the volume attempts to shift a traditionally animated focus on and broaden the scope from merely discoursing with the global North. Where much of the scholarship on African philosophy has tendency to focus on addressing issues associated with the postcolonial task of African self-assertion in the face of or against Euro-modernist hegemony, this innovative book project attempts to map out ways that philosophy and literature can be viewed as mutually enriching disciplines within and for the continent. As such, the volume aims not only to provide a richer and more nuanced appreciation of, as well as extend the debates around, the expansive efficacy and relevance of African philosophy and literature in a current global climate of epistemological decolonization. It also necessarily probes their agential efficacy in the transformational decolonizing and Africanization of institutional(ized) knowledge(s).

Bringing together scholars from the continent and beyond who are working within, or in relation to, the two disciplines, this book of chapters attempts to thread—explicit and implicit—areas of interlocking possibilities and mutual borrowings between the two canons. In developing and establishing these areas, most of the chapters here also engage the latest phase of decolonization which, for obvious reasons, has South Africa at its epicenter, reflecting thus the skewed—geographic and demographic—nature of the debates around, as well as the potentially exclusory or at least representative limitations inherent in, the canonicity of these two disciplines.

Yet in the process of re-imagining the continent (and its subjects) through critically renewed, sophisticated understandings, *African Philosophical and Literary Possibilities* is primarily rooted in and committed to re-interpreting African philosophy and African literature within continental and global, transnational and transitional contexts. As such, in its problematization of African philosophical and literary canons, the volume offers a significant and timely contribution that necessarily disrupts, in order to enhance intra-continental and global intellectual and political decolonization and transformation imperatives. To this end, each chapter in the book explores the efficacy of and possibilities afforded by African philosophy and African literature as morally, ideologically, and socially transformative disciplines.

Oritsegbubemi Anthony Oyowe's "Philosophy and an African Conscience" kick-starts the conversation with a critical inquiry into the efficacy of establishing African philosophy in the first place. Questioning the probity and value of "taking sides with Africa" in this regard, Oyowe examines the role of and prospects afforded by philosophy in developing and articulating a situated African ethics or a "philosophy with an African consciousness." Arguing against the descriptive treatment of Africa as fixed and knowable and maintaining that it might benefit rather from ongoing rigorous appraisal, his contention that the "task of philosophizing, like the stories we tell, is never neutral," anticipates Chielozona Eze's meditation on the enduring utility of African literature to African philosophy as the material inquiry for the African condition. Entitled "African Literature as a Handmaid of African Philosophy," Eze's revisionary interpretation of Chinua Achebe's celebrated canonical novel, *Things Fall Apart*, seeks to shift the focus on and preoccupation with traditional, postcolonial anti-imperialist moral valuations to advance ethical and existential, philosophical questions relevant to the continent itself. In considering Africa's (global) navigational prospects, he poses two significant questions: "What kind of narrative do Africans tell themselves about themselves? Do those narratives help Africans to examine their lives?"

Eze's deliberations are carried forward in George Hull's chapter, "Conflict and Compromise in Three Novels of the Eastern Cape." Focusing specifically on South African writing, Hull maintains that the "question of how one ought to act in response to conflicting legitimate moral values or principles is a subject of theory and debate in philosophical ethics. But it is also a practical question" that arises in everyday South African realities and encounters governed by political and cultural conflicts of value(s). In a close analysis of three (controversial) canonical South African texts set in the Eastern Cape—S. E. K. Mqhayi's *The Case of the Twins* (*Ityala Lamwele*), A. C. Jordan's *The Wrath of the Ancestors* (*Ingqumbo Yeminyanya*), and J. M. Coetzee's *Disgrace*—Hull suggests that the only "adequate responses to some types of moral dilemma are likely to be better modeled in creative literary works than in philosophical analysis." Similarly examining literature's philosophical prospects, Pedro Tabensky's chapter, "Blind Sisyphus: Two Perspectives on Mersault," extends the African canon's traditional geopolitical focus and borders to include the North African philosophical canon. Engaging with the literature of French-Algerian philosopher, Albert Camus, Tabensky considers the ethics of colonial violence and the efficacy thereafter of postcolonial African identity. This is in order to interrogate the delimiting effects of utopian thinking and to propose an alternative way of thinking through and about (contemporary notions of) African emancipation.

Carrying through and differently expanding the theme of alternative ideological methodologies, Pier Paolo Frassinelli and Lisa Treffry-Goatley's chapter, "Digital Media, Literacies, Literature, and the African Humanities," reframes and problematizes the debate around the decolonization of the African humanities by bringing into innovative conversation "the two humanities"—literature and philosophy on one side and digital media studies on the other. Questioning the value of constructs such as literature and philosophy and illustrating the prospective interface of these disciplines with African cultural productions and digital media in particular, they argue that "the humanities need to confront the challenge and grab the opportunities presented by digital media" in realizing Africa's place in a globalized transitional and mutating world. The notion of global mutation and Africa's centrality in this regard is similarly pivotal to Rocío Cobo-Piñero's reading of Nnedi Okorafor's science fiction novel, *Lagoon*. Entitled "African Gaze: Hollywood/Nollywood and the Postcolonial Science Fiction Imagery in Nnedi Okorafor's *Lagoon*," her chapter traces postcolonial Nigeria's fictive and filmic re-interpretation and re-contextualization of what is typically viewed as a (white, male) Western genre. In this way, Cobo-Piñero maintains that an emergent African science fiction and futurist fiction "constitute a powerful counter-discourse to stereotypical images of Africa in the Western imagination, while re-imagining the continent and re-inventing African identities" in ideologically expansive and ontologically inclusive ways.

The sociopolitical and ontological prospects for simultaneously re-imagining Africa and African identities in globally transformational ways find resonance in Aretha Phiri's chapter, "Transgressing Borders: (Re)imag(in)ing Africa(ns) in the World." In a comparative reading of the fiction of celebrated contemporary Afrodiasporic female writers, Taiye Selasi and NoViolet Bulawayo, Phiri suggests that the "less explicitly politicized, idiosyncratic versions of African diasporic cultures" exhibited in their novels, *Ghana Must Go* and *We Need New Names*, respectively, advance less prescriptive and more worldly readings of the continent. Acknowledging the persistence of global asymmetries and extending the traditional diaspora themes of home and exile/belonging and unbelonging, Phiri maintains that these texts necessarily strive toward the transgression of geopolitical and cultural borders in the universal achievement of a just and human(e) world. Differently picking up on this theme, Marzia Milazzo's chapter, "'The Whims of the White Masters': Miriam Tlali's *Between Two Worlds* and the Totality of White Power," offers a cautionary note to the utopian aspirations of global "post" rhetoric by highlighting the enduring realities of structural racism. While Tlali's novel is set in and focuses on apartheid in South Africa, Milazzo's comparative reading of *Between Two Worlds* traces racism's transnational iterations and extends the national articulations of the anti-apartheid Black Consciousness movement to include global, particularly African American experiential resonances. In engaging thus the "synergic relationship between Black Consciousness philosophy and apartheid fiction," Milazzo expands her critique of the "machinations of racism and white people's place in society" to include the canonical disciplines of philosophy and literature in South African academe, where the study of Black Consciousness philosophy and black South African fiction, she argues, continues to be marginalized.

Where Milazzo's chapter provides a somber conclusion to the book, her critique aptly acknowledges and reiterates, as with all the chapters here, the continued need for the reassessment of African philosophical and literary canons. Debating the efficacy of these disciplines within the frame of renewed concerns in South African higher education for the decolonization of its curricula, the chapters in this book effectively guard against "seeing transformation as a place of arrival that, therefore, requires the suspension of critique" (Lange 2014, 12). In generating explicit and implicit, critical and imaginative conversations across the disciplines, *African Philosophical and Literary Possibilities* seeks to further problematize and reinvigorate debates around the intra-continental worth and relevance of transformational African epistemologies. At the same time, in connecting African philosophy and African literature to ongoing, broader questions and debates, the book aims to reposition and reinterpret Africa's social, moral, and political currency within global transformation imperatives.

REFERENCES

Education White Paper 3. 1997. *A Programme for the Transformation of Higher Education*. Pretoria: Department of Higher Education.

Ekpo, Denis. 1995. "Towards a Post-Africanism: Contemporary African Thought and Postmodernism." *Textual Practice* 9 (1): 121–35.

Ekpo, Denis. 2010. "From Negritude to Post-Africanism." *Third Text* 24 (2): 177–87.

Garuba, Harry. 2015. "What Is an African Curriculum?" *Mail and Guardian*. https://www.mg.co.za/article/2015-04-17-what-is-an-african-curriculum.

Lange, Lis. 2014. "Rethinking Transformation and Its Knowledge(s): The Case of South African Higher Education." *Critical Studies in Teaching and Learning* 2 (1): 1–24.

Le Grange, Lesley. 2014. "Currere's Active Force and the Africanisation of the University Curriculum." *South African Journal of Higher Education* 28 (4): 1283–94.

Manzini, Nompumelelo Zinhle and Zinhle Mncube. 2018. "Identity by Race Does Matter." https://mg.co.za/article/2018-05-25-00-identity-by-race-does-matter.

More, Mabogo P. 2017. "Racism and Academic Philosophy in South Africa." http://www.theconmag.co.za/2017/03/03/racism-and-academic-philosophy-in-south-africa/.
Orwell, George. 2008 [1949]. *Nineteen Eighty-Four*. Penguin: London.
Phaphitis, Sharli Anne and Martin H. Villet. 2017. "The Demographic Diversity of Philosophy and the Possibilities for Transforming Philosophy in South Africa." *Transforming Philosophy in South Africa Draft Report*: 1–67. https://docs.google.com/viewer?a=v&pid=forums&srcid=MTI5OTgxMDE5Mjk1NjExMDEzMTIBMDgyMTE3MDM2NzY0MDM0OTY3ODgBV0RUZDlwLWlDQUFKATAuNAEBdjI.
Price, Max and Russell Ally. 2016. "The Challenge of Decolonisation." https://www.news.uct.ac.za/article/-2016-04-05-the-challenge-of-decolonisation-ucts-transformation-journey.
Sides, Kirk B. 2017. "Precedence and Warning: Global Apartheid and South Africa's Long Conversation on Race." *Safundi* 18 (3): 221–38.
Wali Obiajunwa. 1997 [1963]. "The Dead End of African Literature?" *Transition* 75/76: 330–35.
Zeleza, Paul Tiyambe. 2005. "Transnational Education and African Universities." *Journal of Higher Education in Africa* 3 (1): 1–28.

Chapter 1

Philosophy and an African Conscience

Oritsegbubemi Anthony Oyowe

INTRODUCTION

The phrase "philosophizing with an African conscience" was coined by Kwasi Wiredu (Wiredu 1980, x). In its original context, it carries the tone of an injunction to do philosophy in a way that counts as authentically African.[1] One way to get clarity on what that might mean is to directly examine the corpus of Wiredu's own work in African philosophy in order to source it out. As will become clear, his was a philosophy of culture, of African culture. Or, more broadly, it was characterized by a great deal of interest in Africa—its peoples, history, cultures, and futures. Moreover, his methodological preference in connection with that idea of authentic African philosophy goes under the rubric of "conceptual decolonization" (Wiredu 1998). My approach in this chapter, however, is not to comment directly on the particular ideas that define Wiredu's philosophical productions and the methodological preferences he adopted over time, although I shall refer to these along the way. This also means that I do not intend to assess the meaning of the terms "conscience" and "authenticity," and the other philosophical quandaries that comes with doing so.

Instead, I proceed in a somewhat roundabout way, by first substituting talk of doing philosophy with an African conscience with something intuitive and mundane as taking sides in a dispute. Doing so will afford me the context to clarify what I believe motivates Wiredu's call for conscientious African philosophizing. But it will also allow me to say what I believe conscientious African philosophizing is not. In the end, my goal is to show that for Wiredu it was a critical epistemic attitude toward Africa and everything African, rather than a wholesale embrace, that should define the conscience of a contemporary African philosopher.

I anticipate the discussion to unfold in different stages. In the first part, I focus on some reasons why one might frown at the suggestion that one way of doing philosophy should involve us taking sides with Africa. My primary aim will be to consider and set aside these reasons. Although the concerns behind them are sometimes worth keeping in mind, these should not deter us from taking sides. In the second part, I shall consider a deposition by an African philosopher, Polycarp Ikuenobe, and then characterize a way of taking sides with Africa when doing philosophy that I believe veers dangerously in the wrong direction.[2] Moreover, it is at odds with the spirit of Wiredu's injunction and with the overall character of his philosophical productions.

This second part of the discussion actually breaks down into two specific aims. On the one hand, the aim is to show that the conception of philosophy that emerges from Ikuenobe's deposition lacks the critical epistemic attitude integral to Wiredu's appeal to the notion of a conscience. On the other hand, the aim is to show that the image of the philosopher inspired by that deposition is dubious. In particular, I am especially critical of the nationalist undertones and the expectation that the philosopher should not distance himself from the African world about which he speaks. As I go on to show, this image of the philosopher has antecedents in contemporary African literature. Drawing on the work of Kwame Appiah, I trace the origins of this image of the philosopher in the work of Wole Soyinka on the ideological role of the writer.

The lessons gleaned from the foregoing should illuminate a more attractive model of taking sides with Africa, or doing philosophy with an African conscience—one I deem to be closer to what Wiredu must have had in mind. I hope to highlight these lessons along the way. In addition, I focus attention on the pitfalls of the earlier model and underscore the merits of the alternative one. All of this is done in relation to Wiredu's thoughts about how we might undertake conscientious African philosophizing, or otherwise take sides with Africa when doing philosophy.

WHY "TAKING SIDES" MIGHT BE A BAD IDEA

One probable objection to philosophizing with an African conscience, which I interpret here as taking sides with Africa when doing philosophy, is that it is at odds with the method of philosophy itself. This objection may be expressed in two different ways. First, the method of philosophy itself requires contestations, disagreements and the willingness to change one's views in light of good reasons, whereas taking sides with some tradition or worldview not only precludes disagreements but also encourages widespread uncritical consensus and a general unwillingness to revise one's views in light of good reasons.[3]

Alternatively, one might claim, as Kai Horsthemke and Penelope Enslin have done, that because taking sides generates a condition that precludes disagreements, contestations, and discord in philosophical exchanges, the side which a philosopher takes necessarily becomes immune from criticism.[4] Such a situation is unlikely to lead to progress in a philosophical endeavor.

Now, while the focus is on Africa and its peoples and cultures, and many African philosophers often attempt to retrieve what they deem useful resources from Africa's cultural past that can contribute to current developmental goals, taking sides with an African world doesn't preclude criticisms from within and without. Indeed, the above objection seems to me to originate from a rather poor grasp of what African philosophy is about and what African philosophers have been and are doing. There is within the growing literature lively protestations, counter contestations emerging from different and sometimes conflicting understanding of what it means to properly do African philosophy, or what are the most plausible conceptions of democracy or personal identity. And these competing positions are developed by people who see themselves as part of the tradition and those who may define themselves as outsiders. Unless the criticism that African philosophy may become "immune from criticism" is read as shifting attention from the global North, it is hard to see why this is a serious objection. Having said that, I think there is a need to protect African philosophy from the uncritical pursuit of consensus in the practice of philosophy, that is, in its search for and articulation of meaning of concepts and values. The objection, however, seems to assume that the point of philosophy is disagreement, and that consensus is inherently inimical to philosophizing. This seems wrong. What we should guard against, rather, is *uncritical* consensus with respect to answers to philosophical questions.

Another potential objection may be framed as follows. Although philosophy focuses on ideas that are both universal in that they are widely applicable rather than simply the particular concerns of some group and abstract in that they are potentially separable from the original concrete concerns that gave rise to them, the idea of taking sides suggests the opposite. In a different discussion, Ward Jones makes a similar point that we can adapt here. "The universal scope of philosophy," he writes, "appears . . . to be in tension with . . . the directive that philosophers pay attention to their surroundings" (2006, 7–8) or take sides with their context.[5]

Initially, this objection seems convincing, but it is a classic case of a plausible argument that misleads. There is no such thing as universal philosophy, in the sense that it is entirely divorced from a particular context, world, or set of assumptions. The issue then is the degree to which philosophy is universal, and not whether it could be particular, in the sense of focusing one's attention on one's own surroundings—that is, the culture or history of a particular place. To take sides when doing African philosophy will require negotiating the extent to which philosophy, although universal, is also importantly particular. And this is not likely to lead to the "tribalization of philosophy" (Pearce 1992), as some have unjustifiably claimed. In this connection, it is worth noting Bernard Matolino's (2015, 404) observation that the attempt to make the transition from particular African context to the universal global stage has been one sided. A significant number of Euro-American philosophers often look to the traditions of philosophical thought in Europe and nowhere else. That is, although one often finds African philosophers looking to engage philosophically with the traditions in Europe and elsewhere, not often do we find Euro-American philosophers paying attention to the traditions of thought in the global South. As it turns out, the charge that doing philosophy with an African conscience will lead to the tribalization of philosophy is best leveled at Euro-American philosophers who fail to recognize other traditions of thought. To borrow an expression from Chinua Achebe, the task of philosophizing, like the stories we tell, is never neutral.

Finally, taking sides or philosophizing with an African conscience is in conflict with academic freedom. A philosopher working in Africa should be free to not be involved in agendas that are political, social, or in general practical and perhaps non-philosophical. The notion of academic freedom can be put to dangerous uses, however. And often times, it is, as with notions like neutrality and universality, used not only to disguise the deeply ingrained resistance to put Africa—and its cultures and priorities—at the center of intellectual endeavors, but also to implant "offshore" philosophical approaches and methods in Africa. But what is more interesting about this objection is that it appears to deny that one could have justified academic obligations to the context in which one undertakes one's academic work. Academic freedom is desirable obviously, but I do not know that academic bad faith, by which I mean not prioritizing the specific intellectual needs of the place in which one teaches and researches, should be commended. Moreover, it is hard to believe that academic freedom is only valuable when it is put to a predetermined range of uses, and in the interests of the academic. It seems to me that where there is a conflict between academic freedom and one's obligation to context, the latter should win, most of the time. More so, where there are weightier, justice-related considerations, in this case the fact that African voices have been systematically silenced, exercising academic freedom without due regard for them is something we should recoil from. These weightier considerations of justice tip the balance in favor of the freedom to take sides with Africa.

A CONSCIENTIOUS AFRICAN PHILOSOPHY

Consider the following powerful and provocative deposition by an African philosopher, Polycarp Ikuenobe:

> I see myself as a research scholar in the area of or subject matter of Africa; I see myself as a defender of an African perspective, that is, someone who takes pride in the beliefs, views, thoughts of Africa. In this second sense, I am motivated partly by a kind of nationalism (Africanism) and I have an activist attitude in my efforts to defend African ideas. (2006, 42)

It is tempting to read the deposition as Ikuenobe's own personal manifesto. It is in some way a statement of one man's deep convictions about the terms of his calling as an African philosopher. Not only is Ikuenobe unequivocal in his preference for Africa as his primary, or perhaps sole, subject matter in teaching and researching philosophy, but in spelling out the details of his personal philosophical commitments he is also intimating a model of conscientious African philosophy, or so I shall assume.[6] It is worth acknowledging that the importance of centering Africa cannot be overemphasized. African perspectives and voices, although now increasingly receiving attention in the corridors of the academia, have been for a long time relegated to the periphery of philosophical inquiry. Moreover, the early obsession with, and unfortunately protracted debate over, whether and to what extent philosophy could be African had done very little in sustaining the impetus and developing the discourses of a growing field. All these and more should justify an unequivocal statement of intent like Ikuenobe's. Yet, philosophical commitments expressed in the market place of ideas are not just personal; they unavoidably present themselves as raw materials for rigorous scrutiny and criticism. And to the extent that Ikuenobe's deposition suggests more than just centering Africa, rigorously scrutinizing it should be immensely philosophically rewarding.

Specifically two aspects of Ikuenobe's deposition strike me as worth considering. The first concerns the conception of African philosophy lurking behind it. By this I mean that Ikuenobe specifies an agenda for philosophy in Africa, including its aims, modus operandi, and purpose. The second concerns the image of the African philosopher that must accompany that vision—that is, the sort of person the philosopher must be if he is to effectively carry out the terms of the proposed manifesto.

We will focus first on the vision of African philosophy. Although it seems straightforward and simple, it conceals in its simplicity layers of complications. One such complication is that on reflection there is just no unique or distinctive *set* of ideas, concepts, knowledge, and value systems that may be justifiably designated as *African*, particularly in the sense that the items in the set belongs to or are to be found in Africa and nowhere else (Horsthemke and Enslin 2009). At issue here is the implicit suggestion in Ikuenobe's deposition that there is such a set and that it is uniquely African or that African cultures and peoples might collectively claim a monopoly on it. But if, as it seems, ideas typically develop and receive clear articulations out of constant exchanges and borrowings between and among various peoples and cultures, then perhaps, strictly speaking, they could not be the property of any one or group of cultures and peoples. There is another aspect to the problem. Perhaps, there is no predetermined *African* side to take when doing philosophy, since as a matter of fact there is a huge diversity of cultures and massive variation in the ideas, beliefs, and perspectives associated with the ethnic thought-worlds that populate Africa, especially below the Sahara. As such, any meaningful designation of such a set of ideas can only be done on the assumption that these diverse cultures together exhibit some kind of conceptual consensus, a "metaphysical solidarity" or "mythic unity" at a very "high level of abstraction" (Appiah 1992, 82). The point is that if there is no such unanimous set of uniquely African ideas, perspectives, and beliefs, then we are not rationally compelled to adopt this vision of African philosophy. Specifically, the call to "defend African ideas" would be misleading, if not just empty.

But suppose, for the sake of argument, there is a coherent set of African ideas and about which African peoples and cultures are unanimous. One would still have to confront the question of why we should defend that set, since the possibility of such a set doesn't guarantee the plausibility of content of the set. So, in heeding Ikuenobe's call to defend African ideas, we would have to decide whether we are defending the relevant set of ideas because they are African or because they are worth defending. The point here is not that a set of African ideas is in principle indefensible; instead, it is that Ikuenobe's deposition seems to assume that the Africanness of the set and the plausibility of the ideas will always coincide. My sense is that we cannot guarantee that they will. If that is so, a call to "defend African ideas" in advance of assessing their plausibility seems misguided.

It is worth noting that a friend of Ikuenobe—one who is sympathetic to the sentiments expressed in his deposition—might protest, insisting either that the deposition does not face these problems or that it can be amended in a way that avoids these problems. I suspect that the second line of response is the more promising one. At any rate, in what follows I attempt to characterize how a friend of Ikuenobe might attempt to amend the understanding of the deposition to rid it of these worries.

With regard to the possibility of a uniquely African set of ideas, a friend of Ikuenobe might insist that we need not interpret Ikuenobe as claiming that these ideas are unique to Africa, in the sense of being found only in Africa, or are a monopoly of Africans, in the sense that they are exclusively possessed by them. In other words, he might follow Thaddeus Metz in thinking that "in order to count as 'African' something need not be utterly unique to the geographical space of the African continent" (2009, 194). Instead, and more charitably, Ikuenobe's point is just that there is a set of ideas that exhibit a certain degree of salience, in the sense that they are given or have received significant philosophical attention, treatment, or have been prioritized in a way that one does not typically find elsewhere.[7] So, rather than focusing on a unique set, emphasis should shift to the unique relation African peoples may have to that set. What is unique is not the set of ideas themselves but the way those ideas have been engaged, appropriated, redefined, and employed to suit the historical, political, and cultural realities of Africa. This seems reasonable. However, while it solves the problem of uniqueness, it doesn't address the problem of unanimity—that is, whether some set of ideas are unanimously held by African peoples and cultures.

As a further emendation, a friend of Ikuenobe might suggest that the intention is not to focus on whether or not some idea is unanimously held but instead on whether it is just widely shared. That is, notwithstanding the diversity of cultures and variation in beliefs and practices, there may remain a set of common ideas deducible from the diverse set of cultures found in Africa (Nwakaeze 1987, 101). And this would be so even if there are other, less common, conflicting ones coexisting alongside it and that may in some sense be described as African as well. For instance, the idea of community as an axiomatic principle around which much of the theorizing and justification in African cultures turn might be one such element of commonality, irrespective of whether there are individualistic currents in and among African cultures and peoples. Again, this seems to be reasonable.

Notice, however, that at the heart of these emendations is the question of how we should think about the category, African, and consequently what our epistemic attitude toward Africa should be. Interestingly, what has emerged is that whatever else African might mean it is not something we can simply take for granted or assume as already given. To take Africa for granted or treat it as something already given is to engage it in purely descriptive terms. It is to regard it as a fixed category. I want to suggest that one problem with the vision of African philosophy lurking behind Ikuenobe's deposition is that it takes Africa for granted. This is why he freely speaks about the task of defending African ideas and perspectives—the assumption is that these are already *given*. To treat the category of African so unproblematically leads one to envision the philosophical project as the simple one of defending African ideas and perspectives. Not only does this oversimplify the task of philosophizing in Africa today, but also the impulse to think of Africa in this purely descriptive sense is one we should seek to overcome.

This latter point is a key aspect of Wiredu's conception of a conscientious African philosophy. It involves adopting a radically different epistemic attitude toward Africa, specifically treating the category of African, and therefore the set of ideas associated with it, in evaluative terms. Among other things, this means that we should treat whatever purports to go by the name

"African" as something that might benefit potentially from rigorous criticism and ongoing appraisal and/or re-valuation. The result, in his view, is that we would arrive at a vision of African philosophy in which the tasks involved require us to continuously search for and discover which ideas are good for Africa, as opposed to which ones are African ideas. As Wiredu explains:

> Still it would be necessary for us to learn to distinguish, at least conceptually, between the question of what African philosophy is and what it ought to be. A confusion of the two issues has generated a lot of passion that might have been directed towards more useful enterprises. With the best descriptive criteria for what African philosophy actually is, that reality may still be worthless, incapable of helping Africa to master the arts of modern living and holding her own in the comity or (to be closer to the facts) in the competition of cultures. The quest, then, is not just for African philosophy, but for good African philosophy, and I regard what I call conceptual decolonization as a precondition of that objective. (2002, 56)

For Wiredu, our interest in Africa—its cultures, peoples, and history—as a subject of philosophical inquiry should not be about discovering what, if anything, is already there; that is, it is not a search for what African philosophy is (in a kind of matter-of-fact, descriptive sense) but instead a quest for what it should be—which ideas are valuable for the challenges that modern circumstances has put before us. It is certainly not about defending whatever ideas fall under the description, African. On this point, he rather strongly insists that "it is worth repeating that in this project there is no assumption that what comes from Africa is necessarily true, sound, profound et cetera" (2002, 54) and so should be defended. The more complicated philosophical task is to continuously determine which assumptions are worth defending and which ones are truly African, in this evaluative, as opposed to descriptive, sense.

Elsewhere, Wiredu is more explicit about the fact that doing philosophy with an African conscience—which is, as I intimated earlier, equivalent to the search for authenticity—involves adopting a critical and evaluative epistemic attitude toward what may be justifiably regarded as African. His argument is to the extent that authenticity is a prescriptive, as opposed to a purely descriptive, concept, and authentic African philosophy is similarly a prescriptive or normative endeavor. As such, "for a philosophy to be authentically African, it is not sufficient for it to be truly African; it must also be unprejudicial to Africa. Calling a piece of philosophical work authentically African thus implies a certain degree of approbation" (2007, 72). My point has been that if we are to adopt a posture that requires us to regard as African only those ideas, perspectives, or value systems that have passed some test of approval, then the philosophical project cannot be about defending African ideas but instead critically deciding which ones are African ideas. To adopt this position, however, is to commit oneself to the possibility that there may be African ideas—in the sense that they fall under the description African—that may not be worth defending at all.

In addition to the point that we should not treat Africa in a purely descriptive sense—that is, accepting and defending whatever falls under the description African—Wiredu's vision of philosophy also challenges the quest for uniqueness. In deciding which ideas are African and which ones are not, and in working out a philosophical program that can aid African peoples and cultures to confront modern challenges, "it would not be rational," Wiredu writes, "to try to reject everything of a colonial ancestry." In his view, "conceivably, a thought or a mode of inquiry spearheaded by our erstwhile colonizers may be valid or in some way beneficial to humankind. Are we called upon to reject or ignore it? That would be a madness having neither rhyme nor reason" (1988, 17). He goes on to add that the quest for uniqueness as a feature of the African philosophical project betrays "colonial type mentality that regards African philosophy as something that should be kept apart from the mainstream of philosophical thinking" (1998, 17). The implication is that the African philosophy program must involve not just looking inward to indigenous sources of knowledge but also outward to explore what the global knowledge community might have to offer. And to say this is not to say that concepts, values, and perspectives that are rooted in or originating from cultural frameworks in Europe and elsewhere become automatic replacements. A similar critical eye toward them—so as not uncritically to accept—is one of the hallmarks of Wiredu's conceptual decolonization.

THE CONSCIENTIOUS AFRICAN PHILOSOPHER

The other item in Ikuenobe's deposition that I wish to confront concerns the image of the philosopher that accompanies the "activist" vision of African philosophy he envisions.[8] It is the image of the African philosopher as a bona fide member of the African nation and exhibiting enough patriotism to be so regarded. "I am motivated partly by a kind of nationalism (Africanism)," Ikuenobe writes, and by so doing specifies some criterion for identifying a bona fide African philosopher. Roughly, what Ikuenobe seems to be proposing is a special relation between the philosopher and the African world—one that generates a special set of obligations for the philosopher in relation to that world.

There are two aspects to this relation worth highlighting. The first one concerns the philosopher's relation to Africa by way of belonging as opposed to mere presence. In this respect, the allusion to nationalism is not insignificant. This is because it not only evokes the attitude of patriotic devotion to some cause, but also incidentally marks out the borders of belonging perhaps along the lines of race, ethnicity, and nationality. To be a bona fide African philosopher is to fit in neatly with these markers of identity. But with clearly specified conditions of belonging, the result is exclusion—certain others strictly speaking do not belong and could not speak authoritatively for that world. I am not going to dwell on this point; it seems to me obviously problematic to read necessarily into the conditions of participation in the project of African philosophy the implied requirements of racial, ethnic, and national belonging. Moreover, Peter Bodunrin (1981) has argued persuasively, I believe, against the inclusion of these features in the determination of the proper boundaries of the tradition of African philosophy.[9]

Bodunrin's argument is both substantive and comparative. As I see it, his substantive point is that there is no essential link between, on the one hand, intellectual interests, ideas, discourses, and ethnicity, or nationality, on the other. Instead, history presents a picture according to which intellectual interests, ideas, and discourses often migrate and are adapted in various contexts and by various people so that no particular group of people can claim a monopoly on them. As such, if we were to determine some tradition of thought by way of tracking the ethnic and/or national origin of a people, we might leave out crucial details about what constitutes that tradition. So, for example, relying on the criteria of ethnicity and nationality, we might think that the French tradition of philosophy includes every French person and we might be led to think that Ludwig Wittgenstein, originally Austrian, could not be an influential figure in British philosophy—both of which would obviously be a mistake. Comparatively, other traditions of philosophy are best understood not in terms of tracking the ethnic and/or national identity of a people. So, for example, prominent figures in what is called British philosophy have been from beyond the British Isles and that tradition of philosophy does not necessarily include the ordinary Briton. Also, the "thoughts of the ancient Greeks belong to the history of Western philosophy but the ancient Greeks and ancient Britons were mutually ignorant of each other" (Bodunrin 1981, 178). In the same way, the tradition of African philosophy need not be delimited by ethnic and/or national identity.

The other aspect of the supposed relation of a philosopher to the African nation or world concerns the endowment with what may be described as the African personality, about which, it seems to me, Ikuenobe is rather explicit. To be so endowed, and as it emerges from Ikuenobe's deposition is, among other things, to be equipped with the right sort of emotions. More clearly, it is to be appropriately "motivated" and exhibiting "a sense of pride" in relation to Africa and African ideas. It is the image of the African philosopher as a certain kind of person, if he is to speak authoritatively or pass as a legitimate "mouthpiece" for the African world. Interestingly, this image of the African philosopher emerging from Ikuenobe's deposition coincides with the way Africa's post-independent writers have been imagined. It is the image of the writer who, because she is essentially part of the group, in the sense that she *feels* like them, could not possibly be opposed to them. That is, there is little or no possibility of distancing herself from the group.

By the end of chapter four of his widely debated book *In My Father's House: Africa in the Philosophy of Culture* (1992), Kwame Appiah had stumbled upon what he describes as a "novel self." After having noted that this conception of self "is the product, surely, of changes in social life as well as in the technology of the word," Appiah adds that "this novel self is more individualist and atomic than the self of precapitalist societies . . . it is no longer something that we in Africa could escape even if we wanted to. And if we cannot escape it, let us celebrate it" (1992, 84). He was characterizing, in terms of a modern, atomic, and more individualist self, the existential struggle of the African intellectual seeking to break out as it were from the group, tradition, and attempting to release to that world the fruits of independent intellectual engagement.

The context of the foregoing is Appiah's discussion of the ideological role of the writer in Africa or the relation of the writer to the social world she inhabits, with specific reference to the work of Wole Soyinka.[10] Part of Appiah's concern was to explore how African writers, particularly in Anglophone Africa, negotiate the question of African identity—by appealing to their own traditions. Appiah begins by describing the role of African writers as involving the "search for a culture," quite distinct from the purposes of modern European writers who are steeped in a constant search for the individual self. African writers seek to "to develop their cultures in direction that will give them a role"—indeed, a "public role" (1992, 76). They do this, Appiah says, by drawing "*confidently* on the resources of [that] tradition," on Africa's shared metaphysical resources (1992, 79, emphasis mine). Moreover, Appiah sees Soyinka as exemplifying this role, initially (1992, 80). But so too is the African philosopher in Ikuenobe's deposition, in his effort to defend African ideas. To perform this role reliably and effectively, however, he must stand in a nonconflicting relationship with that world; he could not in principle be opposed to or remain skeptical of it, if he is to draw confidently from it. He has to be appropriately motivated and take pride in it. Yet, the expectation to be properly motivated and take pride in that traditional world seems too strong. The African philosopher, like the post-independence writer, is caught up in a particular kind of predicament—the colonial experience has fundamentally altered her relation to that world.

In Appiah's view, the tension between what Soyinka's play shows and what he says about them is fundamentally a tension between a private, independent self and a "public commitment," and ultimately points toward "the challenge of a new mode of individuality" (1992, 78). Soyinka "the individual," Appiah writes, "outside the traditional, more certain world of his Yoruba ancestors, struggles with the Soyinka who experiences the loss of that world . . . the 'I' seeks to escape the persistent and engulfing 'we'" (1992, 83). The tension, and the inevitable transition from the "we" to the "I," is a function "of changes in social life as well as in the technology of the word" (1992, 84). He describes the tension, mediated through "the growth of both literacy and of the availability of printing," as the struggle of the "authorial 'I' to displace the 'we' of the oral tradition" or as the "I" seeking "to escape the persistent and engulfing 'we'" (1992, 84–85).

It seems to me that Appiah and Wiredu, more than Ikuenobe (at least in that deposition), take seriously the consequences for the African philosopher and, by extension, the writer, of the colonial encounter between Africa and Europe. Wiredu notes that "the very concern with authenticity in African philosophy presupposes a background of crisis" (2007, 73). Elsewhere, "colonialism," he writes, "has caused a widespread involuntary intermixing of Western and African intellectual categories in the thinking of contemporary Africans" (2002, 54). The result is an unsettled sense of identity and, therefore, a disruption in one's relation to one's intellectual and cultural world similar to the one Appiah describes. The philosopher can no longer remain certain about that world or the set of ideas ostensibly already given in it. As such the philosopher's role or task is significantly modified so that instead of simply drawing confidently from it he must adopt what Wiredu describes as, the "the rational approach . . . of critical reconstruction," and embody "a critical spirit" (2002, 54). To put the point differently, rather than being endowed with an African personality, as I have characterized it above, one only needs to be endowed with a philosophical personality, or otherwise a "critical spirit" toward whatever passes as African.

CONCLUSION

I wish to conclude by calling attention to another crucial point. The adoption of a critical attitude or a "spirit" toward the African tradition, and to any tradition of ideas for that matter, requires a certain distancing of oneself from those ideas either by way of temporarily suspending belief in them or by simply not taking their truth-value as given. Again, this cautious skepticism toward what is descriptively given as African results in an image of the African philosopher that differs radically from Ikuenobe's. It is the image of the African philosopher in search of truth, or at least a set of rationally defensible ideas that is applicable and responsive to the problems of contemporary Africa. The conscientious philosopher need not be motivated by "some kind of nationalism" or by the need to defend African ideas as such. The proper motivation is to defend ideas that are not harmful to Africa or are usefully applicable to the African situation.

Two implications follow. First, a category of philosophers who may be described as non-African (in the descriptive sense) Africanist (in the evaluative sense) philosophers could be usefully included in the tradition of contemporary African philosophy. This is so because the requirement to embody a critical spirit toward Africa and ideas that are relevant for Africa is something that a philosopher who may fail to meet the descriptive criteria of being African might be able to satisfy. This might become even relevant as philosophers in other philosophical tradition increasingly become aware and take interest in the tradition of African philosophy. Second, to the extent that the philosopher is not uncritically attached to the African world and to the ideas found therein, there is likely going to be a resulting openness to turn a critical eye toward other traditions to learn as much as may be necessary from them. As I understand, Wiredu makes a similar point. Doing philosophy with an African conscience, he says, should not at all lead us to reject "foreign" perspectives or ideas from elsewhere as "possible sources of edification" (2002, 54). This last point is a piece of wisdom that we might quickly lose if we follow Ikuenobe, or at least my interpretation of what his deposition entails for the mission of African philosophy and the vocation of the African philosopher.

If Wiredu is right that "the test of a contemporary African philosopher's conception of African philosophy is whether it enables him to engage fruitfully in the activity of modern philosophising with an African conscience" (1980, x), the conception of African philosophy and the image of the African philosopher that emerges from Ikuenobe's deposition fails that test.

NOTES

1. Or, at least, elsewhere Kwasi Wiredu (2007) seems to interpret the injunction in terms of authenticity as I have done here.

2. This is not at all to imply that Ikuenobe concretely embodies the image of the philosopher I go on to criticize. On the contrary, his work embodies for the most part the sort of critical epistemic attitude I advocate. I have simply found his deposition useful for my present aims.

3. Although not defending the substance of the objection, and in a somewhat different debate, Ward Jones captures the point with the sort of clarity that allows for easy adaption here. "Our methodology," he writes, "is inherently one that requires discord, disagreement, and discussion in order to progress whereas taking sides is inconsistent with this method" (2006, 4).

4. See Horsthemke and Enslin, 2009 as well as Carol Pearce, 1992.

5. Let me quickly note that Jones sees "this tension [as] illusory. Just because a problem is of particular concern to a community does not mean that the problem will be a problem only about the members of that community" (2006, 7–8).

6. It is not important for my purposes to demonstrate that Ikuenobe subscribes to the model I shall be reading off the deposition or that he personally holds the views I shall be aligning with that model; instead, it would suffice if it was obvious that that model could be plausibly deduced from the deposition, whether or not Ikuenobe intends it to be so.

7. This should not preclude the possibility that some ideas may be unique in the sense assumed in the objection. And such occasions may be rare indeed—my point is that we need not define uniqueness in this context in terms of this standard.

8. I am grateful to an anonymous reviewer for impressing upon me that the image of the philosopher suggested throughout the discussion is, without mistake a male philosopher, notwithstanding the grammatical inclusion of female philosophers. The point is acknowledged, although that implication is not at all intended. Even so, one has to acknowledge the ways in which female participation in African philosophy and the substantive inclusion of female authors in philosophical conversations and publications in Africa continue to represent the zero-points of the discipline. So, sadly, the lack of substantive inclusion of female philosophers here is a symptom of a deeper problem in the discipline.

9. It is worth reiterating that I am not at all claiming that Ikuenobe holds this view; instead, I am claiming that this is an (perhaps incidental) outcome of what he explicitly says in the deposition I am examining.

10. In particular, Appiah had two of Wole Soyinka's works in mind—he analyzes Soyinka's "Myth, Literature and the African World" and "Death and the King's Horsemen."

REFERENCES

Appiah, Kwame Anthony. 1992. *In My Father's House: Africa in the Philosophy of Culture*. Oxford: Oxford University Press.

Bodunrin, Peter. 1981. "The Question of African Philosophy." *Philosophy* 56 (216): 161–79.

Horsthemke, Kai and Enslin, Penny. 2009. "African Philosophy of Education: The Price of Unchallengeability." *Studies in Philosophy and Education* 28 (3): 209–22.

Ikuenobe, Polycarp. 2006. *Philosophical Perspectives on Communalism and Morality in African Traditions*. Lanham, MD: Lexington Books.

Jones, Ward. 2006. "Philosophers, Their Context, and Their Responsibilities." *Metaphilosophy* 37 (5): 1–23.

Matolino, Bernard. 2015. "Universalism and African Philosophy." *South African Journal of Philosophy* 34 (4): 433–40.

Metz, Thaddeus. 2009. "The Final Ends of Higher Education in Light of an African Moral Theory." *Journal of Philosophy of Education* 43 (2): 179–201.

Nwakaeze, Peter. 1987. "A Critique of Olufemi Taiwo's Criticism of 'Legal Positivism and African Legal Tradition.'" *International Philosophical Quarterly* 27 (1): 101–5.
Pearce, Carol. 1992. "African Philosophy and the Sociological Thesis." *Philosophy of the Social Sciences* 22 (4): 440–60.
Soyinka, Wole. 1975. *Death and the King's Horsemen*. London: Methuen.
Soyinka, Wole. 1976. *Myth, Literature and the African World*. Cambridge: Cambridge University Press.
Wiredu, Kwasi. 1980. *Philosophy and an African Culture*. Cambridge: Cambridge University Press.
Wiredu, Kwasi. 1998. "Toward Decolonizing African Philosophy and Religion." *African Studies Quarterly* 1 (4): 17–46.
Wiredu, Kwasi. 2002. "Conceptual Decolonization as an Imperative in Contemporary African Philosophy: Some Personal Reflections." *Rue Descartes* 36 (2): 53–64.
Wiredu, Kwasi. 2007. "Philosophy and Authenticity." *Shibboleths: A Journal of Comparative Theory* 1 (2): 72–80.

Chapter 2

African Literature as a Handmaid of African Philosophy

Chielozona Eze

INTRODUCTION

In his *Poetics*, Aristotle differentiates between history and poetry in relation to truth. Poetry is more philosophical and more serious than history: in fact it speaks more about universals whereas history speaks of particulars. It is in its ability to speak more of universals that poetry is closer to philosophy, which occupies the highest place in the search for truth. We understand truth in this sense to be about the human condition; philosophy is the search for understanding of ways of being human.

Earlier efforts to establish the field of African philosophy had concerned itself with various issues, including the question of whether Africa has a philosophy and, if she does, what does it mean? What is its relation to ethnology, religion, anthropology, and Western philosophy? African philosophy had also occupied itself with contesting the Western negative reading of Africa. There are still efforts, as evidenced in conferences and symposia, to determine the nature and scope of African philosophy.

Whereas the field of African philosophy is still evolving, African literature has long established itself, and it comprises works that explore the human condition in Africa. I contend that African literature has provided enough raw materials for any type of critical thinking that philosophy requires. Literature has delivered the human condition to the doorsteps of Africans; all that is required is to interpret it. In undertaking an interpretive encounter with the reality provided by the African narrative, philosophy raises questions of ethical and existential relevance to Africa. This chapter does precisely that; it undertakes a philosophical reading of *Things Fall Apart*, one of the foundational texts in African literature, and challenges the moral premises of African postcolonial reading of the world. In short, I seek to do two things:

(1) I examine the contexts of the foundations of African postcolonial moral attitude. (2) I propose a return to ethics, specifically to a renewed attention to the self as an embodied being in the African world. Echoing Emmanuel Levinas, I propose that ethics, rather than ontology, is the first philosophy in Africa. To that effect, the guiding questions in the second part of my inquiry are those that examine what Africans are to one another, what the African body is to another African, and to the degree to which the pain that a body experiences in Africa commands another African's attention.

RAISING ORDINARY QUESTIONS

In a 2010 interview with his German film producer, popular Cameroonian filmmaker Jean Pierre Bekolo stated that "the whites must come back to Africa" to take charge of affairs (Bekolo 2010). Perhaps his comment was meant as a provocation or a joke. Regardless of Bekolo's intention, the utterance was painfully demeaning to Africa, especially given the humiliating truth of the sociopolitical dysfunction in many African countries and the fact that in most of them, this dysfunction is not always related, at least directly, to the experience of colonialism. Much of it stems from how the leaders relate to the people on whose behalf they might have fought the colonial masters.

The history of postcolonial African politics is replete with erstwhile colonial powers violently intervening in the affairs of the former colonies, contributing in no small measure to the instability in those spaces. Many African states have, however, produced dictators, some of whom have committed acts of violence on the populace that rival, if not surpass, those of the colonial rulers in some countries. For example, Mobutu Sese Seko took over power in Zaire five years after Belgian forces helped overthrow Patrice Lumumba in 1960. He ruled the Democratic Republic of the Congo from 1965 to 1997, investing his political capital in the notion of *authenticité*, an ideology thought to be based on an authentic African experience. In the end, his ideology designed to make politics palpable was nothing more than a ruse for endowing his people with an abstract relation to reality and one another. Most African heads of state have at least one thing in common: their abstract relation to their people. Their politics are bereft of ethical consideration, yet they deploy vocal anti-imperialist, decolonization mantras as a smokescreen for their failure to relate to their people in meaningful ways. Bekolo's ill-advised utterance, however, urges us to reconsider the reality of African lives and various theoretical responses to them, and this prompts the following questions: Is there any relation between the narratives that Africans have about themselves and the degree to which they respond to their world? Can narratives affect how people relate to one another?

There is an urgent need to examine the structure of African narratives that have shaped African attitudes to the world. What kind of narrative do Africans tell themselves and about themselves? Do those narratives help Africans to examine their lives?

LITERATURE AND MORAL CONSCIOUSNESS

Ethics, broadly defined, is a science of morality (Attfield 1996). Morality, in turn, deals with what is right or wrong, permissible or forbidden. Whereas morality might be personal, specific to a people as is culture, ethics is always about the quality of one's relations with others and to oneself and society. Ethics as a relationship is intrinsically a recognition of the other. I use morality and ethics interchangeably to denote both the good life and quality of our relationship to others and moral consciousness.

What, if any, is the relationship between literature and moral consciousness? The degree to which literature induces moral consciousness in an individual is difficult to measure. We know though that literature has affected people's view of the world so much so that the incipient thoughts about human rights are traced back to it. As Lynn Hunt (2008, 34) states, the eighteenth-century-European novels provoked a "torrent of emotions" in their readers because of the way they shed light on the pains of their protagonists. Such writers as Jean-Jacques Rousseau (*Julie or the New Héloïse*) and Richardson (*Pamela* and *Clarissa*) contributed to the thoughts captured in the proclamation of "the rights of man," the cornerstone of the ideas of the French Revolution (1789–1799). The writers put people's identification with the pain of others in easily graspable narrative formats. The declaration of the rights of man in 1789, Hunt argues, presaged the Universal Declaration of Human Rights. The idea is that these novels, among others, broadened consciousness about human rights and dignity.

Literature is about narratives; it is about the stories we tell ourselves. In telling stories, we present not just characters but also worldviews; in reading or listening to stories, we confront others (in the form of characters) and sets of judgment. In texts, readers are asked to imagine the lives of people (characters) they will never meet. This meeting becomes truly ethical when relation is initiated in the form of identification with characters, worldviews, or events, or rejection of the same. Either way, judgment is involved. Every judgment implies responsibility, either acceptance or rejection of what is presented to one. Ethics, as transmitted in literature, as Adam Newton (1995, 12) argues, "signifies recursive, contingent, and interactive drama of encounter and recognition, the sort which prose fiction both crystallizes and recirculates in acts of interpretive engagement." The phrases "drama of encounter and recognition" and "interpretive engagement" capture the essence of literature as philosophy, for it is rooted in the critical examination of the relation of one character to another, or of readers and the world that is presented to them.

There are certain elements in Aristotle's definition of tragedy to which every understanding of narrative as ethics returns directly or indirectly: an "imitation of an action" that "arouses pity and fear" and thus affects a "*katharsis* of such emotions" (Aristotle 1996, 6). Aristotle speaks of how the narrative of the lives of others moves us toward them in the form of empathy, or at least, to examine our moral attitude to them. As Lynne Tirrell (1990, 117) argues, stories help us to "develop a sense of self, a sense of self in relation to others, and the capacity to justify one's decisions. Being a moral agent, after all, involves understanding or at least attempting to understand people." This is perhaps as much as we can expect of literature. Moral agency implies that one is capable of elementary judgment of good and bad. In engaging the world presented to us in a text, we can ask whether the characters could take responsibility for his or her action, which implies the ability to distinguish oneself from others. We also encounter a view of the world and weigh it on the moral scale we know. We ask: Is this person acting in a morally acceptable way? What could he or she have done? What view of the world does the writer present? Is the condition presented in the narrative acceptable or not? In other words, literature affects moral consciousness only indirectly by initiating a thought-process or forms of identification with a world. At the least, it prepares us to ask serious questions in relation to the human condition, which is precisely what philosophy is about.

THINGS FALL APART AND AFRICAN POSTCOLONIAL MORAL VALUATIONS

The goal of this section is to trace the origin and the structure of postcolonial moral valuations in Africa. I locate it in *Things Fall Apart* (1958) considered to be one of the foundational African novels. Indeed, as Simon Gikandi (2001, 3-8) argues, no other African thinker/writer of Achebe's time, shaped postcolonial African culture as discoursed in academia as profoundly as Achebe did. I argue that *Things Fall Apart* initiated the moral attitude rooted in victimhood that is falsely interpreted as resistance. This attitude sadly prevents introspection and intersubjective relationships that are requisite for moral growth. *Things Fall Apart* gave Africa its most eloquent unifying narrative that has rooted African culture and identity in resistance to the West. Most responses to it have been in glowing admiration of its role in redeeming and shaping the African culture (Lindfors 1978). Few have been critical of it for what it neglected to do (Stratton 1994).

Okonkwo is a respected leader in Umuofia; he gained reputation by throwing in a wrestling match the other tribe's hero and by being a hardworking farmer. His people see in him a symbol of resistance and prowess, and when the British colonialists and missionaries invade his people, he takes it upon himself to champion a strong resistance to the invaders. He commits suicide when he realizes that his clan is not willing to join him in his crusade against the colonial invaders. Okonkwo is a hero who embodies his people's pain and valor in the face of the white man's oppression and is, therefore, a figure of resistance to the white man. Okonkwo's death is touching and revealing, just as some aspects of his life are inspiring. His suicide is ultimately thought to confer on him the honor of tragic heroism. The last incident in his life, coupled with his suicide, is designed to heighten the moral impact of the narrative. In the last part of chapter twenty-four, the men of Umuofia have assembled in a marketplace to deliberate on whether to go to war against the white man. Okonkwo is eager to go to war. He spots Egonwanne, a gifted orator whom he fears will speak against going to war. To him, Egonwanne is a coward. The deliberations have hardly begun when five court messengers arrive. They are the white man's Igbo emissaries. Okonkwo confronts the head messenger, who then lets him know that "The white man whose power you know too well has ordered this meeting to stop" (144). Okonkwo draws his machete and cuts off the man's head. The next moment is one of the most consequential in the lives of the Umuofia people regarding their common enemy.

The men of Umuofia do not follow Okonkwo's example. Instead, they are shocked by his actions. Some of them ask, "Why did he do it?" (144–45). He does not express his feelings, but from his demeanor and actions, it is clear that he is disappointed in his people. He knows that they will not go to war against the white man because they let the other four men escape. He walks into a bush and hangs himself. The district commissioner, Obierika, and other Umuofia men are at the scene of the suicide. After gazing sadly at the body of his friend hanging from a tree, Obierika turns to the white man and says, "That man was one of the greatest men in Umuofia. *You drove him to kill himself*" (149, emphasis added).

I have provided this extensive summary to properly establish the context for my philosophical discussions as an example of how African philosophy could use African literature as a material for inquiry about the African condition. Okonkwo's death dramatizes the devastation of the white man's intervention in the life of Umuofia. He is to be admired for his unwillingness to accept humiliation at the hands of strangers, but there is more to his story than the nobility of resistance. To fully appreciate the philosophical reaches of the narrative as a signifier of Africa's efforts to resist colonial invasion, we must ask some questions about the above scenes:

A. Was Okonkwo right in being disappointed in his people?
B. Were the men of Umuofia cowards in not following Okonkwo's example?
C. Did the district commissioner really drive Okonkwo to kill himself?

Okonkwo comes to the meeting of the men of Umuofia with his decision already made. He is not ready to entertain discussions about his people's appropriate course of action, and this implies his disregard for the other men, who are also unready to take the invasion of their community passively. We do not know what Egonwanne would have said, but hearing him out would have been in line with the community's avowed democratic spirit. We also know that the people of Umuofia have not forgotten the fate of Abame village. When a white man appeared in Abame on a bicycle, the people killed the man and tied his bicycle to their sacred tree. Days later, a group of white men discovered the bicycle and knew the fate of their comrade; they destroyed the Abame market and killed everybody in the village. Okonkwo was in exile in his mother's village when this incident took place, but Obierika made sure the news got to him (99), meaning that even Okonkwo should be at least dimly aware of what might happen to Umuofia should they opt for war against an enemy they do not yet understand. Perhaps the next speaker would have reminded Umuofia of Abame. He could have suggested means of dealing with the white man other than all-out war. Why, then, did Okonkwo think that war was the only courageous choice? Was killing a court messenger, who happened not to be the white man, proof of courage? To be sure, Okonkwo's anger at the white man is justified—he has sufficient reasons for this, including him being humiliated along with the other five village leaders. But his rage is impotent and ultimately self-defeating, as his suicide suggests. Did he realize too late that he never understood his people and their invaders? Did his people understand him? Who was Okonkwo to his people?

I now turn to the second question posed above: *Were the men of Umuofia cowards in not following Okonkwo's example?* This question is better answered with another. Would following his example have supported the goal of their meeting, which was deliberation? This returns the spotlight on Okonkwo. The fact that the Umuofia people convene a meeting means that they are seeking a common line of action, or perhaps no action at all. The issue is not whether Okonkwo is right to confront the invaders; it is whether going at it alone and at that time is appropriate and wise. Why would he preempt, or go against, his people's emerging template? What was he trying to prove by taking matters into his own hands? What does his action tell us about him, the anti-colonial hero and leader of his oppressed people? To answer these questions, we must look into his life. The goal is not to appraise him as a good or bad man; it is to understand the structure of his psyche, to analyze what makes him act the way he does, and to understand the consequences of his actions on his community and on the lives of those who depend on him. Of relevance in this regard is the postmortem judgment that Obierika makes of Okonkwo's death, a judgment that raises Okonkwo's cultural value. So, then, we have two important characters, Okonkwo and Obierika, who are easily the two most recognizable features of the community's encounter with the West.

Okonkwo's life is tragic, owing to its uncompromising one-dimensionality and lack of depth. The narrator emphasizes that he is not a cruel man, "but his whole life was dominated by fear, the fear of failure and weakness.... It was the fear of himself, lest he should be found to resemble his father" (9–10) Unoka, who had not been a great man according to his people's measure of greatness—he was not a strong man or a successful farmer, and so was thought to be a weakling. Because Okonkwo does not want anything to do with failure, he denies his father, whom he sees as a symbol of failure. Ruled by fear, Okonkwo is manifestly unable to consider alternatives to any line of action he has chosen. The fear of being seen as weak prevents him from engaging in dialogue and therefore investing productively in the life of the mind. He misses opportunities to turn moments of weakness into strengths.

Okonkwo presents us with a classic example of a personality set on indignation that is falsely interpreted as resistance to oppression or evil. His resistance is defined by what it is against rather than what it is for; ironically, this kind of resistance binds rather than liberates humans from conditions of their oppression, as Judith Butler (1997) argues. He is against his father's frailties but fails to appreciate any of his father's virtues such as care and love of life, even of others. Indeed, by denying his past, he makes self-knowledge impossible. However, all this does not diminish him as one who embodies one of the qualities that his people admire most: self-reliance. He is a self-made man, and in line with his people's notion of achievement and honor, he becomes one of the lords of the clan. Yet, he has little patience with other men who are poorer or weaker. Indeed, everyone is shocked by his "brusqueness in dealing with less successful men" (19). He calls such men women. The narrator is careful to point out that "Okonkwo knew how to kill a man's spirit" (27). Even his household is not spared his brashness. He beats his wives at the slightest provocation because he considers himself a man's man and thus beyond reproach.

Okonkwo is arrogant, and he is a man of physical prowess, a warrior, and an athlete; sadly, his people honor this type of heroism and respect him as one who embodies their strength and superiority to other clans. He, therefore, begins to conflate the need to prove his worth with his people's fears and aspirations. In other words, he reduces his people to the level of his fantasies, and thereby develops a disregard for consensus and community spirit. He evolves an abstract ideological relation to his people, loving group identity more than the individual human beings around him. That group identity, to be sure, is an abstraction. To Okonkwo, that abstraction, or essence, is superior to a community of his people gathered in flesh and blood to deliberate a common approach to their enemy. Thus, in Okonkwo we see the first pitfall of postcolonial African attitude given that he has been identified as a trope of resistance to the white man. But this resistance induces him to develop an abstract relationship to his people.

Okonkwo's privileging of abstraction over real humans has consequences in the lives of those humans, the first of whom are members of his family. His household is held together only by norms and a conception of affinity rooted in blood, not by any form of intersubjective relationship. There is hardly a moment of warmth that can be said to bind father and children. This absence of human warmth has its greatest alienating effect on Nwoye, his son, a person who, according to tradition, should inherit his estates. We understand the contours of the abstract bond between Okonkwo and his family, or the lack of unity between them after it becomes clear to Nwoye that Okonkwo had his hands in the killing of Ikemefuna. Nwoye feels a profound distancing from his father, just as he had once felt from his culture when walking by the forest in which twins are thrown away (43–44). Nwoye's distancing from his father comes full circle when the missionaries settle in Umuofia, and he joins their ranks. When Obierika confronts him about that, Nwoye confirms that he is one of them. The elder asks him about his father, and Nwoye answers pointedly, "I don't know. He is not my father" (103). Sadly, Nwoye completes the circle of ancestral negation that Okonkwo began. The most obvious consequence of these denials is that Okonkwo's family never stood together, and Okonkwo himself is the reason. He fails to fulfill his role in his family tree, which is to be the nodal point between the preceding and succeeding generations. The irony of his inability to keep his family together is difficult to ignore. If he cannot keep his family and lineage from disintegrating, how, then, can he keep Umuofia from the same fate? But he seems ill-equipped to recognize this cognitive dissonance. The explanation for this is simple. He is so obsessed with the notion of resisting the enemy, imagined or real, that he fails to recognize friends and to relate to reality and people in a moral way. So, then, we have a man who exists to resist, but who does not understand what he is resisting. This condition enables the production of magical thinking part of which is the belief that he can defeat the enemy he does not know. The only thing he has working for him is his belief in his virtue derived from his position as an injured person.

One of the sad things about Okonkwo's death is that his son will not miss him, just as Okonkwo did not miss his father. There is, then, a pattern of breaks in tradition and memory transmission. We have three generations (Unoka, Okonkwo, and Nwoye) who have nothing in common: no shared memory, no warmth, and no stories. The lineage, it seems, was not designed to survive as a cultural continuum, and Okonkwo is very much to blame. The sad, troubling truth is that the district officer and the missionaries have little to do with the system that allowed for the absence of warmth and communication between generations. This is either a truth that Obierika was not equipped to comprehend or one that he chose to ignore. I think it is the latter because of the emotive satisfaction such denial provided him, but it would not have diminished him, the wise thinker, to admit to this and other fundamental weaknesses of his culture. Rather, it would have shown his culture's readiness to live more fully within the context of modernity ushered in by the violent encounter with the West.

This disconnect between facts and the judgment that has a tangential bearing on them is, indeed, the beginning of African schizophrenia in moral discourse, a discourse that seeks to maintain the fact of European guilt and the illusion of African innocence, one that proposes to change African reality by changing other people's perception of it. The discourse arising from this moral premise in Africa is necessarily other-oriented. It is to litigate and to prove the other wrong, not to examine Africa's condition critically.

I have established the following: (a) Okonkwo is stuck in the emotional stage of pure reaction, and because of that, his vision is shortsighted, reduced to a permanent readiness to put out the raging fire of the moment. (b) Okonkwo has no internal, independent motivation to do things except when they are associated with his abstract relation to his society, and in most cases, define his people in contrast to an enemy. (c) Okonkwo's perception of the world is based on the implicit and contrastive presence of the other. (d) Okonkwo's arrogance issues from his false sense of moral certainty, which prevents him from taking responsibility for failures and weaknesses. (e) Okonkwo abhors debate and consensus because he cannot engage in what Jürgen Habermas (2001, 116–94) calls communicative action, which is cooperative action undertaken by individuals based upon common deliberation. (f) Okonkwo has no empathy. These characteristics constitute the first part of the postcolonial African moral imagination. The other part is derived from Obierika's judgment of his world. To comprehend this second part, I now return to the last of the three questions I raised earlier: *Did the district officer really drive Okonkwo to kill himself?* Was Obierika right in making this judgment?

Obierika, who is said to be a wise man, stands as the moral and intellectual spokesman of his people. His accusation of the district officer at the scene of Okonkwo's death recalls another judgment about the white people earlier in the narrative, one which I would like to address now. When Obierika visits Okonkwo in his place of exile, Obierika tells him how Umuofia has changed in the seven years of his absence, how the white man has established missions, and how the people of Umuofia are abandoning their old ways of life. The saddest news is that Nwoye has joined the missionaries. Later in their discussion, Obierika observes that the white man has "put a knife on the things that held us together and we have fallen apart" (124). What exactly are the things that held the Umuofia people together?

The Umuofia is a group of people *held together* by a bond of ancestry and norms anchored in feudal structures and religious, even magical, notions of the world. Part of their magical conception of the world produced disastrous consequences in the lives of the people: twins are considered abnormal and thrown into the bush to die; many people who are thought to belong to certain gods are considered inferior by society, deemed outcasts, and barred from active participation in the sociopolitical life of that society (112–13). Because of this form of segregation, there were visible and invisible cracks in society. Many outcasts quickly became part of the new religion, abandoning the old order that has no place for them. Given that certain sectors of the Umuofia society felt disfranchised, can one really argue that the people of Umuofia stood together as a community? Of course, the answer depends on the perspective from which one considers the question. To the privileged members of that society, everything ran just fine; to the less privileged, those who suffered the consequence of their society's rigid feudal ideology, it is a different story. Might the white man have merely provided an outline for a rebellion that was going to happen anyway? Given this constellation, Obierika is not morally justified and intellectually honest in accusing the white man of having put a knife on the thing that held Umuofia together. On the contrary, he seems to be speaking for the privileged class and gender, not for the whole society. How might one of the outcasts, or women whose twins were taken from them, respond to the notion that the white man brought about the falling apart of their society? To ignore the concerns of these groups is to make the mistake of relating to society in the abstract. From their perspective, it appears that the white man could not have come at a more auspicious time. For them, the white man's arrival is the dawn of modernity, a gesture of liberation they cannot miss. Consequently, they form a new society to protect their lives and live with dignity.

The above consideration returns our focus to Obierika, the mind of Umuofia. If Okonkwo had not had a hand in his death, and not only literally, then Obierika's judgment would be apt, but his death seems to be a logical consequence of a life controlled primarily by impulses. I am, of course, not holding a brief for the white man. He is to blame (at least indirectly) for the death of Okonkwo, but so are Okonkwo, Obierika, and Umuofia. Yet Obierika chooses to ignore these other considerations and his own role in the ensuing dysfunction. The judgment—"You drove him to kill himself" (149)—indeed, grants the district officer more power than he actually possesses, but that is not without calculation. Obierika engages in a moral trade-off whereby he grants the white man immeasurable capacity to do evil while he retains the parallel, if implicit, capacity for goodness as the victim. This morally petty game is the template for contemporary postcolonial African thinking, one that Denis Ekpo (1996, 3) has referred to as "ineffectual moral posturing," by which he means the African person's need to prove the colonial masters as evil and himself as the opposite. Even if we admire Okonkwo's instinct for self-protection in the face of invaders, we must hold Obierika to task for his cowardly moral positioning, for his eagerness to blame others for the weaknesses of his world, and, perhaps, for not applying his vaunted superior mind and wisdom on his bellicose younger friend.

Whereas Okonkwo is figurative of Africa's impotent rage, Obierika exemplifies a sneaky desire to exact a moral vengeance. The narrator characterizes Obierika as "A man who thought about things" (125), that is, a wise man, one with insight. Who, then, does this insight serve, those who benefit from the status quo, or the whole society? According to Theodor Adorno (1998, 282), "a critic is one who is able to bring one's judgment according to one's own insight." We understand his notion of the critic as one who discerns. The goal of a discerner and critique, in general, is to challenge a system that makes the flourishing of life impossible. Adorno explains, "Whoever criticizes violates the taboo of unity, which tends toward totalitarian organization" (283). Sadly, neither Okonkwo nor Obierika wants to violate the taboo of Umuofia's totalitarian organization. Neither of them allows for self-reflection and self-criticism, which are essential for moral maturity. Neither of them seems to have regarded the relation to the less privileged members of society as relevant to the moral health and survival of their society. They are rather more concerned with an abstract enemy, and that shapes their imagination and moral framework.

If we take Okonkwo and his family as a synecdoche of the people of Umuofia and admit that his behavior caused a permanent rift in his own family, we come closer to the notion that the people of Umuofia fell apart not only because of the white man's meddling with the system, but indeed, primarily because they failed to hold their community together in the first place.[1] Lack of care for the oppressed and the underprivileged is the cause of things falling apart, or rather, the cause of things never standing together. The white man might have caused the disintegration of the social structures from without, but the disintegration from within was already inherent in the moral frameworks of their society. Regardless of what the white man might have done to them, their core problem remains the modality of their relation to one another, and this can be boiled down to the basic principle of relational ethics.

It is, therefore, true that Achebe shaped the postcolonial African culture. He also established a pattern of dichotomous moral valuations which functions under a simple syllogism, each of whose premises contains an operative concept that viscerally captures at least one central aspect of Africa's painful encounter with the West.

1. *The first premise*: the evil nature of the West. It suffices to mention anything that posits the historical enemy. That includes whiteness, white people, colonial encounter, eurocentrism, capitalism, imperialism, and so forth. It is the "You" in Obierika's address to the district officer.
2. *The second premise*: oppressed, innocent Africans. Here, it suffices to allude to any aspect of African life that has been denigrated by the West, such as culture, aesthetics, religion, or personhood. Sometimes, expressions such as black pain, soul wound, and black experience do that job. The premise contains the "him" in Obierika's judgment.
3. *The conclusion*: authentic Africa. Anything thought to be truly African is welcome—the past, heritage, and so forth. The justification for that worldview has already been taken care of by history, articulated in the first and second premises.

In the African postcolonial imagination, establishing the binary of oppressor/oppressed is crucial, and its goal is to activate guilt, which is more rhetorical than socially or morally functional. It is to win an argument that is of purely emotional value. Besides the immediate emotional jolt, it also fulfills an ideological function: to protect the status quo; this arises when the truth of the African condition must be sought in the conclusion. Sadly, the African imagination or critical consciousness is not primed to examine the human condition in Africa; it is obsessed with the Okonkwo and Obierike-like task of challenging the white man and proving him wrong.

CONCLUSION: RECOGNIZING THE AFRICAN BODY

In the introduction, I stated that I propose ethics, rather than ontology, as the first philosophy in Africa. I go back to one of the determinant scenes in *Things Fall Apart*, specifically to the killing of Ikemefuna, the boy who was raised in Okonkwo's household and who had begun to call Okonkwo father. Ironically, he dies at the hands of the man he has literally adopted as a father. What exactly was Ikemefuna's body to the Umuofia people in general and Okonkwo in particular? Understanding the moral and existential implications of the death of Ikemefuna is at the crux of my inquiry here and, it indeed represents what African philosophy should be about.

To be sure, the Oracle had decreed that Ikemefuna should be killed. So the people were merely obeying the dictates of an abstract force that can be subsumed within tradition. But obeying tradition does not make the killing justifiable; at least it does not exonerate the people from exhibiting a certain degree of co-feeling toward the boy. Perhaps that co-feeling could have helped them to arrive at a more complex attitude to the world than blind obedience to tradition. Philosophy, unlike religion, interrogates oracles.

At any rate, it is not in my interest to judge the people who blindly obeyed their tradition; I am more interested in establishing the absence of complexity in the people's moral attitude. They perceived and judged the world in simplistic, Manichean paradigms. How then does a culture or society evolve from a naïve, if not primitive, moral relationship to a more complex, universal form? It is, I think, by simply seeing humans for what they are: embodied beings and relating to them accordingly, and philosophy can help us achieve that. The Umuofia people did not see one another through that prism. By embodied being, I mean a being the meaning of whose life is not lost in some abstraction, a being whose essence is nowhere other than where he or she stands. It is to be understood in Martin Heidegger's existentialist sense of *Dasein*, being there, being in the world. As Heidegger states (1996, 67), "when we designate this entity [human] with the term 'Dasein,' we are expressing not its 'what' [as if it were a table, house or tree] but its Being." Dasein, or being in the world as a human is different from being in the world as a stone, a plant, or a lower animal. It is true that humans occupy space in the way that other existing things do, but only they can interact with other things in ways that fundamentally change those things and humans as well.

It is to be understood from Heidegger's analysis that Dasein is embodied; it is not a bare ego or a purely psychological subject. The body is a fact of its being. Understood in its most basic form, Dasein is being ourselves, and this form of being is, according to Heidegger, characterized by concern. We are not just located in a place; we are tied to that place by our interactions. Concern goes beyond mere instrumental understanding of it; it is more about care that expresses itself in *being with*. Being in the world, therefore, is being with others and relating to them, not in terms of instrumentality, but in terms of their being an end in themselves—not a means to an end. The implication here is that to deny the other, your Co-Dasein care is to reduce him or her to a thing, *a seinde*.

I borrow this Heideggerian existentialist term, being-with, to characterize what I meant when I stated that ethics should be the first philosophy for Africa. Every philosophy in Africa must begin from the standpoint of recognizing the body, this body in front of me, this body that feels pain just as mine does. This simple exercise is the root of moral consciousness. A person means something only to the degree of his or her relation to other persons. To be is to be in relation, and where relation falls apart, so does being.

Where then does African philosophy go from here? What must it undertake to become useful to Africans? To me, it must ignore the putative gaze of the West. It must not repeat the morally fatal Okonkwo-mistake of centering its vision of the world on the humiliation suffered at the hands of the white man. Only then can it grant the Ikemefunas and the outcasts of their world their due moral attention. Doing philosophy in Africa in this way is surely going to be messy, for it would require resisting the seduction to litigate the past and Western relation to Africa. Nelson Mandela has shown African philosophy that the way forward is to engage Africa the way it is (Eze 2018, 2014). To truly engage in this demanding task, African philosophers must desist from explaining Africa. Rather, it must analyze. Explaining Africa presupposes an audience whose approval African thinkers eagerly await.

NOTE

1. To be sure, that society could have been defeated were there to be a war between it and the colonial masters thanks to the latter's superior firepower.

REFERENCES

Achebe, Chinua. 1958. *Things Fall Apart*. Portsmouth, NH: Heinemann Publishers.
Adorno, Theodor. 1998. *Critical Models: Intervention and Catchwords*. New York: Columbia University Press.
Aristotle. 1996. *Poetics*. Trans. Malcolm Heath. London: Penguin Books.
Attfield, Robert and Susanne Gibson. 1996. "Ethics." In *A Dictionary of Cultural and Critical Theory*, edited by Michael Payne, 178–82. Oxford, UK: Blackwell Publishers.
Butler, Judith. 1997. *The Psychic Life of Power: Theories in Subjection*. Stanford, CA: Stanford University Press.
Ekpo, Denis. 1996. "How Africa Misunderstood the West: The Failure of Anti-West Radicalism and Postmodernity." *Third Text* 35: 3–13.
Eze, Chielozona. 2014. "Rethinking African Culture and Identity: The Afropolitan Model." *Journal of African Cultural Studies* 26 (2): 234–47.
Eze, Chielozona. 2018. *Race, Decolonization, and Global Citizenship in South Africa*. Rochester, New York: The University of Rochester Press.
Gikandi, Simon. 2001. "Chinua Achebe and the Invention of African Culture." *Research in African Literature* 32 (3): 3–8.
Habermas, Jurgen. 2001. *Moral Consciousness and Communicative Action*. Cambridge, MA: The MIT Press.
Heidegger, Martin. 1996. *Being and Time*. Translated by Joan Stambaugh. New York: State University of New York Press.

Hunt, Lynn. 2008. *Inventing Human Rights: A History*. New York: W. W. Norton & Company.
Innes, C. L. and Bernth Lindfors, eds. 1978. *Critical Perspectives on Chinua Achebe*. Washington: Three Continents Press.
Newton, Adam Zachary. 1995. *Narrative Ethics*. Cambridge, MA: Harvard University Press.
Stratton, Florence. 1994. *Contemporary African Literature and the Politics of Gender*. New York: Routledge.
Tirell, Lynne. 1990. "Storytelling and Moral Agency." *The Journal of Aesthetics and Art Criticism* 48 (2): 115–26.

Chapter 3

Conflict and Compromise in Three Novels of the Eastern Cape

George Hull

VALUE CONFLICT IN LITERATURE AND PHILOSOPHY

The question of how one ought to act in response to conflicting legitimate moral values or principles is a subject of theory and debate in philosophical ethics. But it is also a practical question which arises in the lives of people who experience such conflicts. South Africa has for centuries been a site of pronounced political and cultural conflict: adherents of different cultural and religious outlooks have existed alongside one another, competing for power, and—beginning in the seventeenth century, but especially in the nineteenth and twentieth centuries—groups of European settlers have sought to urge, and then impose, their cultural outlooks on indigenous Africans, sometimes using brutal force. It is, therefore, not surprising that the dilemmas arising from conflicting cultural and moral values have featured prominently in much South African fiction writing. In this chapter I examine three novels set in the Eastern Cape region of South Africa: S. E. K. Mqhayi's *The Case of the Twins* (*Ityala Lamawele*), A. C. Jordan's *The Wrath of the Ancestors* (*Ingqumbo Yeminyanya*), and J. M. Coetzee's *Disgrace*.[1] *Twins*, published in 1914, and *Wrath*, published in 1940, were written in isiXhosa; *Disgrace*, published in 1999, was written in English.[2] These novels form part of a multilingual canon of literary works united by their attention to the distinctive types of cultural and value conflict which have arisen in the South African context. Since, as I will discuss, the most adequate response to some types of value conflict may well be a *creative* act, value conflict is an area where philosophical theory and creative fiction can helpfully inform one another.

Mqhayi, Jordan and Coetzee lived through times of profound societal change, and meditated upon the nature of such change in their art. As *Twins* and *Wrath* were being written, the white South Africans (both Brit and Boer) were consolidating their legal supremacy and institutional control over black South Africans (especially those designated "Natives" or "Bantus") throughout the Union of South Africa. By contrast, in the decade prior to *Disgrace*'s appearance, legal *apartheid* was dismantled, Nelson Mandela's African National Congress won a general election, and a new political order in the Republic of South Africa, increasingly dominated by the previously excluded black African majority, was beginning to take shape. When David Lurie's daughter suggests he give her black neighbor, and soon-to-be landlord, Petrus a hand on his farm, Coetzee's protagonist replies: "Give Petrus a hand. I like that. I like the historical piquancy. Will he pay me a wage for my labour, do you think?" (*Disgrace*, 77). Legislation such as the 1913 Natives Land Act had ensured that for most of the twentieth century black people generally had to work as farmhands for white farmers, rather than the other way around (Thompson 2000, 163–65).

Yet the principal focus of all three novels is not *political*, but *cultural* change. In his foreword to *Twins*, Mqhayi draws a connection between these two aspects of social change. "The language and culture of the Xhosas," he writes, "is gradually disappearing because of the Word and the enlightenment that have come among us—which things have come with the nations of the West, the sons of Gog and Magog" (5). Though he understood and cherished them more deeply than most Xhosa people of his generation, Mqhayi thought it would be disastrous if European religion ("the Word") and European standards of procedure and rationality ("the enlightenment") were simply to *supplant* Xhosa traditions, values, and practices. The same can be said of Jordan, who—like Mqhayi[3]—had been both educated at a Christian mission school and thoroughly schooled in the language, beliefs, and customs of his Xhosa forebears.[4] His novel, *Wrath*, hinges on the tensions between the modernizing tendencies of the "school people" (145) and the reverence for custom of the "red-ochre"[5] people (219). These cultural tensions and the racial and ethnic tensions with which they have so often aligned—white *versus* black, Xhosa "of the soil" (208) *versus* Mfengu[6]—remain significant factors in South African life today.

In this chapter, I examine each of the novels in turn, highlighting the role which conflict of moral and cultural values plays within it. While *Twins*' engagement with cultural conflict, because allegorical, remains at a high level of generality, both *Wrath* and *Disgrace* depict vividly some of the types of seemingly intractable dilemma which conflicting values—whether between or within cultures—can generate. I seek to show that applying some conceptual tools of moral philosophy to these novels can increase a reader's appreciation of them as literary works. But value conflict is equally an area where philosophy can learn from literature: creative acts of amends-making and the generation of new valuational syntheses, which philosophical theorists of value pluralism have suggested are the only adequate responses to some types of moral dilemma, are likely to be better modeled in creative literary works than in works of philosophical analysis. I argue that the palpable sense of hope at the end of both *Wrath* and *Disgrace* is explained in each case by the reader's sense of the possibility of compromise which is not purely *instrumental*, but is a *deep*, creative and adequate response to the conflicting legitimate moral claims in play.

CO-OPERATION, NOT COMMAND: S. E. K. MQHAYI'S DECONSTRUCTION OF PRIMOGENITURE

Mqhayi's *Ityala Lamawele* is set toward the beginning of the nineteenth century, early in the reign of King Hintsa of the Gcaleka Xhosa, prior both to the coming of the amaMfengu from Mbho and to the arrival of the British in Xhosaland (Jordan 1973, 108). It follows the course of a law case between two twin brothers which, when we join the action, has been going on for three years (*Twins*, 7). Wele (meaning "twin") claims that his brother Babini (meaning "we are two") has usurped his position as the senior brother and head of the household. Wele's complaint has already been heard in the court of his local headman, Lucangwana (meaning "small door"), who found against him. *Twins* opens in the *nkundla*—the chief's court—at Hintsa's Great Place, where Wele is exercising his right under Xhosa law to appeal his headman's verdict to the senior court (Qangule 1979, 39).

In *Twins*, Mqhayi portrays the formalities and procedures of the precolonial Xhosa justice system in great and illuminating detail (Gérard 1971, 54). We know from his foreword to the first edition that he does this not only for reasons internal to the fictional plot or for antiquarian interest, but also with *didactic* intent. Mqhayi, who had given up his job as a teacher because the missionary-run schools were forcing him to teach a distorted version of South African history (Jordan 1973, 106), means, through his novel, to dispel certain illusions which his literate isiXhosa-speaking contemporaries are likely to have picked up from their mission education. In particular, he means to show that the king is not authorized to deliver arbitrary verdicts according to his whim ("as foreigners believe is the case"), that Xhosa justice is "based upon precedent," and that "the efforts, the pains, and the time" the amaXhosa take over law cases all contribute to the goal of arriving at correct verdicts consistent with relevant precedents (*Twins*, 5).

Accordingly, Mqhayi conveys in full the laborious dialogue in which two court officials interrogate Wele as to the exact nature of his grievance, asking him to repeat several times his incongruous description of Babini as "my elder brother" (*Twins*, 5). We see the court examine every witness who might have information bearing on the case, including the midwives present at Wele and Babini's birth, who use traditional *hlonipha* (avoidance language) in their testimony (Jordan 1973, 108). Significantly, Mqhayi demonstrates to his readers that a justice system without written records can be based on precedents stretching into the distant past (Nyamende 2010, 24). Hintsa has summoned the wise centenarian Khulile of Nqabara to give his opinion to the court. When he does so, Khulile, who went to circumcision school at the same time as Hintsa's great-grandfather, King Phalo, refers to a case from ten generations ago (Nyamende 2010, 24).

Due to its author's didactic intent, *Twins* sometimes has more the feel of—in Clifford Dikeni's words—"a dramatized documentary of an aspect of Xhosa life" (1992, 51) than that of a novel. Yet the didactic purpose of Mqhayi's text also bestows on its plot a depth and resonance which it otherwise would not possess. For it is not only among the *readers* of *Twins* that isiXhosa-speakers who have abandoned, even questioned the legitimacy of, their ancestral customs and values are to be found; one, at least, is also among Mqhayi's cast of fictional characters. Babini, we learn, acting as steward of the household since the death of his and Wele's father, Vuyisile (meaning "cause to rejoice"), has given "to various people" three of the cattle which are owned by the household in common (*Twins*, 44); Babini ought to have consulted with other household-members before disposing of this common property (Dikeni 1992, 95–96). What is more, at "the feast of the initiation ceremony of [his] sister, Nozici," Babini "refused completely" to give food and drink to "the people of other villages" who were attending (*Twins*, 44). Most upsetting of all, Babini has so far neglected to perform the *ukubuyisa*— the lamentation ceremony—for Vuyisile, who died several years ago now. When his "paternal uncles" had come to meet Babini "on the matter of the rehabilitation of the home," following Vuyisile's death, "these men had been driven away even to the present day" (44). It is, then, not only the readers he addresses in his foreword who could benefit from Mqhayi's "documentary" (Dikeni 1992, 51) about Xhosa customs and practices, but also Mqhayi's character Babini, for Babini is one more among the wayward "youth of the Xhosas," whom Mqhayi exhorts in his foreword "to examine conscientiously what will happen when this language and culture disappear completely" (*Twins*, 5).

Once this point is appreciated, its obverse immediately suggests itself: the verdict in the case of the twins is directed not only at Wele and Babini within the action of Mqhayi's novel, but also at the readers of the novel—both those observant of custom and those who are abandoning it. The implicit equivalence between his character Babini and a section of his intended readership is, I suggest, the structural source of the "fascinating power" A. C. Jordan rightly attributes to Mqhayi's text (Jordan 1973, 108). Once this is appreciated, the short novel reveals itself as a Nabokovian hall of mirrors, in which plot points and Mqhayi's lessons for his readers reflect and magnify one another.

Mqhayi stated explicitly, in his preface to the 1931 version of *Twins*, that the 1914 original had been written in allegorical mode (Dikeni 1992, 10). This would in any case have been a possibility worth considering, because at that time the missionary-run Lovedale Press—which represented the best chance for a book in isiXhosa to reach a wide audience—was not willing to publish material its management thought would be detrimental to missionary work. Manuscripts critical of Christianity or white political domination tended to be rejected or ruthlessly edited (Peires 1979). The Press preferred to publish translations into isiXhosa of edifying religious works or retellings of Bible stories in the vernacular. It is against this backdrop that we should understand Mqhayi's decision to prove the capacity of the traditional Xhosa legal system by feeding into it a "legal 'riddle'" (Dikeni 1992, 161) inspired by a story from the biblical Old Testament. Genesis 38: 28–30 tells of the birth of twins to Tamar, who, after being twice widowed, became pregnant by her father-in-law, Judah:

> And it came to pass, when she travailed, that the one put out his hand: and the midwife took and bound upon his hand a scarlet thread, saying, This came out first.
> And it came to pass, as he drew back his hand, that, behold, his brother came out: and she said, How hast thou broken forth? . . .
> And afterward came out his brother, that had the scarlet thread upon his hand.

In *Twins* the only difference is that, instead of tying a thread, the midwife Teyase "took a spear and amputated the last joint of [Wele's] finger, the little finger," when he put his hand out (41), in accordance with the custom of *ingqithi* (Midgley 2010, 233).

Dikeni has suggested one might see the manner of Wele and Babini's birth as a political metaphor, Babini standing for the white settlers who forced themselves upon the lands of the Cape and subordinated the African residents, symbolized by Wele, who had laid a prior claim (Dikeni 1992, 95). This may well be correct. What is more certain—because supported by evidence internal to Mqhayi's text—is that Wele embodies acceptance of traditional Xhosa values, practices and beliefs, whereas Babini embodies the violation and abandonment of these typical of the Christian, urban-minded, mission-educated Xhosas of Mqhayi's day. Not only is Babini associated, through his flouting of custom, with the contemporary Xhosas whom Mqhayi admonishes in his preface, but the particular ways in which Babini flouts custom are also recognizable as types of behavior characteristic of the *amagqobhoka*—the educated converts—who had adopted a "modern . . .

lifestyle" (Midgley 2010, 226). Babini fails to observe important rituals of the Xhosa religion; he does not attribute special authority to the elders of his family; he does not acknowledge an obligation to provide hospitality to a community stretching beyond the nuclear family; he refuses to recognize cattle as communally owned by the household, treating them as his private property and giving them to discretionary friends unknown to the rest of the family.

In the expert testimony he gives to the court at Hintsa's Great Place, Khulile reflects upon the rationale for the custom of bestowing authority on the first-born brother. "The first-born," he asserts, "is authorised to administer the home because he has the experience of having appeared before the other children of his home; he knows certain people better than the others, he has heard grave matters discussed that the others have not heard" (*Twins*, 74). Having laid out what he sees as primogeniture's justification, Khulile notes that it has little force when the first-born preceded his brother only by a matter of minutes. But he also observes that there are proxy measures of wisdom besides age, meaning that, if the justification of primogeniture is that age is a proxy for wisdom, there might in some cases be another proxy which trumps age in determining which brother is best suited to administer the household. In his words, "Is it not actions that cause eldership, as for instance any first-born who isolated himself from his brothers parts with his eldership when he becomes a child by his actions?" (74)

King Hintsa's verdict is a compromise or reconciliatory verdict, crafted in such a way that neither party can be said to have won outright. In large part, this is because it is an answer to a different question from that which Wele had put to the court. Wele had asked the court to rule on whether he or Babini is Vuyisile's heir (*Twins*, 5). Rather than answer this question—except in passing—the King answers a different question: what each of the two brothers ought to do now. To Wele he says, "Proceed and go home, and look after that calf which you had already been looking after, and keep that family of [Vuyisile] which you had already been keeping, and come and report at your home here anything that you see is not right." To Babini, "Go home then, and help your younger brother to keep the family of your home, and the property, and everything. Even at the Great Place here we should see the two of you together. You should obey him and listen to his words" (75).

Building on Khulile's expert testimony, Hintsa is able to shift the emphasis in his verdict away from the question which of the twins has right of command to the matter of the well-being of their household. His overriding message to the brothers is that they must co-operate together in the way which will best enable them to look after the household well. Babini has proved himself less able to manage the household than Wele up to now, despite being the older twin (as Hintsa acknowledges in passing). In order that the household may flourish, Babini should take instruction from Wele for now. But this could change—if Babini were to mend his ways.[7]

At the allegorical level, Hintsa's verdict in *Twins* is a verdict on the question whether traditional Xhosa culture or modern Western culture is entitled to prevail in Xhosaland. The verdict he delivers indicates that this ought not to be viewed as an *either/or* matter. In spheres where traditional Xhosa practices would benefit Xhosaland most, those practices should be adopted; in spheres where modern Western practices would, these should. When traditional Xhosa practices are to be favored, this is not because they were there *first*, but because they have proved their worth—as the Xhosa judicial system is meant by Mqhayi to prove its worth in his novel. Just as Babini and Wele ought to co-operate together for the good of their household, so traditional Xhosa culture and Western culture need to be put to work in tandem so that Xhosaland may flourish. Mqhayi believes this has already been happening to some extent in practice. While Xhosas have certainly taken over beliefs and customs from the white settlers in many spheres, in the sphere of "legal procedure," claims Mqhayi in his 1914 foreword, "[t]he white races took for themselves a considerable share of the customs and laws of the Xhosas" (*Twins*, 5).

CONFLICT BETWEEN INCOMPATIBLE CULTURAL VALUES: A. C. JORDAN'S CRITIQUE OF "ONE-SIDED," PURELY INSTRUMENTAL COMPROMISE

If in *Twins* the conflict between educated, Westernized Xhosa people and traditional, rural Xhosa people—between the *amagqobhoka* and the *amaqaba*—is presented allegorically, in A. C. Jordan's *Ingqumbo Yeminyanya*, published twenty-six years later, it is the novel's explicit theme. *Wrath*'s more fine-grained depiction of the compresence of two cultures in one society focuses our attention on cases in which the values of different cultures *conflict*, prescribing incompatible courses of action. In doing so, it raises doubts about whether the model of cultural co-operation, which seemed so attractive in Mqhayi's high-level allegory, is realizable in practice.

Jordan paints a vivid picture of the two worlds in which both the amaMpondomise and neighboring isiXhosa-speaking peoples existed in the 1930s. On the one hand, there is the world of the mission school, the university and the town. In this world, Xhosas wear Western clothes and drive motor cars; in times of trouble they pray to the Christian God and turn to Christian priests (*Wrath*, 36); such rites of passage as passing exams, graduating, entering university and starting a new job (14–15, 29, 52) chart their progress through life; Xhosas favor Western medicine over traditional medicine

(67); and they are on terms of familiarity with white people, at ease speaking in English. On the other hand, there is the world of the village, the "mealie lands" (95) and the *nkundla*. In this world, Xhosas wear "bright red" blankets (7) and travel on horseback; "tribal custom" (153) and the wishes of the ancestors are to be taken seriously; animals associated with the ancestors, such as the *nkwakhwa* (brown cobra) (168) or an ox from "the ancient stock of the House of Majola" (171), are to be revered; Xhosas practice polygamy (149), scarify their children (172), go to traditional "diviners" and "herbalists" (178) when unwell; they hesitate to hire a car for fear that "[w]hen White people pass by" they will "stop and want to talk to the owner of the car in that strange language of theirs"; and, in any case, as one of Dingindawo's men remarks, "[W]ho is going to drive the car seeing none of us can drive?" (103–104)

Jordan shows us that a few of his characters are able to slip with ease from one world to the other. For example, Mphuthumi, a graduate of Lovedale College, lives and works as a teacher at St. Cuthbert's Mission; but he spends many of his evenings at the house of Ngubengwe, headman of Ngcolisi, of whom he is "a great favourite," "discussing news" and "eating green mealies that were being roasted by the children" (*Wrath*, 57). Mphuthumi is in his element both traveling the countryside with the headman Dabula, and conducting business as secretary of the Teachers' Association (88); equally adept at giving a speech in English on behalf of the teachers welcoming the Chief of the Mpondomise to St. Cuthbert's (137), and delivering a spontaneous praise-poem in isiXhosa to honor his friend Zwelinzima (33). The same cannot be said of Zwelinzima—hidden heir of Zanemvula, late chief of the Mpondomise—or of his fiancée Thembeka. Both were raised in families which have abandoned Xhosa tradition—Zwelinzima by Gcinizibele Majola, who has not seen Mpondomiseland "since childhood," and his wife, MamBhele, an Mfengu who had never "seen her husband's people" (109); Thembeka by her father Khalipha, who has "long since ceased to attach any importance to tribal custom" (153). When the two young lovers mention traditional Xhosa customs to each other, it is to mock them (see, for example, *Wrath*, 136). Zwelinzima, though his inborn charisma and courage inspire allegiance (110, 199), admits in his private thoughts that the Mpondomise people and his position as heir to the chieftainship have "no reality for him"—"no real meaning" (35).

It is not a modernizer, but the traditionalist Ngxabane, an aged but vigorous repository of customary wisdom (comparable to Khulile in *Twins*), who sets in motion the restoration of Zwelinzima to the seat of the Mpondomise chief at Tsolo—occupied since Zanemvula's death by Zwelinzima's maleficent uncle, Dingindawo (meaning "without a seat"). Once Zwelinzima is in place, though, he quickly discovers that Mpondomise traditionalists—not just former backers of Dingindawo, but also Ngxabane (meaning "quarrel")—are to be the greatest obstacle in the way of the program of reforms he has in mind.

Battle lines between the "school people" and the "ochre people" are drawn first over the issue of Zwelinzima's wife (*Wrath*, 154). The modernizers among the leading Mpondomise men take the view that Zwelinzima should be permitted to marry one woman, the woman he loves, in accordance with Christian rites. To the traditionalists, the woman Zwelinzima loves, Thembeka, is unacceptable on two counts: first, she is a commoner (139); second, Ngxabane announces that Zanemvula's "dying-wish," communicated directly to him, was "*that his son, Zwelinzima, should marry the princess royal of the Bhaca!*" (141) Among the traditionalists, some are prepared to compromise—such as Jongilanga of Matyeba, who suggests permitting Zwelinzima to marry Thembeka, on condition that he also marry the Bhaca princess, and that the latter be "the head wife, the mother of the heir" (149). Others are ultimately won over by the modernizers' arguments—for example, by that of Dabula, who makes the case that the chief "must choose a woman who understands him well" (143). Dabula can be understood as—like Khulile in his expert testimony in *Twins*—reflecting on the rationale for a time-honored custom: in former times, a wife's being royal might have been sufficient to indicate she had been brought up with knowledge of "sacred customs" (150) and would understand her husband's perspective and preoccupations; now that the heirs of chiefs are sent to school—itself an uncustomary practice (143)—other qualities are required in a wife if she is to be a good companion to her royal husband.

Ngxabane, on the other hand, will not budge. Indeed, he presents his *uncompromising* stance in defense of custom—here both the custom that a chief must have a royal wife and the custom that a chief's dying wish must be complied with—as a virtue. In his eyes, the arguments of modernizers such as Dabula are pusillanimous rationalizations designed to give cover to a departure from moral principle; as Ngxabane sees it, to budge from strict observance of custom would be a compromise in the pejorative sense, one which leaves one morally *compromised*. Thus, he sees his "unyielding attitude" (Qangule 1974, 42) as justified. Ngxabane expresses his point with a simile: "I have lived my life to the full," he declares, "because I have always adhered to custom, aye, custom, from which the Dabulas would escape, truly like monkeys trying to escape detection by hiding their faces behind tree branches and protesting that 'times have changed'" (*Wrath*, 142). Zwelinzima, for his part, also adopts an uncompromising approach. Refusing to discuss the matter with his counselors, he walks out of the meeting after handing Dingindawo a note saying, "[A]*s long as Khalipha's daughter lives, I will marry no other woman, no matter whose daughter she may be*" (142).

In the end, Zwelinzima and Thembeka get married with no uproar—and Thembeka acquires the name "Nobantu" ("Mother of the People") (*Wrath*, 163). But a few chapters further on, in Chapter 1 of Book IV, we as readers are prompted to think again about compromise: not just about whether Zwelinzima should adopt a more compromising approach but also about the *nature* of compromise. In this chapter, Chief Zwelinzima receives similar advice from three people, all of whom he respects. First, Thembeka's friend Nomvuyo writes advising them "*not to be too hasty in your leadership. If you try to drag* [the Mpondomise people] *too fast, they will drop, exhausted by the wayside, and you yourselves will collapse before you reach the place where you want to take them*" (177). Second, Chief Zwelinzima visits the Chief at Sulenkama, the Great House of Majola, who speaks to Zwelinzima about the people's "belief in witchcraft and diviners" (177). He describes how he allows a "medicine-man" to treat him, though this goes "against his own beliefs," in order to give his "followers . . . confidence in him" (178). He concludes that "[t]he main thing was to inspire this confidence in them so that they would accept his leadership, and then he would be in a position to uplift them and wean them from these very superstitions" (178). Third, at a meeting of the Transkeian Bhunga, Zwelinzima meets with the Thembu Chief, who gives him much the same advice as the Chief at Sulenkama (179).

Commentators often take the Thembu Chief and the Chief at Sulenkama to function in *Wrath* as valuable role models for Zwelinzima: if he had been more like them, and if he had followed Nomvuyo's advice, he would have been a good and successful ruler of the Mpondomise.[8] In my view, this reading is simplistic, and does not accurately capture the role which the advice Zwelinzima receives in this chapter plays in the novel as a whole. I would suggest that a reader cannot help admitting there is much that is right and admirable in Zwelinzima's immediate reaction to the advice of the Thembu Chief at the end of this chapter. "Am I to pretend," he remonstrates, "that I too believe in [the diviners'] practices, just because I want the people to follow me? Oh, NO!" (*Wrath*, 181)

For one thing, Zwelinzima is right to emphasize that doing as the Thembu Chief suggests would involve deliberate deception, and this is surely an ignoble way for a ruler to behave toward his people. But there is more to it than that. A presupposition which Nomvuyo, the Chief at Sulenkama, and the Thembu Chief apparently share is that the cultural practices, customs and beliefs of the Mpondomise traditionalists are all so much backwardness: erroneous views, unjustifiable modes of behavior, habits and customs of no value. All three are proposing that Zwelinzima should engage in a *purely instrumental* form of compromise—a compromise by which he takes part in, or goes along with, practices which in themselves have *no* value or even *negative* value (the Mpondomise customs), for the sake of achieving an outcome which *does* have positive value (his modernizing reforms). This *purely instrumental* type of compromise is familiar from interpersonal negotiations, where two parties may both agree to do something which they regard as of no, or negative, value, but which is viewed as valuable by the other party. If they do so, the other party will reciprocate by doing the same, and thus both parties will end up with more of what they actually value. The philosopher Henry Richardson calls a reciprocal instrumental compromise of this type, reached by negotiation, a "[b]*are compromise*" (2002, 146).[9]

The low or negative estimation of Mpondomise traditions which would justify attempting such a *purely instrumental* compromise accords, by all indications, with Zwelinzima and Thembeka's own thinking. It does not accord, though, with what the implied author[10] of *Wrath* shows us, in his descriptions and narration, is actually the case. The novel's leisurely exposition, through which in the first half of *Wrath* Jordan situates each of his characters in the Western Christian world, or in the traditional village world, or slipping—with more or less agility—between the two, invites us as readers to make comparisons and draw parallels.

While his innovations to prevent disease and soil depletion are certainly welcome, the reader cannot help wondering whether some of Chief Zwelinzima's other modernizing endeavors are really improvements at all. For example, he introduces cricket matches and "Girl Guide and Boy Scout companies" at his "Royal Place" (*Wrath*, 160). Is there any reason to suppose that these are inherently superior as practices which build teamwork and enable participants to demonstrate physical prowess to more traditional Mpondomise practices, such as working together on the land "during the ploughing and harvest seasons" (229) or becoming a fine horse-rider who captains "the young men's horse-riding parties—imikhwelo—at wedding-feasts" (75)? At the "Convention of Transkei Chiefs at Nyandeni" (166), Zwelinzima speaks out on the issue of goat culling. He "summarily dismissed" (176) the objection raised by his people—"ochre men, as well as a considerable number of the school people" (175)—that goats were needed for ritual slaughter as prescribed by diviners and "[a]t the initiation ceremony of novice-diviners." What is more, he then "went on to say that, if he had his way, the diviners who demanded black goats from the people for their medicines should be exterminated along with those goats, for it was they who were misleading the people" (176).

Yet, as readers we cannot help noting that it is not only in the traditional world of the village that people perform rituals prescribed by agents of the supernatural to provoke interventions from the spiritual realm. When he is asked through Mphuthumi to take up the Mpondomise chieftainship, Zwelinzima may not go and see a traditional diviner or seek his ancestors' guidance, but he does go to chapel to pray "to the Father-of-All-Power to give him advice on this matter" (*Wrath*, 36) and seeks guidance from the Bishop (37–38). Jordan's rich, sympathetic portrayal of *both* cultural worlds, with their different beliefs and practices, makes it extremely difficult for a reader to concur with Zwelinzima that the religious ways of the Mpondomise traditionalists are crude errors, his own Christian ways based upon reason and evidence. Furthermore, Jordan takes care to show us that when Zwelinzima can supply a strong, evidence-based argument for a view, the Mpondomise—both "ochre" and "school"—are willing to come around to it. Having heard his argument for general stock limitation (which does not involve culling all goats), on the basis that it will prevent soil depletion, "a large section of those who had previously been sceptical about the measure now supported the Chief very strongly" (175).

Wrath's narrator shows us two cultural worlds, both of which involve beliefs and rituals which guide and orient their adherents, both of which include practices and traditions which are of value, and neither of which is utterly irrational or impervious to reason-based argument; in many respects, he shows us, there is no clear basis for saying that one of the cultures is bad, or backward, and the other good. As readers of *Wrath*, we are thus invited to adopt a *pluralist* (though not necessarily *relativist*)[11] position—a view which says there is, objectively, more than one way of living a good moral life, and that some widely diverging conceptions of the good life are equally morally acceptable.[12]

Consequently, the implied author gives us readers the firm impression that Zwelinzima's uncompromising imposition of Western Christian ways is not just *unstrategic* but "one-sided" (*Wrath*, 242). The latter is the word used by the traditionalist Jongilanga when he criticizes Zwelinzima's approach. He fleshes out the idea metaphorically at the meeting between the Chief and the traditionalist "Mpondomise of the soil" (219), which is held after Nobantu has—in "an act akin to sacrilege" (Nyamende 1991, 123)—beaten to death the *nkwakhwa*, which the Mpondomise believe embodies their ancestor Majola, at the *nkundla*. Given *Wrath*'s thematic resonance with *Twins*, and Jordan's admiration for Mqhayi's literary work (see Jordan 1973, 103–116), the metaphor Jongilanga utilizes is most likely an authorial allusion to Mqhayi's novel:

> Majola, our forebear, gave birth to twins. One of them he dressed in the garments of the White man and the other in the blanket of red ochre. Now the twin in the White man's clothes is the darling of the family, because he is dressed like his father. As for the twin in the red blanket, . . . no matter how loudly he cries, his voice is never heard. (*Wrath*, 220)

As in *Ityala Lamawele*, so here the image of twins is used to convey the fundamental equality in status of the values and practices of two cultures. As in

Mqhayi's allegory, so in Jongilanga's it is used to indicate that in a society with two legitimate cultures the right question to ask is not "Which should take precedence?" but "What should be done in order that people in such a society may flourish alongside one another?"

Chief Zwelinzima thus has reason to act in a way which is *compromising*, in the sense that it strikes a compromise between two cultures which are *both* of value. This is very different from being *compromising* in the sense envisaged by the advice he received in Chapter 1 of Book IV—going along with the putatively backward, worthless culture in the short term in order to be in a position to impose the putatively good, enlightened culture more comprehensively in the long term. There are some simple ways in which Zwelinzima might have acted differently in order to be compromising, in the former sense. Allowing the Mpondomise to retain sufficient goats for their religious ceremonies—and avoiding flippant comments about exterminating traditional diviners—would have been a good place to start. And he might have patronized *both* cricket, the Boy Scouts and the Girl Guides, *and* more traditional Mpondomise pastimes and pursuits at his Royal Place, rather than one to the exclusion of the other. Zitobile Qangule has suggested that the repeated motif of blending Western and traditional in Jordan's description of Zwelinzima and Thembeka's wedding day—guests, "White and Black," arriving "in cars and on horseback" (*Wrath*, 156); the young guests "playing all kinds of games, old and new" (157); telegrams, "some in English, some in Xhosa" (158)—indicates that such a *both-and*, blending, approach fair to both "twins," was a real possibility for Zwelinzima's chieftainship (Qangule 1974, 121): a road not taken.

However, *Wrath* shows us very clearly that in some cases the values and practices of one culture are *incompatible* with those of another—making a straightforward *both-and* approach impossible (and calling the optimistic message of King Hintsa's verdict in *Twins* into question). Zwelinzima's marriage dilemma is the principal exemplar of this phenomenon in the novel. Even readers who do not believe this specific case represents a genuine dilemma[13] may still accept that there will be *other* cases of genuine dilemmas arising from incompatible cultural values, and thus treat it as a placeholder for one of these. If Zwelinzima does right by his Western values, he will marry one woman, the woman he loves. If he does right by the traditional values of the Mpondomise, he will marry a woman of royal blood and be guided by the leading men of the Mpondomise, and the dying wish of his father, in his choice—and should he marry more than one woman, this will bring more glory to his people (Qangule 1974, 50). It follows that if he does right by the one set of values, he cannot avoid doing wrong by the other.[14]

Jongilanga gives best expression in *Wrath* to the idea that in a society with two cultures worthy of respect, a plurality of different values must be acknowledged: his metaphor of two twins and his criticism of Zwelinzima's one-sidedness. It is also, I suggest, Jongilanga who, of all the characters in the novel, best expresses the intractable nature of the dilemmas to which this situation can give rise. Ultimately the most accommodating of the ochre faction, Jongilanga, in a final meeting with Chief Zwelinzima, says that he regrets calling for the children to be withdrawn from school following the nkwakhwa incident; now he means to return to Matyeba and call for the children to return to school (*Wrath*, 243). He is murdered before he arrives—probably on orders from Dingindawo and Mabhozo ("knife wielder") (243–44)—but before that happens he repeats to Dabula a version of the hermetic remark he has already made to Zwelinzima (243): "Zulu, I still maintain that there is no such thing as wisdom in this world. But truth there is, without doubt" (244). Jongilanga makes the remark in connection with his own wrestling with a "dilemma" (243). But, in my view, we can understand what he says as having a broader application, and in particular as applying to Zwelinzima's marriage dilemma. It is *true* that by marrying the Bhaca princess, Zwelinzima would respect Mpondomise custom and his father's dying wish—both of which are genuine, important claims on him; and it is also *true* that marrying one woman, the woman he loves, would be the only proper way to consummate his love relationship with Thembeka in the Western way which orients them both. But simply appreciating these *truths* leaves neither us nor Zwelinzima any the wiser about what he *ought to do*: the *truths* deliver no practical *wisdom*.

Philosophers who accept value pluralism, and acknowledge the intractable type of moral dilemma to which it can give rise, have proposed that in some cases the only adequate way to respond to a genuine conflict of values is with a creative act. Bernard Williams has argued that "[m]oral conflicts are neither systematically avoidable, nor all soluble without remainder" (1973, 179). When an agent opts for the course dictated by one true value rather than another, they may rationally feel "regret" for the course not chosen; and in the best case the agent will feel "creative regret" (175), in the sense that the regret will "receive some constructive expression" (179), such as a creative way of making amends to parties wronged by the lights of the value not honored. Differently, Henry Richardson has described how in some circumstances parties within a community will not be able to agree on a way to live together unless one or both sides modify the final ends which they see as having ultimate value. This he calls "[*d*]*eep compromise*," as it is a "change in one's support of policies . . . that is accompanied and explained or supported by a change in one's ends that itself counts as a compromise" (2002, 147). If, motivated by mutual respect and a commitment to living together, two parties both adjust their ultimate values, this is likely to give rise to new practices and ways of ordering life which could not easily have been anticipated, because the parties will have generated a new synthesis at the level of the fundamental ends they pursue.

Wrath ends in disaster. Rather than achieving a creative response to the conflict they are in the midst of, Zwelinzima and Thembeka are rendered numb, unable to function, and take to wandering the countryside absently (251–52). Finally, Thembeka hurls herself and their child, Zululiyazongoma (meaning "rumbling heavens"), into the Bedlana river. Not only she and her son die but also Zwelinzima's cousin, Vukuzumbethe (meaning "rise and strike"), who dives into the river in an attempt to rescue them (264). A week later, Zwelinzima commits suicide by throwing himself into the same river.

Despite these catastrophes, the short epilogue to Jordan's novel, entitled "Umso" ("dawn" or "illumination"), strikes an unmistakable note of hope. Mphuthumi and Nomvuyo have married and had a child.

> What a dispute there was between the parents over his name! The father thought he should be Thembekile, while the other insisted that his name be Zwelinzima. Finally there was peace and harmony when the parents agreed to call their son Zwelethemba, "Land of Hope." (277)

This short report leaves the reader with a sense of optimism, even elation, quite disproportionate to its literal meaning or contribution to the plot. The three short sentences, I would suggest, function as a literary chord, whose notes and overtones recall to the reader's mind all the indications Jordan has provided that the situation of the amaMpondomise is not irremediably tragic, that a compromise acknowledging the equal value of the two cultures present in their society—a *deep compromise*—is after all possible. The birth of a child is a creative act, bringing something new into the world. In this instance the new creation is presented to us as a blending, a synthesis, of two valuable things: the names of Thembeka and Zwelinzima, Nomvuyo and Mphuthumi's dearest friends while they were alive, are amalgamated equally in something new, the name of their child. This amalgam chimes with the repeated motif of blending in Jordan's description of the royal wedding. The new synthesis, we are explicitly told, is the result of a compromise which ends a "dispute," creating "harmony." Finally, the child is born to Mphuthumi (meaning "mover" or "shifter"), the character who we have seen throughout the novel is most able to slip nimbly between the "red ochre" world and the "school" world. Jordan's brief, nicely crafted epilogue suggests that, though Zwelinzima and Thembeka did not find it, or even seek it, there does exist the potential for a new synthesis in the Mpondomise society which will enable school people and red ochre people to live together in a way which acknowledges both their cultures equally: a form of *wisdom*—to borrow from Jongilanga's formulation—which cannot simply be read off the existing, conflicting, *truths*, because it involves the creation of a *new truth*.

CREATIVE ACCOMMODATION IN THE FACE OF VALUE CONFLICT: PARSING THE OPTIMISM OF J. M. COETZEE'S *DISGRACE*

In *Disgrace*, set in the mid-1990s, cultural conflict is a more muted theme than in *Twins* and *Wrath*. Yet J. M. Coetzee's novel, like Jordan's, hinges on the moral dilemmas that arise from the claims of distinct moral values and its characters' different responses to these.

Like Zwelinzima and Ngxabane in *Wrath*, the protagonist of *Disgrace* displays an *uncompromising* attitude; also like Zwelinzima and Ngxabane, he sees his uncompromising stance as a badge of honor. David Lurie, an adjunct professor of communications (*Disgrace*, 3) at Cape Technical University, has had an impulsive affair with a student, Melanie Isaacs, who eventually accuses him of harassment (41). Called to appear before a committee of inquiry at the university, he declares himself guilty as charged (49). But when asked to issue a statement—a public apology—in mitigation of the charges to which he has confessed, he refuses.

Coetzee's novel is composed in *style indirect libre*. This narratorial convention generates a perspective tethered to, but not utterly restricted by, the consciousness of the novel's protagonist.[15] Crucially, though David's perspective on events is our primary point of reference, the narratorial perspective can encompass more features than David himself is directly aware of. There is thus potential for dramatic irony.

Commentators on *Disgrace* often fall into the trap of assuming that David Lurie's perspective is the perspective of the novel—of the implied author. Yet, as is frequently the case with novels composed in the free indirect style, one of the tasks of a reader of *Disgrace* is carefully to separate out that which we are told David thinks about unfolding events from that which the narratorial perspective shadowing David's perspective shows us is actually the case. For our purposes now, there are two aspects of the novel for which it is essential to effect this separation.

The first is David's version of what took place between him and the committee of inquiry at Cape Technical University. Following the scandal, David goes to stay with his daughter, Lucy, who is in her twenties and lives as a smallholder on a farm outside Salem, near Grahamstown, earning money by taking the flowers and potatoes she grows around her house to market. Lucy suggests that David ought to have stayed in Cape Town to stand up for himself (*Disgrace*, 88), to which her father replies, "You miss the point, my dear. The case you want me to make is a case that can no longer be made, *basta*. Not in our day. If I tried to make it I would not be heard" (89).

Earlier novels by Coetzee have featured characters who genuinely cannot make their case or tell their story: most notably *Foe* (Coetzee 1986) and *Life & Times of Michael K* (Coetzee 1998 [1983]).[16] It is, then, very tempting for a reader to fall in line with David's self-conception and view him as fatally misunderstood by the administered society of the 1990s—what he calls "the great rationalization" (*Disgrace*, 3)—where managerialism and moralism have blinded people to the values which only the "moral dinosaur" (89) David Lurie can still discern.[17]

However, we must resist this temptation, because the novel shows us that David is perfectly able to articulate his case to himself (and us), to Lucy, and to the committee. To Lucy he says: "My case rests on the rights of desire. . . . On the god who makes even the small birds quiver" (89). To the committee: "I was not myself. I was no longer a fifty-year-old divorcé at a loose end. I became a servant of Eros" (52). Surely Lucy is not misunderstanding him when she replies with the pertinent question, "So males must be allowed to follow their instincts unchecked?" (90) Nor is Desmond Swarts, on the committee, when he replies, "Don't you think . . . that by its nature academic life must call for certain sacrifices? That for the good of the whole we have to deny ourselves certain gratifications?" (52)

Lurie has not been misunderstood. In both cases, what his interlocutor is driving at is that the legitimate claim arising from the value of passion or eroticism or impulsive adventurousness—which of course *are* important and valuable things—exists alongside *other legitimate claims* of *other values*.[18] If desire has rights, then so do other things, and their respective rights sometimes come into conflict.[19]

The second aspect of *Disgrace* where it is crucial to separate the implied author's perspective from the character David's relates to Petrus, a black African man in his forties who works for Lucy, but has also acquired land of his own adjacent to hers, and is becoming a successful farmer. On arriving home one day—in fact, minutes after their conversation about the rights of desire—Lucy and David are met by two men and a boy (91), who commit a horrific crime: they assault David, steal Lucy and David's possessions, and rape Lucy inside her house.

David quickly becomes convinced that Petrus was complicit in the crime: even if he was not the primary instigator, he helped in some way, or at least "knew something was in the offing" and could have warned Lucy, but didn't (118). It is hard to find a commentator on *Disgrace* who does not assume that David's opinion is correct.[20] Yet, I submit, the evidence presented to us in the novel does not support this view.

As regards Petrus' general character, we know that David has had a negative, aversive attitude to him from the beginning. He notes his "shrewd eyes" (64), and later builds more colorfully on this initial impression: "A plotter and a schemer and no doubt a liar too, like peasants everywhere" (117). Immediately after the attack, Lucy's neighbor Ettinger adds his own sweeping prejudice to David's. "Of the absent Petrus, Ettinger remarks darkly: 'Not one of them you can trust'" (109). But those who actually know Petrus the individual, as opposed to generalizing about peasants or black people, tell a different story. Lucy's best friend, Bev Shaw, tells David: "You underestimate Petrus. Petrus slaved to get the market garden going for Lucy.... [S]he owes him a lot." And: "Petrus is a good old chap. You can depend on him" (140). Bev's impression chimes with what we see of Petrus: even David has to admit he is a hard worker (117), and when Lucy is in no state to take her flowers to market following the attack, Petrus goes in her stead (116).

Petrus was absent on the day of the attack, that much is certain. But is it grounds for suspicion? Well before the attack, we learned from Lucy that Petrus has another wife and children in Adelaide, and visits them from time to time (64). When Petrus does return, it turns out he has an even better excuse for having been away: he was fetching a lorry full of building materials for his house, and sheep to be slaughtered for the party to celebrate his marriage to a second wife. As to whether—as David remarks—"he ... took good care not to be in the vicinity" (140) on the day of the crime, one could equally speculate that the rapists chose that day to strike because they knew Petrus would have stopped them had he been present.

At Petrus' party, Lucy spots the youngest of the attackers. David, his suspicions confirmed, confronts the boy and then demands of Petrus, "Do you know who this is?" The dialogue continues: "'No, I do not know what this is,' says Petrus angrily. 'I do not know what is the trouble. What is the trouble?'" (132) Later, after it has emerged that the boy, Pollux, is the brother, or kinsman, of one of Petrus' wives (200), David misremembers the exchange, saying to Petrus, "You told me you did not know him. You lied to me" (201). But the actual dialogue—as just quoted—suggests that Petrus, whose first language is isiXhosa, had misunderstood David's question, not lied.[21]

From the moment of the confrontation at Petrus' party, David—quite understandably—urges Lucy to adopt an uncompromising approach. She ought to call the police on Petrus, effectively breaking off her relations with him, and make sure that Pollux is arrested. The language he uses echoes that which he has used to describe his interaction with the committee of inquiry in Cape Town, inviting us to compare the two situations.

Discussing with his ex-wife Rosalind his refusal to make a public apology as required by the committee of inquiry, David says, "I was standing up for a principle" (188). On the farm, talking to Petrus about the need for Pollux to be arrested, he says, "[T]here is a principle involved" (137). The way David sees things, to compromise on a matter of principle in either of these cases would demean one so much that—as he says of the "compromise" offered to him by the committee of inquiry—"I would prefer simply to be put against a wall and shot" (66). Similarly, in a short note to Lucy about her decision to stay on the farm without calling the police on Petrus, he writes: "[T]he road you are following is the wrong one. It will strip you of all honour; you will not be able to live with yourself" (160). Earlier he has said, "[Y]ou will never be able to hold your head up again" (133).

But there also runs through *Disgrace*, in counterpoint with David's attitude, a much more positive view of compromise. Desmond Swarts, on the committee of inquiry, tells David that the committee sees itself as trying to work out a compromise which will allow him to keep his job (54). When David tells his daughter of the compromise offered to him which he rejected, she responds: "You shouldn't be so unbending, David. It isn't heroic to be unbending" (66). More generally, there is a language of accommodation apportioned among several of the other characters which contrasts with David's all-or-nothing formulations. When David first arrives at Lucy's farmhouse, he asks:

"Is this what you want in life?"
"It will do," replies Lucy quietly. (70)

Bev, talking to David about Lucy after the attack, says: "It will be alright. Petrus will take her under his wing" (140). Later: "'It will be all right,' she whispers. 'You will see'" (162). Petrus uses the same language, to David's exasperation, after the attack: "Yes, I know what happened. But now it is all right" (138).

I have argued above that we must look at Petrus' behavior following the attack with an open mind, not assuming it is that of a guilty party. Petrus refuses to hand Pollux over to the police, as David has been urging him. Why?

In the first place, he may have reasonable doubts about whether Pollux is guilty. As far as we are made aware, only David—who Petrus hardly knows—has accused Pollux of being one of the attackers, and Pollux himself has denied this (132). Second, even if his guilt is granted, Pollux is a child, which must reduce his moral responsibility and liability to some considerable degree. Petrus makes this point to David: "He is too young, you cannot put him in jail" (138). Even though he had originally registered the attackers as two men and a boy (91), David now changes his tune, claiming that Pollux looks more than eighteen (138). Third, another significant factor in mitigation is that Pollux is mentally handicapped: "there is something wrong with him," as Lucy puts it (200), and David later agrees (207).

Fourth, Pollux is a family-member to Petrus. "He is my family, my people," as he says to David (201). The thoughts David shares with us over the next page or so suggest he has heard this as a statement of *racial* solidarity—"*[m]y people*" against "*his people*" (201)—: an egregiously uncharitable interpretation of Petrus' words, given that Lucy has just informed David that Pollux is a brother of Petrus' wife (200). When somebody is a family-member, one has special obligations toward them: one must look after them, as Petrus puts it (201), perhaps also give them the benefit of the doubt in cases where one would not to a non-family-member.

In the fifth place, Petrus, as a man of forty or forty-five years (64), will have attained adulthood during the worst years of *apartheid* pass laws, bannings, army raids, and targeted police violence. We may surmise that, if Petrus has not himself had run-ins with the police, he will at any rate have acquired at second hand a pretty shrewd idea of what sorts of thing tend to happen when the South African Police take in a black boy or young man for interrogation to assist them with their inquiries.[22]

David takes Petrus' unwillingness to hand Pollux over to the police to be proof of his complicity in the attack. A careful reader of *Disgrace* is more likely to wonder whether it could possibly be morally justifiable for Petrus to hand over his under-age, mentally handicapped brother-in-law, on nothing but the say-so of a man he hardly knows, to a police force internationally renowned for torturing and murdering black boys and young men in custody.

Whereas David cannot see the moral force of the considerations which motivate Petrus' refusal, we are shown that Petrus *does* appreciate the moral force of the point David keeps stressing. "I want those men to be caught and brought before the law and punished. Am I wrong? Am I wrong to want justice?" David asks. Petrus' reply is: "No, you are not wrong" (119). As before the committee of inquiry, so in conversation with Petrus, David is quite able to make his case, and his case is heard and understood. Like Desmond Swarts earlier, Petrus appreciates the legitimacy of David's claim: it is right that wrongdoers be punished. But, also like Desmond Swarts, Petrus appreciates that there are *other* legitimate claims of *other* values in play, which, since they pull in a different direction, are not straightforwardly to be reconciled with that of the value of punishment.

Attempting to get David to see things from his point of view, Petrus says: "And I, I am the one who must be keeping the peace. So it is hard for me too" (137). One obvious sense in which Petrus must keep the peace is that he needs to prevent the tension between individuals following the attack from escalating into open conflict, even further violence. But we can see now that there is another sense in which he must keep the peace. To borrow from Mqhayi and Jordan's metaphorical repertory, Petrus must keep the peace between *twins*—that is, between competing values, which, though in each case genuine, pull in different directions. He must keep the peace between a legitimate demand for punishment, on the one hand, and, on the other hand, the mitigating factors of minority and mental handicap, as well as a family-member's obligation not to subject a fellow family-member to a real risk of torture, or even murder, at the hands of the police.

Following the attack, Lucy chooses not to leave the farm or lay charges against Pollux and/or Petrus, but to seek a "'modus vivendi'" (Kossew 2003, 161) with Petrus and his family where she is. In view of the moral complexity of the situation, as unpacked above, we should beware of seeing this as a *purely instrumental* modus vivendi—a "[b]are" (Richardson 2002, 146) or *strategic* compromise dictated by the power dynamics of the situation. Though she has been the victim of a horrific crime, it is Lucy herself who tries to make David see some of the reasons why handing Pollux over to the police is not obviously the right thing to do: his mental handicap, and the fact that Petrus has family obligations to him (*Disgrace*, 200). In addition, she is unwilling to let David call the police on Petrus and thereby "destroy" things for Petrus, given that "[i]t's not Petrus's fault" (133) and—as we know from Bev—she owes him a lot for his work getting the market garden going (140).

Moreover, in the most controversial passage of Coetzee's novel, Lucy makes clear that she sees the moral imperative to make redress for past injustice as having some bearing on her situation. Segregation and *apartheid* during the twentieth century worked to the relative benefit of white people like David and Lucy, but to the relative disadvantage, and indeed oppression, of black people like Petrus and his family. This idea comes to expression in a very unsettling form, when Lucy says to David of her rape: "What if . . . what if *that* is the price one has to pay for staying on? Perhaps that is how they look at it; perhaps that is how I should look at it too" (158). It is important to see that we readers can—and indeed must—reject the idea that this is how Lucy should think of the wrong that her rapists did to her, without rejecting the notion that the moral imperative of redress has some bearing on her situation following the crime. The idea that a concern not to perpetuate historical injustice could rightfully play a role in Lucy's choice not to call the police on Petrus, causing great setbacks for him and his dependents, certainly cannot be rejected out of hand.

Like the epilogue ("Umso") to *Wrath*, the last scene involving Lucy in *Disgrace* strikes a palpable note of hope and optimism. As in *Wrath*'s epilogue, the tone is partly sustained by a motif of *new life*: it is summer, "[a] season of blooming," the bees are "in their seventh heaven" (216), and Lucy herself is pregnant—from the day of the attack. Yet it is not only at the biological level that something new is coming into being at the end of *Disgrace*, but also at the social, interpersonal level. Lucy is arriving at a new accommodation with Petrus and his family—a compromise recognizably guided by the diverse moral considerations we have seen are in play in this relationship. Following her ordeal, Lucy and her child are from now on to be officially protected by Petrus (204)—he "will take her under his wing" (140). She will sign the land over to Petrus, to whom she owes so much. But she is to retain her independence: the house remains hers, and no one—including Petrus—is to enter it without her permission (204). She will continue to live as she has up to now, as an independent smallholder. The arrangement is to be called a *marriage*—these are the *lobola* (bride price) terms Lucy commissions her father to communicate to Petrus (Van Wyk Smith 2001, 33). But it is no normal marriage, either by traditional Xhosa standards or by those of "[*u*]*s Westerners*" (202)—in David's phrase. No doubt, David continues to regard the arrangement as a shabby departure from principle—a compromise in the pejorative sense, which leaves one *compromised*: "How can you even contemplate it?" he had said (203). But we readers, taking our cue from the signs of new life, can justifiably take it to be a very different type of compromise: a new synthesis in response to the plurality of conflicting values in play.

Following a horrific experience, Lucy—rather than running away, as David did from Cape Town—elects to stay in the home she has made for herself on the farm and try to feel her way into a new accommodation. At the end of *Disgrace*, it is far from certain that the accommodation will succeed. Nonetheless, this scene, in a much more concrete way than the epilogue to *Wrath*, leaves us with an indication that it will be possible for the individuals on the farm to respond to value conflict, not with paralysis or evasion, but with a creative attempt to find a deep compromise. Despite its harrowing material, *Disgrace*, a novel written during the uncertainty of the 1990s democratic transition, embodies a tangible optimism about South Africa's future.

A DISTINCTIVE LITERARY CANON

South Africa's history and present-day circumstances provide a wealth of fascinating—sometimes harrowing—case studies for philosophical thinking about the plurality of values, the types of conflict to which this plurality gives rise, and the nature of compromise as a response to value conflict. It is, then, no surprise that some of South Africa's greatest literary works incorporate and reflect upon these philosophical themes. The South African literature which explores value conflict and value compromise constitutes a literary canon which crosses linguistic boundaries—in Mqhayi's case, crosses genre boundaries too. It is a canon unified by the distinctive social and historical context to which it is a response.

This chapter has sought to demonstrate that *The Case of the Twins*, *The Wrath of the Ancestors* and *Disgrace* are novels which repay interpretation through a philosophical lens. But it has also sought to show that in this distinctive South African canon, the philosophical and the literary cannot always be cleanly separated from one another. When the only adequate response to a dilemma arising from value conflict is a creative act which brings something new—not fully predictable—into being, the next step in a creative process and the resolution of a dilemma in philosophical ethics may well be all of a piece.[23]

NOTES

1. Some of the action of *Disgrace* takes place in Cape Town and George, in the Western Cape.

2. I have worked from Collingwood August's translation of *The Case of the Twins*, and the translation of *The Wrath of the Ancestors* by A. C. Jordan himself together with his wife Priscilla P. Jordan. I refer throughout to Mqhayi 1966 [1914], Jordan 1980 [1940], and Coetzee 2011 [1999] with the abbreviations *"Twins," "Wrath,"* and *"Disgrace,"* respectively.

3. Mqhayi was born in 1875 at Gqamahashe, on the Thyume River, and educated at Lovedale College (Gérard 1971, 53); but from 1885 to 1891 he and his family lived in Centane, where Mqhayi, though receiving no Western education, learned about the Xhosa judicial system at the *nkundla* of Chief Nzanzana (Dikeni 1992, 24). Although a Christian, Mqhayi went to circumcision school (*op. cit.*, 31), and later achieved distinction as an *mbongi*—or praise-poet (Jordan 1973, 112).

4. Jordan was born in 1906 at the Mbokothwana Mission in Tsolo district (where much of the action of *Wrath* takes place). He grew up in a Christian family, studied at Fort Hare University College, taught at Kroonstad High School in the Orange Free State, and in 1946 was appointed as lecturer in African Languages at the University of Cape Town (Gérard 1971, 82–83, 88).

5. A reference to the ochre body paint and red-dyed blankets worn by traditional Xhosa people.

6. This ethnic tension escalates into open hostility in *Wrath* (206–210). Though *Twins* is set before the coming of the amaMfengu to the lands of the Gcaleka Xhosa, J. H. Soga suggested the novel might be intended to demonstrate how King Hintsa used justice to protect the amaMfengu (Nyamende 2010, 19).

7. As a matter of fact, Babini does "reform after the lawsuit" (Midgley 2010, 236), whereupon "Hintsa presented him with cattle calling him an obedient young man" (Dikeni 1992, 76). (This episode is not included in the Collingwood August translation of *Twins*.)

8. For example, Peter Midgley writes: "The Thembu chief has learned to negotiate the divide which Zwelinzima still needs to cross. . . . What he realises is that he has to walk the tightrope between tradition and book-learned knowledge with care, and this is something that the young and inexperienced Zwelinzima does not acknowledge until it is too late" (2010, 229).

9. "Bare compromise," writes Richardson, "thus does not involve any reconsideration of what is worth seeking for its own sake, only a willingness to accept less satisfactory means to the ends one started with" (2002, 147).

10. I follow Wayne Booth (1988) in distinguishing between the *implied author*, whose intentions can be inferred purely from evidence internal to the text, and the *real-life author*.

11. For a pithy statement of the distinction between these two views, see Berlin 1998 (11–12).

12. Joseph Raz's classic statement of "moral or value-pluralism" affirms "the existence of a plurality of incompatible but morally acceptable forms of life," and claims "not merely that incompatible forms of life are morally acceptable but that they display distinct virtues, each capable of being pursued for its own sake" (1986, 395–96).

13. For example, readers who think that polygamy or arranged marriages are unacceptable in all circumstances.

14. Compare Qangule's commentary on this episode: "Traditional and modern values come face to face and make incompatible demands. . . . Western love requires what traditional attitudes forbid. The competing powers are both in themselves right, the claim of each is equally justified, but the right of each is transformed into a wrong, because it ignores the rights of the other faction" (1974, 52).

15. Coetzee himself has written, "The key characteristic of free indirect speech is that the presence of a narrating intelligence is not asserted: the narrator slips behind or into the intelligence of the character" (1988, 123).

16. I discuss this recurring theme in Coetzee's novels in Hull 2013.

17. David Attwell is an example of a commentator too willing to credit David Lurie's take on the committee of inquiry: "These are puritanical times. Private life is public business" (*Disgrace*, 66). Attwell writes that "the episode involving Lurie's hearing . . . suggest[s] that what exists of the public sphere is an exercise in Foucauldian power intent on destroying the concept of private life" (2002, 338). In fact, though, the charges Lurie faces—sexual harassment (*Disgrace*, 41) and falsifying the mid-term test mark of a student with whom he has been having an affair (40–41)—plainly pertain to his professional role, not his private life.

18. In contrast to this interpretation, Adriaan van Heerden echoes David Lurie's version, claiming that David's "core values . . . do not register on the radar of the committee of inquiry" (2010, 48).

19. Again, compare Qangule's commentary on *Wrath*: "The competing powers are both in themselves right, the claim of each is equally justified, but the right of each is transformed into a wrong, because it ignores the rights of the other faction" (1974, 52).

20. Derek Attridge writes: "It comes to seem likely that [Petrus'] absence during the attack was no coincidence, and that his long-term plan is to reduce Lucy to a condition of dependency" (2004, 171). Suresh Raval attributes to "Petrus and Lucy's rapists" the goal of "possessing Lucy in sexual and material terms" (2008, 157). Adriaan van Heerden concurs, echoing David Lurie's impression when he calls Petrus "an avaricious and cunning manipulator" (2010, 57). There are many other examples.

21. Another possibility is that Petrus had deliberately answered a question different from that posed to him by David, so as not to have to state Pollux's relationship to him right away. Either way, the exchange did not take place as David remembers, or claims to remember, it; either way, Petrus did not lie to him, as David now claims.

22. See Thompson 2000 (235–36). For a vivid flavor of the policing experienced by black people in rural areas during *apartheid*, see Steinberg 2002 (89).

23. The interpretations of literary works laid out in this chapter were first presented to a meeting of the Coetzee Collective in the English Department at the University of Cape Town on August 21, 2013, and to a conference on Transformation of Higher Education and the Formation of the Canon in African Philosophy and African Literature in the Philosophy Department at Rhodes University, Grahamstown, on May 30, 2016. I am grateful to Carrol Clarkson and Uchenna Okeja, respectively, for invitations to speak on these occasions, and to the participants at both events for their comments. To Thabisa Xhalisa I am indebted for introducing me to *Ityala Lamawele* and *Ingqumbo Yeminyanya*, and discussing these novels with me. The published secondary literature on Jordan and Mqhayi's novels is sparse compared to the profusion of published work on *Disgrace*, but several unpublished Masters theses and PhD dissertations stored in the University of Cape Town Library contain high-quality commentary on which I have gratefully drawn, as indicated in the text. Siyasanga Hayi and Phumeza Mlokoti generously assisted me on matters of meaning in isiXhosa. For written comments on drafts of this chapter, I thank Carrol Clarkson, Kathy Luckett, Nicoletta Michaletos, Aretha Phiri and Hedley Twidle.

REFERENCES

Attridge, Derek. 2004. *J. M. Coetzee and the Ethics of Reading: Literature in the Event*. Chicago and London: University of Chicago Press.

Attwell, David. 2002. "Race in Disgrace." *Interventions: International Journal of Postcolonial Studies* 4 (3): 331–41.

Berlin, Isaiah. 1998. *The Power of Ideas*. London: Pimlico.

Booth, Wayne C. 1988. *The Company We Keep: An Ethics of Fiction*. Berkeley: University of California Press.

Coetzee, J. M. 1986. *Foe*. Johannesburg: Ravan Press.

Coetzee, J. M. 1988. *White Writing: On the Culture of Letters in South Africa*. New Haven and London: Yale University Press.

Coetzee, J. M. 1998 [1983]. *Life & Times of Michael K*. London: Vintage Books.

Coetzee, J. M. 2011 [1999]. *Disgrace*. London: Vintage Books.

Dikeni, Clifford. 1992. "An Examination of the Socio-political Undercurrents in Mqhayi's Novel *Ityala Lamawele*." Master of Arts thesis submitted to the Faculty of Arts, University of Cape Town.

Gérard, Albert S. 1971. *Four African Literatures: Xhosa, Sotho, Zulu, Amharic*. Berkeley, Los Angeles and London: University of California Press.

Hull, George. 2013. "Coetzee in His Castle." *The London Magazine* (October/November): 107–116.

Jordan, A. C. 1973. *Towards an African Literature: The Emergence of Literary Form in Xhosa*. Berkeley, Los Angeles and London: University of California Press.

Jordan, A. C. 1980 [1940]. *The Wrath of the Ancestors (A Novel)*. Translated by A. C. Jordan with Priscilla P. Jordan. Alice: Lovedale Press.

Kossew, Sue. 2003. "The Politics of Shame and Redemption in J. M. Coetzee's *Disgrace*." *Research in African Literatures* 34 (2): 155–62.

Midgley, Peter. 2010. "Renaissance Men: Ntsikana, A. C. Jordan, S. E. K. Mqhayi and South Africa's Cultural Awakening." In *Grappling with the Beast: Indigenous Southern African Responses to Colonialism, 1840–1930*, edited by Peter Limb, Norman Etherington and Peter Midgley, 215–43. Leiden and Boston: Brill.

Mqhayi, S. E. K. 1966 [1914]. *The Case of the Twins*. Translated by Collingwood August. *The New African* (January, March and April): 5–8, 41–44, 74–76.

Nyamende, Abner. 2010. "The Conception and Application of Justice in S. E. K. Mqhayi's *Ityala Lamawele*." *Tydskrif vir Letterkunde* 47 (2): 19–30.

Nyamende, M. A. B. 1991. "Who Really Cares If the Ancestors Are Angry? A. C. Jordan's *The Wrath of the Ancestors 'Ingqumbo Yeminyanya'*." *South African Journal of African Languages* 11 (4): 119–24.

Peires, Jeffrey. 1979. "The Lovedale Press: Literature for the Bantu Revisited." *History in Africa* 6: 155–75.

Qangule, Zitobile Sunshine. 1974. "A Study of Conflict and Theme in A. C. Jordan's Novel *Ingqumbo Yeminyanya*." Master of Arts thesis submitted to the University of South Africa.

Qangule, Zitobile Sunshine. 1979. "A Study of Theme and Technique in the Creative Works of S. E. K. L. N. Mqhayi." Doctor of Philosophy dissertation submitted to the Faculty of Arts, University of Cape Town.

Raval, Suresh. 2008. "In Search of an Ethics in a Troubled Society: Coetzee's *Disgrace*." In *J. M. Coetzee: Critical Perspectives*, edited by Kailash C. Baral, 145–60. New Delhi: Pencraft International.

Raz, Joseph. 1986. *The Morality of Freedom*. Oxford: Clarendon Press.

Richardson, Henry S. 2002. *Democratic Autonomy: Public Reasoning about the Ends of Policy*. New York: Oxford University Press.

Steinberg, Jonny. 2002. *Midlands*. Johannesburg and Cape Town: Jonathan Ball.

Thompson, Leonard. 2000. *A History of South Africa*. Third edition. New Haven and London: Yale University Press.

Van Heerden, Adriaan. 2010. "Disgrace, Desire, and the Dark Side of the New South Africa." In *J. M. Coetzee and Ethics: Philosophical Perspectives on Literature*, edited by Anton Leist and Peter Singer, 43–63. New York: Columbia University Press.

Van Wyk Smith, Malvern. 2001. "From 'Boereplaas' to Vlakplaas: The Farm from Thomas Pringle to J. M. Coetzee." In *Strangely Familiar: South African Narratives on Town and Countryside*, edited by Chris N. van der Merwe, 17–36. Parow: ContentLot.

Williams, Bernard. 1973. *Problems of the Self: Philosophical Papers, 1956–1972*. Cambridge: Cambridge University Press.

Chapter 4

Blind Sisyphus
Two Perspectives on Meursault
Pedro Tabensky

NORTH AFRICAN PHILOSOPHICAL CANON: COLONIALITY, REVOLUTION, AND THE ABSURD

Albert Camus was a philosopher, novelist, playwright, editor, and activist hero of the French resistance movement during World War II; he was also the recipient of the 1957 Nobel prize in literature, which he obtained three years before his untimely death in a car accident in 1960. His passing came two years before the end of the bloody Algerian War (1954–1962) in which Algeria gained its independence from France, largely thanks to the efforts of the *Front de Libération Nationale* (FLN). A *pied noir* (translated "black foot"), that is, an Algerian of European ancestry, a Frenchman of North Africa,[1] Camus' existence was peculiar, as peculiar as the fact that the Mediterranean part of Algeria, his birthplace, was considered by France to be an integral part of itself rather than a colonial outpost, despite the fact that most people living there did not have French citizenship. Camus' sensitivities were largely French, but his heart was in Algeria. And, atypically for a *pied noir*, his concerns were for Algeria as a whole, including the Arab and Berber majority, those generically described by Camus as "Arabs," rather than merely for the inward-looking insular and, in general terms, highly racist *pied noir* community. And his concerns were genuine, as evidenced by his journalistic writing, particularly regarding the French-caused famine of the Arab and Berber population in Kabylia. Indeed, these articles brought his journalistic career to an end in Algeria as they incurred the wrath of local authorities.

Perhaps controversially, I include Albert Camus in what could be described as the North African philosophical canon, with Albert Memmi and Frantz Fanon. Camus, however, would perhaps not be so happy with being classified as a member of this canon, among other things, because he balked at being described as a philosopher. And he would also balk at being put in the same category as Fanon, as he was one of the fiercest critics of revolutionary violence while Fanon, one of its great apologists, famously defended the idea that revolutionary violence is a "cleansing force" (1963, 94). Memmi lies somewhere in between, somewhat closer in spirit to Camus than to Fanon, for he did not think of murder as a solution. But that is precisely the point: despite the fact that they never engaged with each other's work (Memmi engages with the work of both, but not in ways that are directly useful to our present concerns), Camus and Fanon were both dedicated to understanding the same cataclysmic event that put an end to French colonial ambitions over the largest country in Africa.

Both Fanon and Camus died before the end of the war, before the "suitcase or the coffin" expulsion of almost all *pieds noirs* from Algeria, and before the revenge massacre of tens of thousands of *harkis*—Muslims who fought on the side of the French during the war—and their families. This happened with the rise of a new reign of bickering commanders and "police interrogators," to borrow from David Macey (2012, xv), that would have welcomed neither Camus nor Fanon in the new Algeria.

What connects the three authors listed above is a deep preoccupation with overcoming colonial rule or at the very least diminishing its nefarious impact on Algeria. Memmi refers to Camus as the "Colonizer of Good Will" (1957, 95–96), living an impossible double-life: a Frenchman of North Africa—a *pied noir*—and a man committed to ending iniquity.[2] Edward Said (1994, 169–85) is also sympathetically critical of him. He sees him as part of the colonial canon. And Muslim Algerian author Kamel Daoud (2015) echoes some of Said's concerns in his novel *The Meursault Investigation*, a novel I will discuss in some detail in the pages that follow. Thomas Meaney (2013) summarizes Camus' position on Algeria during the war of liberation as follows: "The crisis in Algeria, for him, did not stem from the fact of the French presence, but rather from the form it took." In other words, Camus was less concerned about ongoing French presence than he was with the injustices brought about by the French. He perhaps naively believed that the best solution for Algeria was a kind of French protectorate where *pieds noirs* and Muslims could live side-by-side as equals.

INTRODUCING HARUN, THE WRETCH

Kamel Daoud's critical yet sympathetic literary engagement with Camus' philosophy and literature in *The Meursault Investigation* (2015) does much to locate Camus in his Algerian context, and he follows a line of inquiry initially explored by Memmi and Said. In this section I explore Albert Camus' philosophy in light of Daoud's literary engagement with Camus' philosophy and literature. Daoud's novel is at once a celebration and a critique of Camus by a Muslim Algerian who explores the extent to which Camus' philosophy of the absurd can help us understand contemporary Algeria's predicament embodied in the failed life of Harun, the protagonist of Daoud's novel. Camus' inability "to remain on a universal plane" (2004, 211) blinded him to the possibility that someone like Harun—portrayed as an Algerian victim of colonialism and neocolonialism—could live an irredeemably wretched life, swallowed up by an abject history, unable to find a "solution to the absurd" (2013 [1942], 7), to borrow Camus' phrase. Contrary to what Camus would probably think, one cannot imagine Harun happy. He is unable to find a solution because there is no solution. Harun's here and now proscribes the possibility of happiness.

But before engaging with some of the details of *The Meursault Investigation*, we will need to explore some key features of Camus' exuberant and often bewildering thought, which form the backdrop of the novel through which Daoud explores the contemporary Algerian situation.

SISYPHUS

Camus thought even Sisyphus could achieve the happiness that eluded Harun. Sisyphus—a character based on the Greek myth of the same name—is Camus' absurd hero in his first philosophical treatise, *The Myth of Sisyphus* (1942). Camus' Sisyphus stoically embraces the absurd, accepts his fate solemnly, and without nostalgia finds meaning and purpose, not in his condition alone—which is deeply unpropitious—but in his attitude to his condition, in his refusal to accept the command of his absurd condition, that is, his refusal to capitulate to necessity. He is condemned for defying the gods to a life of futile toil, endlessly and without respite to push a stone up a mountain only to see it come rolling down again once he has reached the top. This interminable cycle turns Sisyphus into an absurd hero because he is human and, as such, he is able to envisage alternatives that he deems better than his present futile—even ridiculous—condition (judged as such from his own perspective). A dung beetle rolling a ball of dung uphill is no Sisyphus, for a dung beetle is incapable of envisaging and so is unable to experience the absurd, to experience the clash between the actual and the envisaged. A dung beetle cannot hope.

The absurd or, better put, the experience of the absurd, is only possible for creatures that hope. It is in relation to this that he has to choose between two possible fates: capitulation or reckoning. He knows that he is condemned and that he cannot change the situation to which he is fettered. So, rather than being defeated by his condition, his defiant scorn ennobles him, turns him into a praiseworthy hero who is able, not so much to overcome, but to struggle with dignity. And his reckoning is that of a happy man whose defiant "No!" implies the "Yes!" of someone who recognizes a world of ennobling value present all along at the center of his being. In Camus' words: "A man who says no: but whose refusal does not imply a renunciation. He is also a man who says yes as soon as he begins to think for himself" (2013 [1942], 1).

"One must imagine Sisyphus happy," Camus tells us (2013 [1942], 89). But, we must ask, can we really imagine him so? Perhaps we can, but perhaps also Camus' image of Sisyphus expresses macho insensitivity. To be sure, defiance has its place, but clearly there are stark limits to the possibility of happiness.

Harun has been checkmated by history and so can be nothing but a wretch unable, despite his deeply thoughtful disposition, to find a solution to the absurd. Like Sisyphus and unlike Meursault, at least for most of his life, Harun lucidly faces the absurd, but he is defeated by his circumstances, namely colonial and neocolonial Algeria. And the question naturally arises in light of Harun's failed life: Ought one truly to imagine Sisyphus happy?

Sisyphus, "proletarian of the gods" (2013 [1942], 87–88), refuses to go to pieces. Yet the possibility of going to pieces is inexpungible. He must struggle to keep it together, and he does so because he is passionately wedded to concrete existence, indeed to living "without appeal" (2013 [1942], 45), without, that is, the need for consoling evasions of an imagined tomorrow that will distract us from living in the only place life can be lived, in the here and now. Before being condemned by the gods to push the stone, "he lived facing the curve of the gulf, the sparkling sea, and the smiles of earth" (2013 [1942], 87). Sisyphus is portrayed as a man of this world as it appears to us, avoiding consoling distractions. This is indeed a central theme in Camus. As he explains:

> I want to know whether, accepting a life without appeal, one can also agree to work and create without appeal and what is the way leading to these liberties. I want to liberate my universe of its phantoms and to people it solely with flesh and blood truths whose presence I cannot deny. (2013 [1942], 74)

Sisyphus, Camus tells us, has learned to embrace his tragic condition by avoiding—but never fully eliminating—tempting distractions that drag the possibility of desperation with it, stemming from a denigration of life born of the stark contrast between what is and what could be. If he hoped for the impossible, he would lose the will to carry on, the will to live a life of honor—a necessary condition for happiness according to Camus—despite the futility of his efforts. So he pushes hope for the impossible aside, thus liberating his "universe of its phantoms and to people it solely with flesh and blood truths," truths, that is, that "the heart can feel . . . before they [the truths in question] become clear to the intellect" (2013, 5). These are the truths that Camus describes in "Nuptials at Tipasa," where he recommends that we inform our lives by a "strange certainty" that comes about when one is "fitting into things," concrete things such as the sensual landscape of Tipasa where one is "greeted by the song of the world," the "great free love of nature" that "absorbs me completely" (1970, 95–96). Having at least partially forgotten "the smiles of the earth"—given that he is averse to nostalgia and any other distractions that militate against a focus on the actual—Sisyphus presses forward with purpose, despite the impermanence and futility of his efforts: "The struggle itself towards the heights is enough to fill a man's heart" (2013 [1942], 89). He fits into his stone, becoming one with it.

"[S]truggle . . . is enough to fill a man's heart" if, Camus thinks, the heart is properly directed to the actual, rather than fully invested in an imagined tomorrow or swallowed up by a blinding routine, as was Meursault. This is of course not true of all struggles; for some circumstances are irredeemable, and we shall see toward the end that, oddly, Camus does not properly consider possibilities of this variety. Our passion for life necessarily drags unfulfilled desires with it, primarily our desire that all or much that is good shall forever remain with us, including the good of life itself. The fear of impermanence, that everything will escape us like sand between the fingers, is arguably one of the greatest fears of those who have become conscious of their predicament, and this is particularly so for those who have much to lose. Happiness drags its shadow with it. Camus says: "There is no sun [happiness] without shadow, and it is essential to know the night" (2013, 89). Perhaps, but the night can also drown the light.

Sisyphus is no longer nostalgic or, better put, he is no longer consumed by nostalgia, by hopes for something outside of the realm of "flesh and blood truths." He has come to realize the value of struggle to the end, even while knowing that in the end he cannot win. So he turns away from distractions and looks toward the task at hand in the domain of the actual. The value of struggle and the value of achievement come apart in his mind, for he is committed in the first instance to life, to the actual, to being fully present in the present, straining every nerve, consumed by the task, a task that is at once redemptive and futile.

Sisyphus is driven by a "yes" and by a "no": the Nietzschean life-affirming "yes" (*amor fati*) and the "no" that refuses to surrender to his fate while at the same time remaining faithful to his mission.[3] Sisyphus' "no" implies a refusal to succumb to wishful thinking, to buy solace at the price of trickery, the false hope that finally the stone will remain on top of the mountain and that he will be able to walk away a man no longer condemned.

And it implies a refusal to end it all, motivated by placing too much value on success of the sort that militates against being present in the present, as embodied beings fully absorbed in the business of being alive, rolling our own stones.

Sisyphus embodies Camus' vision of how we should live in light of our condition. Following Nietzsche's footsteps, Camus argues that we can avoid false comforts brought about by misplaced hopes and the possibility of desperation that emerges when one dedicates the actual to a disembodied future that undermines our ability to appreciate life and the living, by living with dignity with what is at our disposal rather than yearning for "the mirage of the Eternal City" (2000, 247).

Sisyphus does not want the stone to come rolling down, but he recognizes that this is not something he is going to be able to change, and he turns his frustration into a form of a life-affirming protest. The form that his protest against the inevitable takes is attitudinal. He cannot change his predicament, but he can change his attitude to it. By adopting the attitude that he did toward his situation, Sisyphus lets his divine assailants know that he cannot be defeated by their sentence; that he, like Oedipus—fated to murder his father, marry his mother, father his siblings, and who rips his eyes out in an act of desperation once the truth is revealed to him—cannot in the end be defeated by the inevitable.

NAGEL ON ABSURDITY

We should ideally passionately embrace life, Camus avers—effortfully find contentment in it, something that will invariably drag disappointment with it. Indeed, part of the task of living well, according to Camus, involves finding a rickety balance between accepting the actual and envisaging alternatives, something that philosopher Thomas Nagel thinks should motivate irony rather than Camus-style scorn. Nagel thinks that his views actually contradict Camus' views on "defiance and scorn" (1971, 726). But I think Nagel helps add clarity to Camus' views while at the same time failing fully to appreciate the importance of what is at stake. According to Nagel,

> We cannot live human lives without energy and attention, nor without making choices which show that we take some things more seriously than others. Yet we have always available a point of view outside the particular form of our lives, from which the seriousness appears gratuitous. These two inescapable viewpoints collide in us, and that is what makes life absurd. It is absurd because we ignore the doubts that we know cannot be settled, continuing to live with nearly undiminished seriousness in spite of them. (1971, 719)

For Nagel, the absurd emerges because we are forced to take ourselves seriously from the perspective of our own daily lives and yet, *sub species aeternitatis*, the grounds for seriousness are not available, which is why he recommends an ironic stance on life. Seriousness and skepticism clash in us—given that all justifications start with premises which are themselves unjustified, meaning that our grounds for belief are always shaky and, yet, we have no choice but to take ourselves seriously—inviting us unavoidably to continue to engage with life with "energy and attention . . . making choices which show that we take some things more seriously than others," but to do so without taking ourselves too seriously. But this invitation to develop what we could describe as a form of moral light-heartedness cannot be sustained and would indeed be preposterous in extreme situations, say, at the coalface of injustice or in the face of deep loss. In such circumstances, irony has no place and Camus-style scorn is warranted. The right attitude is not Nagel's skepticism that flows from the fact that all chains of reasoning lead us down an interminable path, but to recognize with Camus the extent to which the ethical is unrenounceable. Camus has little interest in ultimate justifications. Instead he is interested in clarity of vision stemming from sensitive observation of what cannot be renounced, of what shows itself vividly to us when we are properly disposed.

Camus' concern with the absurd is precisely the concern regarding the contradiction between knowledge of the facts and a desire for transcendence. Disappointment emerges as a consequence of the fact that we are creatures burning with desire for transcending our current predicament, and also burning with desire to relish in the wonder of actual existence. "[T]he capacity to transcend ourselves in thought" (1971, 727), as Nagel puts it, puts us at odds with the world, something that Camus acknowledges. The brute fact, for instance, that death happens does not in and of itself put us at odds. Non-human animals are not at odds. Rather, it is the often-visceral belief that we do not want to die—informed by hope for what is not—and the knowledge that we will that puts us at odds. And this accounts for the experience of the absurd. Nagel recommends good humor and Camus recommends defiance.

BLIND SISYPHUS

Meursault, protagonist of *The Stranger*, is a *pied noir* Sisyphus who only comes to terms with his condition in his prison cell, while awaiting his own encounter with the blade, accused of casually murdering an anonymous "Arab" (Harun's brother, according to Daoud). He is, prior to his epiphany, a man "divested of illusions and lights" and hence he "feels an alien, a stranger" (2013 [1942], 7). Meursault lacks something that defines Sisyphus' existence: "passions of this earth" (2013 [1942], 87). He did not live "facing the curve of the gulf, the sparkling sea, and the smiles of earth" (2013, 87). Instead, his life was characterized by mindless routine, by apathy and indifference, indeed, by distance from the actual.

His life is one of disenchantment, simply passing time and wedded to nothing. But Meursault's sense of the passing of time is vague, out of focus. One is tempted to say that it is unstructured insofar as it is neither informed by false comforts nor by the feeling of the absurd. *The Stranger* can be read as providing an alternative solution to the problem of nihilism, of the absurd, to Fyodor Dostoyevsky's, who, according to Camus, trades lucidity for consoling evasion.[4] Dostoyevsky famously holds that without God life would be senseless, so he cannot but believe in his existence. Without religion Dostoyevsky avers, we risk going down Kirilov's nihilistic path. Kirilov is one of the characters in Dostoyevsky's *Demons* (2008), the character that most emphatically embodies Dostoyevsky's idea of a "logical suicide," an idea also explored in essay form in his *The Diary of a Writer* (1919, 538–42). Kirilov's is not, in the first instance, the desperate kind of suicide driven by overwhelming passions. It is, rather, suicide born of the conviction—mistaken according to Camus—that, given that reality does not furnish us with pre-given meanings, life is not worth living.[5] Kirilov "feels that God is necessary and that he must exist. But he knows that he does not and cannot exist" (Camus 2013 [1942], 77). According to Dostoyevsky, without faith we are condemned to utter absurdity, to a nihilistic world dispossessed of a guiding light from afar. He explains:

> If faith in immortality is so necessary to the human being (that without it he comes to the point of killing himself) it must therefore be the normal state of humanity. Since this is the case, the immortality of the human soul exists without any doubt.[6]

Meursault, like Kirilov, lives without consoling evasions. He lives without hope for a promised land but, unlike Kirilov, he remains ignorant of his condition until the very end of the novel. In fact, for most of his life Meursault lives for nothing. He lives in exile, divorced from life. He feels the weight of the absurd born of this divorce, but is unable to come to terms with it, at least not until the end of the novel, when it becomes clear to him that he is a condemned man, something that brings him to lucidity and to the happiness of he who, like Sisyphus, has come to terms with his fate. Before then he lives a "mechanical life" (2013 [1946], 12).

Before realizing that he is condemned to death by a court of law, Meursault is unable to take responsibility for his life. He floats over events like a ghost, indifferent to them. Meursault casually observes that "I'd rather lost the habit of noting my feelings" (2013 [1946], Loc. 741). Everything to him carries the same weight: the death of his mother or of the anonymous "Arab" who he casually murders on a beach in Algiers, and his affair with Marie, his lover. He does have an inner life that responds weakly and passively to outside stimuli. He seems to stand away from his life as if it did not belong to him, as if he were the captive of Algerian suffocating heat and cutting light, which he perceives as threatening until the end of the novel, where he finally comes to terms with his predicament and starts grasping the beauty embodied in Mediterranean light. His life abruptly comes into focus in light of his non-evasive confrontation with his own mortality, once he has given up on the idea of a successful appeal, once he realizes that he "was caught in the rattrap irrevocably" (Camus 2013 [1946], Loc.1289). The terrible light and heat that motivates the murder gives way to nature's sublime beauty.

Meursault is, as the original French title of the book suggests, a foreigner, a stranger, an outsider. Things happen to him, but nothing touches him. Meursault unthinkingly stands at a distance from life, unable to take responsibility for it. And hence he is blind, enveloped in a surreal cloud of incomprehension. Even the thirst to comprehend escapes him. From his perspective, everything is unreal. He is the embodiment of nihilism, that which needs to be overcome if one is going to live facing the absurd without "false comforts." Meursault indifferently states that: "'But,' I reminded myself, 'it's common knowledge that life isn't worth living, anyhow'" (Camus 2013 [1946], Loc. 1338–39).

"ARAB-NESS"

"Arab-ness is like Negro-ness," Harun tells us: it "only exists in the white man's eyes" (2015, 60). Meursault kills one casually—as if the blazing sunlight of Algeria had pulled the trigger—and nobody in the hermetically sealed *pied noir* world condemns him for this. Meursault murders under a "stifling sky" (Camus 2013 [1946], 23) from which a "shaft of light shot upward from the steel, and I felt as if a long, thin blade transfixed my forehead" (Camus 2013 [1946], Loc. 1338–39). This sky that shows vividly to him that he is an outsider and that he needs to choose whether to die or to stay, rather than remaining in a limbo of indifference. This sky illustrates the "confrontation between the human need and the unreasonable silence of the world" (2013 [1942], 22). His murder is merely the excuse to punish him for greater sins that are not typically punishable by law. The "Arabs" merely form the backdrop of Camus' novel. An insignificant murder. Hardly a murder at all. If the victim were French, that would be a different matter altogether. Indeed, he is condemned to death for being indifferent to his mother's death, for casually starting an affair with Marie the day after the funeral. From the perspective of his judges, his true crimes are against *pieds noirs*. The Arab, the real victim, the one whose life was extinguished by four bullets, is anonymous, a nobody, a mere excuse for Meursault finally to take responsibility for his life, in his cell, as he awaits his encounter with the violent blade. Nobody, not even Meursault, gives a damn about the death of the anonymous "Arab." He is condemned for not abiding by the rules of his social milieu. A blind man condemned by blind men. He floats over the landscape indifferently while his executioners are shackled by the weight of the unquestioned, of the collective expectations of a condemned community.

Meursault overcomes nihilism in the end; he moves from indifference to the feeling of the absurd and to finally finding a solution to it. He takes a stand when he attacks a caretaker of metaphysical hope—a priest who visits him in the hope of converting him, By doing this he seals his commitment to the actual and, in this coming down from the safe place of indifference, he recognizes the need to take a stand. But he never overcomes the fact that he is a *pied noir*, indifferent to the end to the fate of the Arab. He is a condemned man who remains in his heart a member of a condemned community that has disowned him for not giving a damn for those who they think matter. Meursault reflects in his cell:

> And I, too, felt ready to start life all over again. It was as if that great rush of anger had washed me clean, emptied me of hope, and, gazing up at the dark sky spangled with its signs and stars, for the first time, the first, I laid my heart open to the benign indifference of the universe. To feel it so like myself, indeed, so brotherly, made me realize that I'd been happy, and that I was happy still. For all to be accomplished, for me to feel less lonely, all that remained to hope was that on the day of my execution there should be a huge crowd of spectators and that they should greet me with howls of execration. (2013 [1946], Loc. 1448–52)

Meursault hoped for an appeal, hoping to regain his lost freedom. But "that great rush of anger"—finally a sign of commitment to life, when he took a stand against the priest—freed him from this attachment to the impossible, to the idea "of circumventing the machine, learning if the inevitable admits a loophole" (Camus 2013 [1946], Loc. 1275–76). His mortality became a reality to him and, relatedly, his angry refusal to accept subterfuge, brought him into his present, forcing him finally to take responsibility for his life, to take a stand.

But what kind of man was Meursault, who was largely indifferent to the fact that he committed a murder, who didn't spare a moment's thought for the Arab? Can Camus consistently claim that he is of this world in the way he envisaged one ought to be, that he learned in the end to be in the now, if he is unable to grasp the humanity of the man whose life he casually extinguished? Camus would probably reply in the negative if asked this question directly, and it is conceivable that, by doing so, he would come to realize that his philosophy is inconsistent with his commonplace *pied noir* prejudices.

WRETCHED SISYPHUS

Daoud's *The Meursault Investigation* is a rewriting of *The Stranger* "from right to left," from an "Arab"—who, the narrator complains, even "Arabs" call "The Arab"—rather than a *pied noir* perspective (2015, 7). We had to wait decades until the writing of this novel—set in an Algeria that has already excised *pied noir* and French iniquity only to rediscover new forms—to rediscover (apparently, for we cannot be certain that the narrator is not making the whole thing up) what the victim's name is, to discover that he had a life, that he is somebody to others rather than the mere excuse for *pied noir* introspection.

Musa's brother, Harun—the narrator—sees himself as a "bottom-feeder," a wretch. His situation seems irredeemable. The stone that he is rolling uphill is his brother's corpse, helped along by his embittered mother who wishes that it was Harun who died on that fateful day when Meursault shot Musa on account of the blazing sun. Harun is born of the misfortunes of Muslim Algeria: conquest, mass murder, criminality, dependency, inhumanity, and bilious resentment. He lives without hope, irreligiously, confronted with the reality of his situation in raw form and committed, as was Meursault in the end (even if only imperfectly), to stare reality in the face. And it seems that nothing can change his perspective on his circumstances. He has become entirely incapable of love or of passionate commitment to anyone or anything, living inside a body that may as well be someone else's. He is an old man, fully aware that his days are numbered, and he looks back at a failed life with brutal honesty, interested only in "flesh and blood truths" or, as Harun puts it: "As for me, I don't like anything that rises to heaven, I only like things affected by gravity" (2015, 69).

Somehow, despite his tragic predicament, Harun clings to life. But, given his circumstances, we cannot imagine him a happy Sisyphus. And he concludes that "All things considered, my life has been more tragic than your hero's [Meursault]" (2015, 88). *The Meursault Investigation* is a respectful critique of Camus. Following the footsteps of earlier critiques such as Memmi and Said's, Daoud accuses Camus of having what could be characterized as a colonial sensitivity.

The epigraph of *The Meursault Investigation* by the Romanian pessimist, Emil Cioran, gives the reader a direction from the very start: "The hour of crime does not strike at the same time for every people. This explains the permanence of history." Or, as Harun, the protagonist, puts it: "The truth is that Independence only pushed people on both sides to switch roles" (2015, 11). Although *The Meursault Investigation* is meant to be a rewriting of *The Stranger* "from right to left," it is more explicitly focused on history than Camus' first novel, strongly suggesting that Daoud is also interested in the material developed in *The Rebel* and elsewhere, where the political dimension of Camus concerning with "flesh and blood truths" is explored, and how such truths are undermined by establishing relationships to ideals that make it so that the actual is understood merely as a means. Daoud's narrator states:

> It was a Monday in March 1963. The country was in full celebration mode, but a kind of fear underlay the rejoicing, for the beast fattened on seven years of war had become voracious and refused to go back underground. A muted power struggle was raging among the conquering commanders. (2015, 123)

The novel is largely about the post-independence "hour of crime" or the switching of roles, about how the "hour of crime" of Muslim Algeria followed on from French Algeria's hour. And, more specifically, it is about Harun's "hour of crime," when he is forced by his mother to murder Joseph for being a *pied noir*, thus avenging the murder of his brother.

As with Meursault, Harun is a condemned man. He believed that he "was practically the murderer's double" (2015, 131). But he was not really. Meursault is indifferent to the murder till the end while Harun is consumed by the *roumi* or foreigner's murder. But he, unlike Meursault, is crushed by circumstances—a "bottom-feeder," in his own words (2015, 25)—indeed, by history as expressed in the passage from Cioran. The absurd is more real for Harun than for Meursault. The history of terror repeats itself. And he can find no peace, no happiness. All is dark in his life.

Harun is right to think that, from Meursault's perspective, the murder of his brother is inconsequential. The murder figures only vaguely in Meursault's mind. He is self-obsessed and seems till the end not to care much about others (although he shows some interest in his mother toward the end, but the care is abstract, the care of a detached onlooker rather than a son). Harun, on the other hand, confronts the absurd but is unable to make anything positive of it. He wallows in the muck, "bottom-feeder" like. The murder of Joseph proscribes any possibility of happiness, whereas for Meursault it is the beginning of the path toward the peculiar happiness of a man who is soon to be decapitated. And the narrator of Daoud's novel accuses Meursault of "heading for a mystery" rather than actually caring about "flesh and blood truths": "That's denial of a shockingly violent kind, don't you think? As soon as the shot is fired, the murderer turns around, heading for a mystery he considers worthier of interest than the Arab's life" (2015, 46).

Daoud seems rightly to be critiquing Camus, using Camus against himself. Camus, the philosopher who spends his philosophical life critiquing lovers of distractions and evasions, is being accused of "heading for a mystery," of caring too much about abstractions and too little about "flesh and blood truths."

Harun rolls his stone uphill, a broken man, condemned, and miserable. He lives for very little, crushed by the weight of history, committed to the actual, and hence wretched. He seems committed to his resentments:

> The crime forever compromises both love and the possibility of loving. I killed a man, and since then, life is no longer sacred in my eyes. After what I did, the body of every woman I met quickly lost its sensuality, its possibility of giving me an illusion of the absolute. (2015, 91)

Although apparently endorsing much of Camus' philosophy of "flesh and blood truths," Daoud seems to think that Camus falls prey to what he thinks we must always shun, namely subterfuge. There seems to be something of the National Geographic aesthetic in Camus' writing where even the most horrendous events seem to be "heading for a mystery." Even Sisyphus is "heading for a mystery." In Harun's words:

> Have you seen the way he writes? He's writing about a gunshot, and he makes it sound like poetry! His world is clean, clear, exact, honed by morning sunlight, enhanced with fragrances and horizons. The only shadow is cast by "the Arabs," blurred, incongruous objects left over from "days gone by," like ghosts. (2015, 2)

Camus' aesthetic approach to the problem of the absurd blinds him to the fact that happiness demands more than merely the right attitude. Circumstances must be minimally adequate. Harun's circumstances are not. His "flesh and blood truths" are crushing. A poetic attitude toward his life is not available to him, and the novel's style is expressive of this. One must imagine Harun crushed by the weight of his stone, in short, by the abject history of Algeria, past and present.

Harun was not even granted the strange privilege of being condemned for the murder of Joseph. His act was met with indifference as was the indifference of the court that tried Meursault for not caring about the death of his mother. Joseph is a mere *roumi*, a mere foreigner, no one that anybody should be concerned about in the new Algeria. *Roumi*-talk replaces Arab-talk. Were he to have been condemned to death, perhaps he would have achieved Sisyphean enlightenment.

The Meursault Investigation is a novel about crime, about crime that is a response to French criminality. It is a story that shows that the happiness that Camus recommends is not available to all. And the fact that he did not see this shows that Camus contradicts his own philosophy and heads "for a mystery."

REBELLION'S DISCONTENTS

Despite the criticism outlined above, Daoud endorses central ideas developed by Camus. Daoud's strategy is to use Camus in order to critique him. *The Meursault Investigation* is, among other things, a literary endorsement of Camus' views on political violence, developed most extensively in *The Rebel*. Here Camus returns to ideas developed in *The Myth of Sisyphus*, but takes them from the personal to the political. *The Rebel* can be read as a plea to shun abstract thinking that disregards "flesh and blood truths." He argues that the focus on any virtuous political rebellion must prefer "a man of flesh and blood" rather than "an abstract concept of man." "Real generosity toward the future lies in giving all to the present" (2000 [1951], 257), Camus argues. At the heart of Camus' concern with virtuous rebellion is a rejection of the instrumental logic that forfeits the present and its people to an ideal future, an object of hope that distracts us from full immersion into the present. This is precisely the sort of hope that leads to "resentment," for it amounts to a denigration of the actual for the sake of the ideal, that is, it places the actual at the service of an idea rather than the other way around.

But it is tempting to prefer the abstract to the concrete when circumstances are so bereft that happiness becomes impossible unless informed by subterfuge or, relatedly, by an abstract vision of a better tomorrow. Indeed, circumstances of this sort are precisely those that led to the FLN revolt that ended French colonial rule in Algeria. The bloody Algerian War (1954–1962), as it is known, cost hundreds of thousands of lives on all sides of the divide, and the net result was the replacement of one sort of tyranny for another. Camus was one of the most famous voices against FLN and French violence. He thought that the status quo could largely be preserved for *pieds noirs* while at the same time improving the circumstances for "Arabs," and that this could only be achieved if France remained in power, at least in an administrative capacity. Daoud does not side with the FLN and is quite critical of it, as suggested by Cioran's "hour of crime" passage. He endorses Camus' view that violence for the sake of an abstract ideal can lead to nothing good for it denigrates the actual.

The problem is that the actual circumstances of those living Harun-style lives cannot sustain a virtuous Sisyphus, a possibility that Camus does not seem to consider fully enough. In this regard and as discussed above, Camus seems strangely to be aligned with the Stoics, who believed that one could be happy on the wheel because a happy person just is a virtuous person, a person with the right attitude to life, something that ideally floats free of external conditions.[7] So *The Meursault Investigation*, unlike *The Stranger*, is an unqualifiedly tragic novel that shows the extent to which history can irredeemably crush individuals. And the history of Algeria, where French terror was replaced by bickering commanders, exemplifies the impossible burdens that history can place on our shoulders. Harun is not only an "Arab" Meursault. He is a Sisyphus that we cannot imagine could ever be happy. Consequently, Harun's life is irrevocably clouded by the experience of the absurd. Nothing in Harun's life allows him to find a "solution to the absurd." He cannot, contrary to Camus' Sisyphus, cultivate an attitude that would allow him to live happily in the world that he inherited.

NOTES

1. *Pieds noirs* were forced to leave Algeria after the war. Almost none are left in Algeria today, not surprisingly given that they were confronted with the chilling choice between "the suitcase or the coffin," between exile or death.

2. In "Camus or the Colonizer of Good Will" (1957) Memmi discusses the tragic predicament of the leftist colonizer—epitomized by Camus—who was in the "impossible historical situation" of having to choose between being a *pied noir* and having leftist commitments. See also Memmi (2003, 63–88).

3. Although inspired by Nietzsche's notion of life affirmation, Camus argues that Nietzsche's "yes" is not accompanied by the "no" of the rebel (and, by contrast, the "no" of the revolutionary is not accompanied by the "yes" of affirmation). Camus believes that there is an ideal mean between affirmation and denial (2000, 39–53).

4. See particularly Camus (2013 [1942], 75–81).

5. A key aspect of Camus' discussion of Kirilov is to show that logical suicide entails a commitment to unrenounceable values meaning that Kirilov's gesture is expressive of a misunderstanding and, more generally, this is true of all varieties of logical suicide and not just Kirilov's.

6. Quoted in Camus (2013 [1942], 80).

7. Camus' Mediterranean philosophy seems to be in tension with his Stoic tendencies in a way that is similar to the tension that Martha C. Nussbaum (1994) finds in Nietzsche's writing. Moreover, Camus' Stoic tendencies seem to militate against the basic idea that happiness is a function of deep involvement with the actual. If this is how we should live, something I am in broad agreement with, then one can always in principle suffer reversals that can destroy our ability to be happy. Arguably, to be invulnerable to reversals involves imperviousness to our surroundings. Now, Camus is not quite demanding that Sisyphus be impervious. Rather, he is inviting Sisyphus to recalibrate once he is fettered to the stone. This indeed seems to be good advice, but I think it is unreasonable for Camus to expect that the best among us can always recalibrate.

REFERENCES

Aronson, Ronald. 2004. *Camus & Sartre: The Story of a Friendship and the Quarrel That Ended It*. Chicago: University of Chicago Press.
Camus, Albert. 1960 [1943]. "Letters to a German Friend: Second Letter." *Resistance, Rebellion and Death: Essays*, 12–19. New York: Vintage.
Camus, Albert. 1970 [1938]. "Nuptials in Tipasa." *Lyrical and Critical Essays*, 93–103. London: Vintage.
Camus, Albert. 1970 [1938]. "Summer in Algiers." *Lyrical and Critical Essays*, 114–30. London: Vintage.
Camus, Albert. 2000 [1951]. *The Rebel*. London: Penguin Books Ltd. Kindle Edition.
Camus, Albert. 2013 [1942]. *The Myth of Sisyphus*. London: Penguin Books Ltd. Kindle Edition.
Camus, Albert. 2013 [1946]. *The Stranger*. London: Vintage Books. Kindle Edition.
Daoud, Kamel. 2015. *The Meursault Investigation*. London: Oneworld Publications. Kindle Edition.
Dostoyevsky, Fyodor. 1919 [1873–188]. *The Diary of a Writer*, 538–42. New York: George Braziller.
Dostoyevsky, Fyodor. 2008 [1871–72]. *Demons*. London: Penguin.
Fanon, Frantz. 1963. *The Wretched of the Earth*. New York: Grove Press.
Meaney, Thomas. 2013. "The Colonist of Good Will: On Albert Camus." *The Nation*, September 16. https://www.thenation.com/article/colonist-good-will-albert-camus/
Mecey, David. 2012. *Frantz Fanon: A Biography*. London: Verso.
Memmi, Albert. 1957. "Camus ou le Colonisateur de bonne Volonté" ["Camus or theColonizer of Good Will"]. *La Nef* 12 (December): 95–96.
Memmi, Albert. 2003 [1957]. *The Colonized and the Colonizer*. London: Earthscan Publications Ltd.
Nagel, Thomas. 1971. "The Absurd." *The Journal of Philosophy* 68 (20): 716–27.
Nussbaum, Martha C. 1994. "Pity and Mercy: Nietzsche's Stoicism." In *Nietzsche, Genealogy, Morality*, edited by Richard Schacht, 139–61. Berkeley, CA: University of California Press.
Said, Edward W. 1994. *Culture and Imperialism*. New York: Vintage Books.

Chapter 5

Digital Media, Literacies, Literature, and the African Humanities

Pier Paolo Frassinelli and Lisa Treffry-Goatley

MEDIA CONVERGENCE AND CYBORALITY

This chapter reframes the debate about the decolonization of the African humanities by looking at the relations between what has been called "the two humanities": "literature, history, and philosophy on one side and communication and media studies on the other" (Miller 2012, 2).[1] We problematize the notion that digital media spell doom for African literature and, with it, for the humanities in Africa (by which it is usually meant a traditional configuration of the humanities—"the study of literature, of art, of language and of philosophy" (Weber 2000)—that the West exported to its colonial outposts). Versions of this argument include perturbations that "African readerships are under siege" by "the cost of books, varying degrees of general literacy, inadequate library services and the seductions of the web and social media" (Ojwang and Titlestad 2014). The latter are held responsible, in particular, for the decline of modes of attention attuned to "older forms of 'deep' and refined literature," in favor of "visual salience, speed, brevity and the predominance of surface over depth." In this view, the steady fact and information flow of new media has rendered the pastime of reading fiction, with its affects and "stylistic or literary pretensions to beauteous form, [...] seem evermore superfluous" (de Kock 2015).

Nor are lamentations about the decline and marginalization of literature, literary studies, and, more broadly, reading unique to recent discussions about African literature. They have become a kind of ritual for some literary scholars, who have taken to equating their own loss of centrality in the academy, as well as that of the study of their preferred expressive forms, with digital barbarism and the looming terminal crisis of the humanities. We thus have South African English literature departments that embrace Nicholas Carr's techno-pessimist views on "the effect of the internet on our thought processes," whereby "we touch on ideas and then our attention shifts," to defensively argue "that it is not reactionary or Luddite to stress the importance of sustained and careful reading of literary works" in what is otherwise becoming "a world of browsing."[2] Not to be out-gloomed, South African Nobel laureate John Maxwell Coetzee portrays a world where the yes-or-no binary thinking that he says governs the logic of digital devices "extends further and deeper into our daily existence." As "one can only foresee a further and deeper takeover of mental life—at least among human beings," it "is up to the poets" to "keep our children from the single vision of YES or NO" (2016, 1152). Of course, as Coetzee comments in another piece on keeping "humanistic studies alive in a world in which universities have defined themselves out of existence," to conceive of this as anything other than a Quixotic pursuit "would be laughable" (2013, xii–xv).

If one googles "crisis of the humanities," one now gets about 47,500,000 results (August 4, 2019), including an article by U.S. poetry scholar Marjorie Perloff that starts by noting that "One of our most common genres today is the epitaph for the humanities" (1999). The role of the internet features prominently in this kind of melancholic writing. As media studies professor Kathleen Fitzpatrick writes in *Profession*, the annual publication of the Modern Language Association of America, anxieties about the effects of digital media abound among literature scholars, and they often translate into apocalyptic declarations of the decline not only of literature and literary studies, but also of a reading culture as such. Fitzpatrick points out that this techno-pessimism is borne out of blindness "to signs of literary culture's continued proliferation, including the increasing number of devices and platforms and services through which we read today." She also reminds us that this kind of anxiety about technology is nothing new. The Greek philosopher Plato worried that writing would produce forgetfulness—if you can write things down there is no need to remember them—while the English poet Alexander Pope described the invention of printing as a "scourge for the sins of the learned" (2012, 41–42). Even narratives about literature being shunted aside by other media go back to the advent of visual media such as movies or television, long before the rise of the internet. Fitzpatrick makes the point that "reading, especially of texts other than the sacred, was always an activity dominated by those with time to spend at leisure." Secondly, she notes that the dismal vision of a present where literature is relegated to the margin of cultural life by digital media is overstated. Contemporary narratives of cultural decay and of the decline of reading have more or less overt ideological motivations. Their subtext is usually something like "'No one reads [anything good] anymore' or, even more pointedly, 'No one reads [anything (I think is) good] anymore'"—statements that leave "the speaker's evident value judgments and personal taste unspoken in what winds up simply presented as bald fact" (2012, 42). An example of this can be found in the first article we quote about the lack of a "general, established and dependable reading culture" on the African continent, which goes on to lament that today "Most reading is tabloid or ecclesiastical in content. Even this version of reading seems to be declining with the widespread accessibility of Pentecostal and pirated DVDs. South African publishers—once a relatively secure bastion for fiction—lapse each month further into cookbook and self-help titles" (Ojwang and Titlestad 2014).

In 2018, the South African top ten selling categories, taking all publishers into account, were: (1) genre fiction; (2) religion; (3) children's and young adult fiction; (4) general fiction; (5) biographies and autobiographies; (6) personal development; (7) preschool and picture books; (8) food and drink; (9) children and adult nonfiction; and (10) the world/ideas/culture: general interest.[3] In fact, religion, cookbooks, and self-help titles sell consistently well across the world, so this is a global phenomenon rather than a South African "lapse." But it is still a small minority that we are talking about—in South Africa, book buyers are estimated to be about one percent of the population.[4] Local fiction authors consider themselves fortunate if they sell one thousand copies of a novel and any text that sells in excess of a few thousand copies is effectively a best-seller. Which is not to say that this readership is not significant or valuable, or that there should not be attempts to expand it through a better public library system, but we ought to be realistic about its size. Nor do we want to suggest that book readership in South Africa—and across the African continent more broadly—is or has ever been uniform. In South Africa, book publishers and their readerships have complex and multi-faceted political and social histories, imbricated with those of colonialism and apartheid but also with resistance to them and with the transition to democracy (Mpe and Seeber 2000). An initiative such as the Abantu Book Festival, which was launched in Soweto in 2016, in reaction to the white middle-class normativity of the Franschhoek and other South African literary festivals, testifies to the existence of a young, engaged, and politically switched-on black readership.[5] The popularity of the pop-up bookshop at the Abantu Festival, which offers a range of fiction and non-fiction titles by African writers and publishers, also points to a readership that is interested in books from and on the continent.

It is not that people, including African people, who are active online, do not read, and write, anymore. The digitally connected tend to read and write a lot. It is just that they often read and write short, small size chunks of text: WhatsApp messages, tweets, and Facebook and Instagram posts. The key shift is that digital media users bypass the divisions between the written, the visual, the oral, and the aural. We read and write texts, look at images, play videos, and listen to music or speech on the same device, often at the same time. We have created ways of communicating in which the written, the visual, the oral, and the aural are constantly mixed and remixed. The results are hybrid and complex messages that produce their own discourses, modes of engagement, codes and forms of attention (Frassinelli 2019, 16–17 and 67–71).

In media theory, this goes by the name of "convergence"—convergence of modes, or media convergence—a term first introduced in the 1980s to name the "blurring [of] the lines between media, even between point-to-point communications" (Pool 1983, 23). Media convergence is what happens when "Televisions resemble computers; books are read on telephones; newspapers are written through clouds; films are streamed via rental companies; and so on. Genres and gadgets that once were separate are linked" (Miller 2012, 95). Digital media and cyberspace have blurred the lines between different forms and modes of cultural production, transmission, and consumption. Ngũgĩ wa Thiong'o has theorized the implications of this convergence of modes for African literature. In particular, he has highlighted the challenge cyberspace poses to the "aesthetic feudalism" that in modern Western culture and its colonial outposts established a hierarchy between the written and the oral whereby the latter, "even when viewed as being 'more' authentic or closer to the natural, is treated as bondsman to the writing master. With orality taken as the source for the written and orature as the raw material for literature, both were certainly placed on a lower rung in the ladder of achievement and civilization" (Ngũgĩ 2012, 63).

The multimodal and transmedia forms of expression and communication that we encounter online interrupt the hegemony of writing and open up new possibilities for its hybridization with the oral:

> The lines between the written and the orally transmitted are being blurred in the age of internet and cyberspace. This has been going on for some years with the writing down of the orally transmitted; the electronic transmissions of the written as spoken through the radio and television; or simply the radio as a medium of speech. But it has surely accelerated with all corners of the globe becoming neighborhoods in cyberspace. Through technology, people can speak in real time face to face. The language of texting and emailing and access to everything including pictures and music in real time is producing a phenomenon that is neither pure speech nor pure writing. The language of cybejrspace may borrow the language of orality, twitter, chat rooms, we-have-been-talking when they mean we-have-been-texting, or chatting through writing emails, but it is orality mediated by writing. It is neither one nor the other. It's both. It's cyborality. (Ngũgĩ 2012, 84)[6]

DIGITAL MEDIA, LITERACIES, AND AFRICAN LITERATURE

Media convergence and cyborality are especially apt points of entry into the work of some of the best-known contemporary African writers, not in the least because of their engagement with different media, and especially their digital media presence. The first example that comes to mind is the internet celebrity status of Nigerian novelist Chimamanda Ngozi Adichie. By October 2019, Adichie's talk "The Danger of a Single Story" had hit over twenty million views on ted.com and over five and a half million on YouTube, with well over one thousand comments for each video, while her TedxEuston talk "We Should All Be Feminists," sampled in Beyoncé's 2013 single "***Flawless," was scoring over five and a half million views on YouTube. Similarly, Teju Cole's fame is associated not only with his books, but also with digital media interventions such as the 2014 "Time of the Game" Twitter experiment. In it, Cole asked his then 160,000 followers to tweet photos of their TVs showing the soccer world cup with a caption indicating where they were watching the game and what time it was. It resulted in "a synchronized global view of the World Cup" that aggregated "over 2,000 different photos of people's TVs showing the World Cup" (Meyer 2014). Cole's entire writing career has marched in step with the evolution of digital and social media. His first book, the novella *Every Day Is for the Thief* (2007), was first published online as a blog. Then came his Twitter fame, which coincided with the success of the novel *Open City* (2012). He has since moved to Instagram (Cole's Twitter account has been dormant since 2014), where he gained traction by producing a photo essay using reposted images of the Mona Lisa.[7] And another well-known example of this kind of media crossing is that of Binyavanga Wainaina's hugely popular 2005 *Granta* essay "How to Write about Africa," which "grew out of an email" about a special issue on Africa that a pissed-off Wainaina had sent to the editor when he was a graduate student in England. Consisting of an edited version of the original email, the essay "became the most-forwarded story in Granta history" (Wainaina 2010).

Digital media also find their way into and out of African authors' books. Again, the best-known example comes from Adichie's *Americanah* (2013), whose main character, Ifemelu, sets up a blog called "Raceteenth or Various Observations about American Blacks (those Formerly Known as Negroes) by a Non-American Black." Her anonymous blog postings, typed in a different font from the rest of the text, provide a counterpoint to the unfolding story, in which Ifemelu first migrates to the United States and then comes back to Nigeria, where she starts a new blog, "The Small Redemptions of Lagos" (2013, 418–23). Adichie has explained that the blogs were meant to create a seemingly non-fictional space within the narrative: "I wanted this novel to also be social commentary, but I wanted to say it in ways that are different from what one is supposed to say in literary fiction" (Adichie and Rifbjerg 2014). The second blog would have a short life of its own outside the covers of the book. Between August 27 and November 2, 2014, a series of posts on topics ranging from everyday life in Nigeria to responses to the representation of Africa in Western media were uploaded, as if Ifemelu had written them, to the website https://americanahblog.com/, where they are still accessible.

The impact of digital media on this body of literature in fact goes beyond this or other uses and references. Contemporary narratives of migration by African authors have articulated the complex relations between the rupture produced by migration and the role and limits of new communication technologies in bringing separate worlds together (Toivanen 2016). The phrase "new-media-driven narratives" has been used to describe how novels such as *Americanah* and NoViolet Bulawayo's *We Need New Names* (2013) address "issues of affect and access, which the influence of expanding virtual networks on social relations is making increasingly visible" (Isaacs 2016, 174). U.S. critic Caren Irr theorizes a new subgenre she labels the "digital migrant novel"—in which she includes the "African migration fiction" of Teju Cole's *Open City*, Chris Abani's *Virgin of Flames* (2007), and Dinaw Mengestu's *The Beautiful Things that Heaven Bears* (2007)—where digital media provide a representational template and spatial sensibility that enable the move "from the discrete geography of nations to the overlapping and virtual spaces of communication technologies" (2013, 26).

But digital media are not only the playground of African and diasporic literary stars who use them as narrative devices or to enhance their visibility. What Shola Adenekan calls "the internetting" of African literature dates back "to the mid to late 1990s, when many young African writers, wanting to escape the politics of book publishing, began to publish poetry, short stories, and essays on African listservs, personal blogs and creating writing websites" (2016, 3). Today, "there are dozens of poetry and creative writing communities online." They testify both to the possibilities opened up by digital media for hybridizing written and oral forms of expression and to their complex imbrication with the offline world:

> Poetry posted on Facebook may be performed for members of the public in the real space of Lagos and Nairobi, and the recording of those performances may be posted on YouTube and Facebook for consumption by the online public. Young poets such as David Ishaya Osu (Nigeria), Dami Ajayi (Nigeria), and Redscar McOdindo K'Oyuga (Kenya) publish poems almost every week on Facebook, many of which later form part of print collections. These works may also appear as part of a collection of a creative book project. These processes arguably involve reshaping the text for different formats, and through this

process the creative piece is unfixed and susceptible to changes. (Adenekan 2016, 2)

Digital media have offered a platform for the production, circulation, and reception of diverse texts and performances through modes of delivery that make them travel outside of the literary establishment and move away from canonical literary forms.

In June 2019, the number of African online users was "already larger than in Latin America (448 million) and at current growth rates could eclipse Europe (719 million) as internet penetration on the continent grows" (*Business Insider SA* 2019). Still, a note of caution about the scale and reach of these developments is in order. In June 2019, less than 40 percent of Africa's population used the internet, contrasting with more than 60 percent of the population in the rest of the world (*Business Insider SA* 2019). Although internet penetration and mobile telephony are growing exponentially in Africa, giving many access to digital and social media platforms, the digital divide remains a reality linked to class, age, gender, geographical location, and language—"the majority of Internet sites [are only] available in English or other colonial languages" (Mutsvairo and Ragnedda 2019, 14). Smartphones and data are still unaffordably expensive for the continent's poor. For instance, at the time of writing, in South Africa only 32 of over 58 million citizens have internet access, while the cost of data is more expensive than higher-income countries such as Australia (Mutsvairo and Ragnedda 2019, 15).

African digital literary networks are largely middle-class and elite spaces. As Adenekan underscores, the "poets, novelists, critics, and consumers of [African literary] works [that circulate online] are people with the language capability to enjoy them. They can afford fast and reliable internet, are often based in metropolitan centres of Africa, Europe, and America, and some even spend much of their time in these places." The listservs that Adenekan surveys, such as ConcernedKenyanwriters, Krazitivity, USA-Africa Dialogue and Ederi, do not exceed a few thousand active users (2016, 4). There is no disputing the digital divide on the African continent, where a minority of people have access to digital technologies—to devices, software, data, effective connection and digital literacy skills, computers, and other proficiencies. Where people only have access to the cheapest type of devices—"dumb" or "feature" cellphones—they are more likely to be using them for oral communication than enjoying the other affordances of digital media. It is not just a matter of access but of meaningful and effective access, unimpeded by the cost of data and lack of digital literacy skills.

Even so, despite unequal access to digital technologies, and despite the current constraints on digital connectedness in Africa, digital media can and do play a significant role in promoting reading practices and cultures across the African continent, in a multiplicity of Africa's languages. Examples of this can be found in work promoting early reading—critical to developing life-long readerships—by Nal'ibali, a national reading campaign in South Africa, and African Storybook, a multilingual digital publishing literacy initiative based in South Africa and active in several other African countries.[8] Using traditional and digital publishing technologies, both Nal'ibali and African Storybook create, circulate, and support the use of a variety of multimodal materials and materials that can be used multimodally. Nal'ibali does this in South African languages, and African Storybook in a wider variety of African languages.

Launched in 2012, Nal'ibali means "here's the story" in isiXhosa, one of the eleven official languages of South Africa. It is a national campaign to promote reading in South African languages. As their website notes, "Nal'ibali fully promotes reading and writing in mother tongue languages. All children and adults need to understand what they are listening to, or reading, for it to be meaningful and enjoyable."[9] There is a clear link made here between writing and speaking/listening, with a dialogic relationship—rather than a binary one—between the two. As Ngũgĩ wa Thiong'o states about the possibilities opened up by the internet and cyberspace, "writing and orality are realizing anew the natural alliance they have always had in reality" (Ngũgĩ 2012, 85).

Nal'ibali's activities are multifaceted and include reading clubs, materials development and publishing, materials distribution, radio broadcasts, flagship events and competitions, and a media campaign that uses newspaper adverts and supplements, different types of social media and marketing, radio stories and storytelling events. The stories harvested from Nal'ibali's Story Bosso competition are a case in point for the alliance between the written and the oral championed by Ngũgĩ. Launched in Khayelitsha, Cape Town, in 2015, and run annually until 2019, Story Bosso is a "multilingual storytelling talent search," with South Africans of all ages invited to submit audio or video clips of themselves reading aloud or telling their favorite stories.[10] There are also a series of pop-up auditions among reading groups and communities in the provinces of Eastern Cape, KwaZulu-Natal, Mpumalanga, and the Western Cape. Story Bosso spans media, modes, and languages, and includes community events and storytelling sessions by well-known South African storytellers such as Sindiwe Magona and Gcina Mhlophe. From a start of around 2,000 entries in 2015, there were more than 6,000 entries in the years 2016–2018.[11] This goes to show the interest in storytelling and oral narratives, especially in languages other than English, which is hardly surprising given the powerful local oral traditions. But what makes it significant is that it is within the context of a national reading campaign: it is a multilingual celebration of both oral and written forms of human creative expression. The stories are available for free as audio files, but they can also be developed into print books or even animations.

The Nal'ibali website offers a variety of open access print and aural materials, which "may be freely downloaded, shared and reprinted."[12] It is possible for anyone with access to submit a story to the website for review and publication on the "Story Library" page. Most of the stories are written by local writers. The majority of stories are available in six official South African languages—those languages with the largest groups of speakers—and some are available in all eleven languages. The Nal'ibali website currently hosts 649 multilingual stories and 102 story cards across all languages. Additionally, Nal'ibali has distributed 550,340 books and 37.3 million copies of its bilingual reading-for-enjoyment reading supplement since the campaign was launched in 2012. The website also offers "featured books" and "recommended reads," which tend to be commercially published fiction and nonfiction books, mostly from local publishers—indicating a mutually supportive relationship between the reading campaign and the local publishing industry.

Our second example of the role of digital technologies in promoting reading practices is the African Storybook initiative, which "aims to address the shortage of contextually appropriate books for early reading in the languages of Africa." Its objective is "for all young African children to have enough enjoyable books to read in a familiar language to practise their reading skills and learn to love reading."[13] Central to the initiative is a website that is a repository of openly licensed digital storybooks written by African educators in a multiplicity of languages ranging from Acholi (Uganda), Afaan Oromo and Amharic (Ethiopia), Akwapem Twi and Asante Twi (Ghana), to isiXhosa (South Africa), Yoruba (Nigeria), and Zarma (Niger). The vision of the website is "Open access to picture storybooks in the languages of Africa. For children's literacy, enjoyment and imagination." Storybooks are freely available for reading online, and for downloading as PDF or EPub files. In addition to storybook publishing produced by African Storybook itself, the website enables any registered user to create and publish her own storybooks, and also to translate and adapt storybooks published by anyone else on the website. At the time of writing this chapter, a total of 6,847 digital storybooks have been published on the website, in 184 languages—mostly indigenous African languages, but also English, French, and Portuguese. Some of the languages represented previously had little-or-no reading material published specifically for children. The total number of storybooks available on the website consists of those classified as original, plus the number of translated or adapted versions of the original storybooks. In addition to original and translated/adapted, there are two further categories of storybooks—those that are created and published by independent users of the website ("community storybooks"), and those that are created and published with African Storybook resources ("ASb approved storybooks," which have gone through a basic editorial process and are illustrated by artists commissioned by African Storybook). This represents a shift from publishing being the preservation of expert professional publishers to publishing being accessible to anyone with a computer who has access to online publishing tools (and the ability to use them).[14] The story manuscripts illustrated by African Storybook-commissioned artists and published by African Storybook staff have been developed and written mostly in workshops with teachers, librarians, and education students in Uganda, Kenya, South Africa, Lesotho, Ethiopia, Ghana, Nigeria, and Rwanda. In other words, the majority of storybooks are authored by non-professional writers who create the storybooks for their contexts of use. Contributors of stories are asked to write in their preferred language, and to submit two final texts—the story in an indigenous African language and in English (either the writer or someone else from the community translates as necessary). The English storybooks are seen as the "seed texts," which can be accessed and translated/adapted by translators with proficiency in that language. This means that one illustrated storybook in one language can potentially be used by many different readers because it is possible to replace the written text on the digital pages and publish new translations and adaptations of any storybook. For example, one of the early storybooks published in Lusoga and English ("Omusaadha omuleeyi einho"—"A Very Tall Man") has been translated—mostly via the English version—into over forty-five African languages, as well as into multiple non-African languages (via Global African Storybook).[15] This storybook—and others with similar high numbers of translations and adaptations—is a good example of the affordances of online open license digital publishing for multilingual cultural production.[16] We are reminded here of another initiative by *Jalada Africa*, an online journal out of Nairobi that published a short story originally written in an African language and subsequently translated into thirty other African languages. Titled "Ituĩka Rĩa Mũrũngarũ: Kana Kĩrĩa Gĩtũmaga Andũ Mathiĩ Marũngiĩ," and authored by Ngũgĩ wa Thiong'o, the story was published in March 2016 in Gĩkũyũ and translated into English as "The Upright Revolution: Or Why Humans Walk Upright." According to Mũkoma wa Ngũgĩ, this is "the most translated African language story" and the translation initiative an important contribution to "decolonization" (2016).

The examples of "internetting" of African literature, as well as of Nal'ibali, the African Storybook, and the *Jalada Africa*'s translation initiative illustrate some of the possibilities at the interface of literature, digital media, literacy, storytelling, and African cultural production. They also underscore the complexity of theorizing reading practices and creative expression in contexts where linguistic diversity and plurality are the norm, thereby inviting us to question what, in African contexts, constitutes the value of constructs such as "literature," "literacy," and even "language."

CONCLUSION

Some key issues emerge from our overview of digitally mediated African literature and of other forms of African cultural production and digital publishing. Given the limited space of a single chapter, we can only present them in the barest outline, as an invitation to further conversation.

Our first (obvious but worth restating) point is that the humanities need to confront the challenge and try to grab the opportunities presented by digital media. This however is not the same as what is meant by the moniker digital humanities, which mainly refers to the application of computational tools and methods to traditional humanities disciplines such as literature, history, and philosophy. Our point is that we need to rethink disciplinary divisions in the humanities and move beyond what has been called "the two humanities" (Miller 2012, 2). The first is the traditional humanities that people talk about when they refer to the crisis of the humanities—declining enrolments, institutional marginalization, and loss of relevance and public interest—while the second, communication and media studies, is a fast growing area in the contemporary academy (Miller 2012, 1–14). One way of starting to undo this division on the side of traditional humanities is by dealing not only with texts, but also with the media, technologies, social relations, and political economy involved in their production, circulation, and consumption, as well as with other forms of oral, aural, visual, and multimodal cultural expression.

By and large, literary scholars have been reluctant to engage with publishing models and technologies, media platforms, and the political economy and social life of their objects of study—we write from experience: for instance, one of us had a detailed discussion of a digital publishing model dismissed by a literary scholar as "tautological." Literary studies' most typical scholarly engagement is textual analysis, what Keyan Tomaselli describes as "a post-Leavisite type of personal relation to the text under study" (2012, 32), with scant attention paid to how the texts one studies are produced, circulated, and consumed, how much they cost, and who reads (or not reads) them and why. As Toby Miller writes about the United States, "Undergraduate and graduate students and professors in literature generally inhabit and leave the university knowing how to analyze fictional texts in a formal and social way. But they are typically ignorant of where those texts physically come from or end up and what happened to them in between" (2012, 104). As far as we can tell, the state of literary studies and curricula in South Africa, from where we write, is not substantially different.

On the part of literary scholars, taking on the challenge of digital media also requires being open to question what, in African contexts and elsewhere, constitutes the value of a construct such as "literature." As we argued at the beginning, narratives of the marginalization and crisis of literature, literary studies, and of the humanities tend to be premised on the valorization of a very narrow canon of texts and expressive forms. Embedded in this type of melancholic writing are negative value judgments about other forms of writings, textualities, and media that are today part of the everyday life of a great number of people. Here too, we agree with Toby Miller that the "historic task of history and literature, what Stuart Hall nominates as 'a humane, critical discourse designed to deepen the social awareness of a wider readership,' must be transferred to additional media forms and liberated from its banal reliance on aesthetic narcissism" (2012, 95).

One phrase that describes this kind of media crossing is "comparative media studies," which "typically includes not only text but also film, installation art, and other media forms" (Hayles and Pressman 2013, vii). Writing from within literary studies, Katherine Hayles and Jessica Pressman introduced this label to the discipline as an answer to its need to catch up with the digital world: "we now find ourselves in situations where print-born assumptions linger and intermingle with practices such as social media networking, tweeting, hacking, and so on, to create highly diverse and heterogeneous social-technical-economic-political amalgams rife with contradictions and internal inconsistencies" (2013, x). From this perspective, a comparative focus on media is a way of rescuing literary studies from its self-defeating emphasis on the uniqueness of its object of study by highlighting "its connections to the real world and to other fields of intellectual inquiry" (Hayles and Pressman 2013, xv). In communication and media studies, the phrase is associated with the Massachusetts Institute of Technology's Comparative Media Studies program, which focuses on "media practices across historical periods, cultural settings, and methods in order to assess change, design new tools, and anticipate media developments" and also supports a "studio and workshop curriculum featuring the techniques and traditions of contemporary fiction, poetry, creative non-fiction, journalism, digital media, video, and games."[17]

With reference to African literary and cultural studies, we have mentioned Ngũgĩ wa Thiong'o's coinage of the term "cyborality," from which he derives "cyborature" to name the permutations of orature and literature in the age of internet and cyberspace (2012, 85). We have also commented on the digital media presence of African literary stars, as well as on the more diffuse "internetting" of African literature since the 1990s (Adenekan 2016), and on its forms of inclusion and exclusion. It has long been argued that African cultural production cannot be straitjacketed into high- and low-culture binaries inherited from Western modernity (Barber 1987). Digital media and their remixing of genres and modes, as well as their breaking the boundaries between content producers and consumers—whence the new coinage prosumers—provide platforms and spaces for rethinking the relation between African literature and "popular" expressive forms, their publics and modes of production, circulation and fruition (Yékú 2017). They also ask questions as to what it means to be "literate" in the world we live in.

As we have seen, affirmations of the value of literary works, as well as questions about their status in the age of digital media, are predicated on evaluative criteria to do with the depth, seriousness, and refinement of the forms of attention and reading practices they foster and require. In *Keywords* (1983), Raymond Williams reminded us of how the word "literature" came into the English language to name "polite learning through reading. [...] Thus a man of literature, or of letters, meant what we would now describe as a man of wide reading." The meaning was then transferred to the texts from which polite learning is acquired. It is this etymology that laid the basis for the future specialization of literature to certain kinds of texts and writing. The term "literature" has been built into an evaluative criterion that has been repeatedly challenged but remains constitutive of the value judgments that continue to be attached to it. Meanwhile, literacy, which shares with literature a common etymology associated with reading, has become a "social concept" used "to express the achievement and possession of what were increasingly seen as general and necessary skills" (1983, 184–88). This social turn is reflected in the developments of applied linguistics, which in the last few decades has adjusted to the norms of multilingualism and to the mundane practices of translation that they have engendered.

Saussurean linguistics from early-twentieth-century Europe influenced generations of language scholars in the northern hemisphere with a definition of language that excluded everything outside of the system of language itself and of the inherent form and structure of the system. This shaped a long-dominant conceptualization of a language as something self-contained: "the notion of languages as separate, discrete entities [and] bounded, impermeable autonomous systems" (Creese and Blackledge 2010, 554). The shifting geopolitics of the late twentieth century saw a social turn in applied linguistics and the emergence of new theoretical paradigms about language and literacy that foreground bilingual and multilingual norms. As a result, there has been a shift from a monolingual conception of language as an autonomous system, to a focus on language and literacy as social practices. These approaches seek to theorize the complexity of plurilingual societies, where "literacy practices are enmeshed within and influenced by social, cultural, political, and economic factors, and literacy learning and use varies by situation and entails complex interactions" (García, Bartlett and Kleifgen 2007, 207). In Suresh Canagarajah's words, "The struggle now is to find new metaphors and constructs that would capture multilingual communication" (2007, 933). In multilingual communication, "speakers are engaged in a negotiation of multiple identities which cut across traditional language boundaries" (Makalela 2013, 113). This is the same negotiation that Ngũgĩ wa Thiong'o sees as the task of translation practices between African languages, which have the potential to play "a crucial and ultimate role of enabling mutuality of being and becoming even within a plurality of languages" (2018, 131). This in turn suggests the need for a social turn in trying to find new constructs for discussing creative expression in plurilingual and pluriliterate societies.

These are complex, changing, and textured times for the humanities, old and new. The internet and digital and social media do indeed signal momentous changes. In addition to the study of written texts and other multimodal expressive forms within their sociocultural lived contexts, conditions of production, and value chains, a social and communicative turn in literary and cultural studies, comparative media studies, or whichever new name we might want to give to this kind of transdisciplinary work, would entail reconsidering and reimagining its objects of study outside of sedimented norms of aesthetic value. This would enable it to open up to a multiplicity of forms, formats, and platforms, genres and categories, media, and modes of production and reception. What the examples in our discussion have illustrated is that more work in Pan-African and transnational contexts, with multilingual, plurilingual, and translanguage considerations and applying multimodal and multimedia approaches, can support and is sustained by current struggles to decolonize the African humanities.

NOTES

1. This chapter was jointly conceived, structured, and conceptualized. For the purpose of academic attribution, we indicate that Pier Paolo Frassinelli wrote paragraphs 1–3, 5–11, 22–26, while Lisa Treffry-Goatley wrote paragraphs 4, 12–21, 27–29.

2. See https://www.wits.ac.za/sllm/disciplines/english-studies/. One wonders whether the irony of committing these thoughts to the department's website is lost on its members.

3. This information is sourced from Nielsen BookScan South Africa data for 2018. Nielsen BookScan provides sales statistics on book purchases through traditional retail outlets such as bookstores. See http://www.sapnet.co.za/nielsenbookscan.php.

4. See http://sabookcouncil.co.za/national-book-week/nbw-faq/. However, we should highlight the limitations of what we know about the reading practices of non-book-buying readers and others not targeted by publishing market research.

5. See http://www.abantubookfestival.co.za/.

6. Russell Kashula has coined the related term "technauriture" in "response to the intersection of orality, the written word and digital technology" (Kashula and Mostert 2011, 3; see also Kashula 2004; and Kashula and Mostert 2009). He and Andre Mostert define technauriture as "an attempt to capture the 'three-way dialectic between primary orality, literacy and technology,' moving the debate beyond what has essentially been a dichotomous tension between the oral and written word, to a discourse that includes the implications of technology as a general and alternative category" (Kashula and Mostert 2011, 4).

7. In his latest book, *Known and Strange Things* (2016), Cole critiques the thematic and aesthetic standardization of social media photography—billions of images of "pets, pretty girlfriends, sunsets, lunch" manipulated with "the same easy algorithms" (154)—even as he acknowledges the new criteria of optical discrimination and pleasure afforded by the increased access and exposure to photographic images, including art photography uncredentialled by the art gallery or book (157–59).

8. See http://www.nalibali.org and http://www.africanstorybook.org.

9. See http://nalibali.org/about-us.

10. See http://nalibali.org/story-bosso/what-story-bosso.

11. See http://nalibali.org/news-blog/news/congratulations-to-our-story-bosso-winners. Winners of the 2017 Story Bosso campaign can be heard at https://soundcloud.com/user-657906137.

12. See http://nalibali.org/terms-use.

13. See www.african storybook.org. African Storybook is an initiative of the South African non-profit organization, Saide (https://www.saide.org.za).

14. https://storyweaver.org.in is another example of an open license website offering tools for independent storybook publishing in multiple languages.

15. For a link to "Omusaadha omuleeyi einho"—"A Very Tall Man," see www.africanstorybook.org/reader.php?id=918&d=0&a=1. For more information about the Global African Storybook Project, see https://global-asp.github.io/.

16. This economy of scale in (re)publishing storybooks on the African Storybook website—along with the fact that language communities not considered viable by commercial publishers can be served—is enabled by an open license publishing model. All storybooks on the African Storybook are published under a Creative Commons CC BY license, and have the following license notice on the back cover: "You are free to download, copy translate or adapt this story and use the illustrations as long as you attribute in the following way." Thus, the core collection of approximately 400 original illustrated picture storybooks published by the African Storybook initiative is available to anyone to translate or adapt online or offline (and then upload) in any language that has a written form (and, ideally, that has a keyboard). It means that, in theory at least, anyone with internet access and the relevant digital literacy skills is able to publish a children's storybook in any language, in a simple book format in digital form that is also ready for printing.

17. See http://cmsw.mit.edu/about.

REFERENCES

Abani, Chris. 2007. *The Virgin of Flames*. London: Vintage.
Adenekan, Shola. 2016. "New Voices, New Media: Class, Sex and Politics in Online Nigerian and Kenyan Poetry." *Postcolonial Text* 11 (1): 1–21.
Adichie, Chimamanda Ngozi. 2009. "The Danger of a Single Story." https://www.ted.com/talks/chimamanda_adichie_the_danger_of_a_single_story https://www.youtube.com/watch?v=D9Ihs241zeg https://www.youtube.com/watch?v=hg3umXU_qWc.
Adichie, Chimamanda Ngozi. 2013. *Americanah*. Fourth Estate: London.
Adichie, Chimamanda Ngozi. 2013. "We Should All Be Feminists." https://www.youtube.com/watch?v=hg3umXU_qWc.
Adichie, Chimamanda Ngozi, and Synne Rifbjerg. 2014. "*Americanah* International Author's Stage," May 20. https://www.youtube.com/watch?v=b8r-dP9NqX8.
Barber, Karin. 1987. "Popular Arts in Africa." *African Studies Review* 30 (3): 1–76.
Beyoncé. 2013. "***Flawless." Ft. Chimamanda Ngozi Adichie https://www.youtube.com/watch?v=IyuUWOnS9BY.
Bulawayo, NoViolet. 2013. *We Need New Names*. London: Chatto & Windus.
Business Insider SA. 2019. "This Startling Graph Shows How Many Africans Are Now Using the Internet—Far More than in North America, and on Track to Beat Europe," July 24. https://www.businessinsider.co.za/internet-users-in-africa-2019-7.
Canagarajah, Suresh. 2007. "Lingua Franca English, Multilingual Communities, and Language Acquisition." *The Modern Language Journal* 91: 923–39.
Coetzee, John Maxwell. 2013. "Foreword." In *Academic Freedom in a Democratic South Africa*, by John Higgins, xi–xv. Johannesburg: Wits University Press.
Coetzee, John Maxwell. 2016. "On Literary Thinking." *Textual Practice* 30 (7): 1151–52.
Cole, Teju. 2011. *Open City*. New York: Random House.
Cole, Teju. 2014 [2007]. *Everyday Is for the Thief*. New York: Random House.
Cole, Teju. 2016. *Known and Strange Things*. London: Faber & Faber.
Creese, Angela, and Adrian Blackledge. 2010. "Towards a Sociolinguistics of Superdiversity." *Zeitschrift für Erziehungswissenschaft* 13 (4): 549–72.
de Kock, Leon. 2015. "An Era in Which Fact Is More Desired than Fiction." *Mail & Guardian*, July 24. https://mg.co.za/article/2015-07-23-an-era-in-which-fact-is-more-desired-than-fiction.
Fitzpatrick, Kathleen. 2012. "Reading (and Writing) Online, Rather than on the Decline." *Profession* n.s.: 41–52.
Frassinelli, Pier Paolo. 2019. *Borders, Media Crossings and the Politics of Translation: The Gaze from Southern Africa*. New York: Routledge.
García, Ofelia, Lesley Bartlett, and Jo Anne Kleifgen. 2007. "From Biliteracy to Pluriliteracies." In *Handbook of Applied Linguistics*, *Volume 5: Multilingualism*, edited by Peter Auer and Li Wei, 207–28. Berlin: Mouton de Gruyter.
GSMA. 2017. "The Mobile Economy: Sub-Saharan Africa." https://www.gsma.com/mobileeconomy/sub-saharan-africa-2017/.

Hayles, Katherine, and Jessica Pressman. 2013. "Introduction. Making, Critique: A Media Framework." In *Comparative Textual Media: Transforming the Humanities in the Postprint Era*, edited by Katherine Hayles and Jessica Pressman, vii–xxxiii. Minneapolis, MN: University of Minnesota Press.

Internet World Stats. 2019. "Internet World Stats: Usage and Population Statistics." https://www.internetworldstats.com/stats1.htm.

Irr, Caren. 2014. *The Geopolitical Novel: U.S. Fiction in the Twenty-first Century*. New York: Columbia University Press.

Isaacs, Camilla. 2016. "Mediating Women's Globalized Existence through Social Media in the Work of Adichie and Bulawayo." *Safundi: The Journal of South African and American Studies* 17 (2): 174–88.

Kaschula, Russell. 2004. "Imbongi to Slam: The Emergence of a Technologised Auriture." *Southern African Journal of Folklore Studies* 14 (2): 45–58.

Kaschula, Russell, and Andre Mostert. 2009. "Analyzing, Digitizing and Technologizing the Oral Word: The Case of Bongani Sitole." *Journal of African Cultural Studies* 21 (2): 159–76.

Kaschula, Russell and Andre Mostert. 2011. "From Oral Literature to Technauriture: What's in a Name?" World Oral Literature Project, University of Cambridge, Cambridge, https://www.repository.cam.ac.uk/bitstream/handle/1810/237322/WOLP_OP_04.pdf?sequence=1&isAllowed=y.

Makalela, Leketi. 2013. "Translanguaging in Kasi-taal: Rethinking Old Language Boundaries for New Language Planning." *Stellenbosch Papers in Linguistics Plus* 42: 111–25.

Mengestu, Dinaw. 2007. *The Beautiful Things That Heaven Bears*. London: Penguin.

Meyer, Robinson. 2014. "When the World Watches the World Cup, What Does That Look Like?" *The Atlantic*, July 15. https://www.theatlantic.com/technology/archive/2014/07/when-the-world-watches-the-world-cup-what-does-it-look-like/374461/.

Miller, Toby. 2012. *Blow Up the Humanities*. Philadelphia, PA: Temple University Press.

Mpe, Phaswane, and Monica Seeber. 2000. "The Politics of Book Publishing in South Africa: A Critical Overview." *The Politics of Publishing in South Africa*, edited by Nicholas Evans N. and Monica Seeber, 15–42. Scottsville: University of Natal Press.

Mukoma wa Ngũgĩ. 2016. "A Revolution in Many Tongues." *Africa Is a Country*, April 26. http://africasacountry.com/2016/04/a-revolution-in-many-tongues/.

Mutsvairo, Bruce, and Massimo Ragnedda. 2019. "Comprehending the Digital Disparities in Africa." In *Mapping the Digital Divide in Africa: A Mediated Analysis*, edited by Bruce Mutsvairo and Massimo Ragnedda, 13–26. Amsterdam: Amsterdam University Press.

Ngũgĩ wa Thiong'o. 2012. *Globalectics: Theory and the Politics of Knowing*. New York: Columbia University Press.

Ngũgĩ wa Thiong'o. 2018. "The Politics of Translation: Notes Towards an African Language Policy." *Journal of African Cultural Studies* 30 (2): 124–32.

Ojwang, Dan, and Michael Titlestad. 2014. "African Writing Blurs into 'World' Literature." *Mail & Guardian*, April 14. https://mg.co.za/article/2014-04-03-african-writing-blurs-into-world-literature.
Perloff, Marjorie. 1999. "In Defense of Poetry. Put Literature Back into Literary Studies." *Boston Review: A Political and Literary Forum*, December 1. http://bostonreview.net/books-ideas/marjorie-perloff-defense-poetry.
Pool, Ithiel de Sola. 1983. *Technologies of Freedom*. Cambridge, MA: Belknap Press.
The Small Redemptions of Lagos. 2014. https://americanahblog.com/.
Toivanen, Anna-Leena. 2016. "Emailing/Skyping Africa: New Technologies and Communication Gaps in Contemporary African Women's Fiction." *Ariel* 47 (4): 135–61.
Tomaselli, Keyan. 2012. "Alter-Egos: Cultural and Media Studies." *Critical Arts: South-North Cultural and Media Studies* 26 (1): 14–38.
Yékú, James. 2017. "'Thighs Fell Apart': Online Fan Fiction, and African Writing in a Digital Age." *Journal of African Cultural Studies* 29(3): 261–75.
Wainaina, Binyavanga. 2005. "How to Write About Africa." *Granta*. https://granta.com/how-to-write-about-africa/.
Wainaina, Binyavanga. 2010. "How to Write About Africa II: The Revenge." *Bidoun*. https://bidoun.org/articles/how-to-write-about-africa-ii.
Weber, Samuel. 2000. "The Future of the Humanities: Experimenting." *Culture Machine* 2. http://www.culturemachine.net/index.php/cm/article/view/311/296.
Williams, Raymond. 1983. *Keywords: A Vocabulary of Culture and Society*. Revised Edition. New York: Oxford University Press.

Chapter 6

African Gaze

Hollywood/Nollywood and the Postcolonial Science Fiction Imagery in Nnedi Okorafor's Lagoon

Rocío Cobo-Piñero

INTRODUCTION: AFRICAS OF THE IMAGINATION AND POSTCOLONIAL FUTURITY

In 2013, *Paradoxa* devoted a special issue to African science fiction.[1] In his introduction to the issue, Mark Bould presented an overview of the place that Africa has always had in the science fiction imagination. In this genre, Western authors tended to represent the trope of colonial expeditions to the African continent under the guise of scientific advancement, or in order to portray Africa as a space for lost race tales, which sometimes included white supremacist terror, like Edgar Rice Burroughs's *Beyond Thirty* (1916).[2] Bould contends that African American author Pauline Hopkins reworked the pattern of such fiction by placing African American and African characters at the center of her novel *Of One Blood, or, the Hidden Self* (1903). Hopkins would pave the way for other African American science fiction authors such as Octavia Butler and Samuel R. Delany, among others. In a later study, Bould (2015) presented a comprehensive account of works by African writers since the Second World War that can be read from a science fiction perspective. However, it is at the turn of the twenty-first century that science fiction really experienced a boom on the continent, accompanied by a rising interest among academics; the aforementioned issue of *Paradoxa* and the *Cambridge Journal of Postcolonial Literary Inquiry* 2016 special issue on African science fiction underscore the new position of Africa in the genre.

African filmmakers are also placing Africa at the vanguard of planetary discourse, creating a new wave of cultural product that signals the continent as a site from which to imagine the emergence of future worlds. Artists who are looking at Africa through a futurist frame include Kenyan director Wanuri

Kahui's *Pumzi* (2009), a speculative short-film set thirty-five years in the wake of the Third World War in a desolate landscape in East Africa, and *Crumbs* (2015) by Miguel Llansó, a Spanish, Addis Ababa-based director who has marketed his latest project as "the first ever Ethiopian post-apocalyptic, surreal, sci-fi feature length film" (Hugo 2017, 47). Many African and African diaspora writers are also breaking new ground by drawing on the conventions of global speculative frameworks. *Moxyland* (2008) and *Zoo City* (2010), written by the South African author Lauren Beukes, advance futuristic visions of dystopian new world orders from local points of view, while the anthology entitled *AfroSF* (Hartmann 2013) features African writing imbued with some of the key characteristics of the sci-fi genre, such as time travel, advanced technology, interstellar journeys, and alien creatures.[3] These themes and genre conventions are part of the 2015 online issue of *Jalada Africa*, entitled "AfroFuture(s)," a collection of short stories that reflect on the constitution of an African form of futurity.[4] This budding opus of experimental cultural production attests to the ways in which "African aesthetics" have become, as Matthew Omelsky (2014) asserts, "more mutant and global than ever, poised to move into radically new speculative and imaginative terrain" (38). Among this growing body of work are the writings of Nigerian American author Nnedi Okorafor, recipient of the 2011 World Fantasy Award for Best Novel for *Who Fears Death* (2010) and of both the 2016 Nebula and Hugo Awards for her novella *Binti* (2015). She has also received the Wole Soyinka Prize for Literature in Africa for the young adult novel *Zahrah the Windseeker* (2005), and the Cark Brandon Society Parallax Award for best speculative fiction by a person of color for *The Shadow Speaker* (2007).

Alina Rettová (2017) rightly points out that it is essential to shine the spotlight on the idea of the future because "Africa is often portrayed as a continent without future, a continent of innocent ignorance about time [...] a continent of the past, of perennial traditions that determine the present" (159). African sci-fi and futurist fiction constitute a powerful counter-discourse to stereotypical images of Africa in the Western imagination, while re-imagining the continent and re-inventing African identities. Kodwo Eshun (2003) importantly underlines in this sense the power structures at play in the act of envisioning narratives of the future: "The powerful employ futurists and draw power from the futures they endorse, thereby condemning the disempowered to live in the past" (289). This is the reason why the so-called Afrofuturist artistic movement is so pertinent for its reimagination of alternate worlds with regard to racial politics and belonging: "it is seen as a way to make sense of the past and its relevance to a black political present" (Barber 2018, 136). Coined by cultural critic Mark Dery in his influential essay "Black to the Future" (1994), the term initially described "speculative fiction that treats African-American themes and addresses African-American concerns in the context of twentieth century technoculture" (180). However, Sofia Samatar (2017) envisions a more pan-African mode of futurism and speculation, rather than one confined by geopolitical borders. Precisely due to its initial restrictions to the African American scope and experiences, Okorafor was reticent to consider herself an Afrofuturist author. As she wrote in her essay "Organic Fantasy" (2008), almost every story she writes is set in Nigeria, the country from which her Igbo parents migrated in 1969. Additionally, Okorafor envisions Nigeria as a fertile ground for science fiction in the present, an idea that her novel *Lagoon* (2014) develops in innovative ways.

According to Patricia Melzer (2006), popular culture's fascination with science fiction derives from "the combination of strangeness and familiarity" (4), two of the elements that comprise the particularities of the genre. She further notes that "This tension between the 'known' and the 'unknown' is at the heart of science fiction. It creates a reading process based on strangeness, which places familiar issues into strange territory" (2006, 4). What the various definitions of science fiction have in common is, in some sense, the encounter with difference and alterity. The figure of the alien in science fiction—extraterrestrial, technological, human-hybrid, or otherwise—has often been connected with the concept of the "Other" in postcolonialism (see Ashraf Masood et al. 2011; Hoagland and Sarwal 2010; Langer 2011; Smith 2012. Jessica Langer (2011) clarifies that the major difference between science-fictional aliens and postcolonial aliens is that the latter group shares at all times a fundamental connection: they are all human beings. Nevertheless, "colonial discourse has often placed the human other in a similar position to the science-fictional other, in that it has 'dehumanized' or significantly 'alienated' the colonized" (Langer 2011, 85). This is a major reason why science-fictional representations of aliens and alienness can be so effective in conceptualizing the ways in which otherness functions in our world.

One of science fiction's most pronounced definitional markers is imperialism. Since early Western science fiction coincided with the age of imperialism, H. G. Wells (1866–1946), Jules Verne (1828–1905), and others wrote of voyages underground, under the sea, and into the heavens, thus reproducing the "otherworldliness of the colonies," which provided "a new kind of legibility and significance to an ancient plot" (Rieder 2008, 6). Keeping these foundational discursive patterns in mind, it is clear that the genre allows postcolonial writers to engage in a cognitive process that disrupts what Rieder calls the "colonial gaze" (2008).[5] He argues that "the colonial gaze" establishes a cognitive framework that bestows knowledge and power on the subject who looks, while denying or minimizing access to power for its object, the one looked at. In traditional science fiction, the male white Western narrator would typically occupy the dominant colonizing role to control the indigenous inhabitants of the colonized land. I intend to consider how this pattern is reworked and overturned when the ones who are looking are African subjects.

A second purpose of this chapter is to explore how Okorafor's novel *Lagoon* (2014) discursively constructs othered selves in postcolonial Nigeria through an imagined landing of a spaceship in Lagos. I also address another distinctive feature of postcolonial science fiction: its hybridity and the blending of scientific discourse with other indigenous genres and traditions. The exuberant and inventive imagery of *Lagoon* combines Nigerian mythology with fantasy, speculative fiction, and characters that speak solely Pidgin English. These components not only serve to decolonize science fiction but also offer critical views on race, gender, religion, ecology, and class. Hence, intersectionality is at the core of this hybrid speculative fiction with overt commentary on the legacies of colonialism (the opening explanation of the Portuguese origin of the name Lagos is one such instance) and criticisms of global capital through accounts of the oil trade or the 419 cyber fraud, as well as claims for a more gender inclusive society that does not discriminate against women and the LGBTQ community in Lagos.

Taking into consideration that Okorafor acknowledged in a note at the end of the novel that she started writing it in direct response to science fiction blockbuster *District 9*, where the representation of Nigerians was highly biased and stereotyped (2014, 301), the following section discusses the dialogue between Hollywood and Nollywood industries on the basis of science fiction. I specifically focus on the exhibition "African Gaze: Hollywood, Bollywood and Nollywood Film Posters from Ghana," presented in March 2019 at Brunei Gallery in London, and curated by Karun Thakar. While the collection comprises a wide range of genres from the three film industries, I select for analysis the posters that depict science fiction and fantasy films through local resignification. The third section delves into Okorafor's *Lagoon*, where I establish symbolic and cultural connections between the imagery in the cinema-inspired artwork and the novel.

HOLLYWOOD-NOLLYWOOD ON DISPLAY IN WESTERN AFRICA

Nigeria, and Lagos in particular, is home to Nollywood, the world's second-largest film industry (after Bollywood) in terms of the number of titles produced per year, but it has mostly steered clear of science fiction.[6] Noah Tsika (2013) claims that *Kajola* (2010) was the first Nollywood sci-fi movie and the most expensive to date. He situates it within two traditions: primarily the U.S. urban sci-fi movies and the Nigerian literary fiction that contain science-fictional elements and Nigerian particularities. Another recent Nollywood sci-fi product is *Hello, Rain* (2018), based on Okorafor's short story "Hello, Motto" (2011). While Nollywood sci-fi is relatively new, the visual and artistic dialogue began much earlier. African art scholar Charles Gore (2019) explains that the late 1980s saw the emergence in Ghana and Nigeria of exuberant new visual modes of expression in a local and innovative film industry, especially in the ways movies were promoted by vivid hand-painted billboard posters on sack or canvas. These arresting images, usually seven or eight feet high, were displayed by the roadside or in prominent public places to alert movie goers to the release of new films being screened by mobile video clubs such as Princess Osu and Pal Mal Video, who would load VCRs, diesel generators, and projectors onto trucks and take the latest films to communities without access to cinemas. These colorful movie posters were often commissioned by local mobile entrepreneurs responsible for taking the movies to a range of communities. The cloth posters could be rolled up and transported easily as they crisscrossed the country. Highly skilled artists joined this effort to create striking images to command the attention of passers-by: "the intense competition between films enhanced the creativity and imaginative possibilities realized by the artists in the film posters and established their individual renown" (Gore 2019, n.p.). In the early 2000s, however, this artistic practice declined with the growth of digital technology.

Media producer Mark Shivas started a collection of more than one hundred movie posters in the late 1990s during one of his trips to Accra, inspired by the extraordinary artwork of one of the films he had produced, *The Witches* (figure 6.1). Starring Angelica Houston, the 1990 U.S. fantasy comedy features witches who masquerade as ordinary women. The movie poster highlights the monstrous and evil elements of the Grand High Witch, depicted with disproportionately large claws, a huge crooked nose, and a freshly burnt body that emerges from the flames of hell. What makes these posters remarkable is that the artists were not just reproducing the original prints but adding indigenous cultural iconographic symbols and ideas. Shivas and the curator of the exhibition at Brunei Gallery were particularly attracted to the African posters portraying Hollywood films, which were familiar yet outlandishly different, through the Ghanaian street artists' inventive rendition and re-interpretation of the source elements.

In terms of filmic inspiration, Okorafor has acknowledged elsewhere how Nollywood films have influenced her writing; *Lagoon* contains frequent sarcastic comments about the highly charged representations of women as seductive and treacherous witches in Nollywood.[7] The hand-painted poster that announces the 1998 Nollywood production *Sakobi: The Snake Girl* (figure 6.2) renders one such depiction: a supernatural, ruthless, and sexualized

Figure 6.1 *The Witches.* Courtesy of © Karun Thakar Collection.

mermaid-like figure, half woman and half snake, who gobbles men to the bone. Her posture, holding one arm up with her hand facing the viewers, and the other down with her hand next to the hip, resembles that of a Hindu goddess. The imagery of the poster adapts the iconic Western African deity Mami Wata ("Mother Water" in Pidgin English), a powerful water divinity, half woman and half sea creature.[8] Contemporary images of Mami Wata mostly portray black women with long hair and snakes circling their torsos.

Figure 6.2 *Sakobi: The Snake Girl.* Courtesy of © Karun Thakar Collection.

For some, Mami Wata provides good fortune through monetary wealth, while others believe that she aids in matters of fertility and procreation. Additional popular beliefs associate her with "irresistible powers of seduction" with potentially lethal outcomes (Drewal 2008, 60). Ytasha Womack (2013) explores the influence of Mami Wata in Afrofuturistic black art and argues that, "according to the myth, when she is not sea bound, she walks the streets of modern African cities and has 'avatars' that do the same. She gives wealth to her followers" (2013, 86). At the bottom right of the movie poster, a black man holds a Voodoo artifact to call upon occult forces.[9] As I will argue in the next section, the presence of Mami Wata is central in *Lagoon*, populated as well by other hybrid sea creatures.

Figure 6.3 *Species.* Courtesy of © Karun Thakar Collection.

The representation of female sexuality as deviously enticing and fatal is also part of the 1995 U.S. science fiction horror film *Species* (figure 6.3). The plot revolves around a motley crew of scientists and government agents who try to track down Sil, a seductive extraterrestrial-human hybrid, before she successfully mates with a human male. Susan George (2001) claims that science fiction films in general respond to this kind of "powerful female sexuality and 'alien-ness' [...] *Species* plays out the dominant trope of 'the monstrous feminine, the evil destructive woman' who is punished at the end through death" (180). The poster on canvas highlights the alien nature of the blond woman, whose white skin turns green below her breasts. The image of her naked body combines robotic machinery with a monstrous extraterrestrial claw, completed with four sharp tentacles that raise from her back. Even though for the most part the rendition of the creature is very similar to the original, the artist of the canvas included two extra elements at the bottom left. The first one is a naked white baby, whose umbilical cord comes out from its mouth. This additional component directs the viewers to the ultimate aim of the alien creature: reproduction. The other is a rat, which represents both the animal species and a laboratory rat. The trope of alien reproduction and hybrid creatures is at the core of Okorafor's *Lagoon*, where she explores the interaction of humans in Lagos with an advanced animal species.

The last canvas reproduces the 1993 science fiction movie *Jurassic Park* (figure 6.4). The franchise blockbuster, an adaptation of Michel Crichton's homonymous novel, delved into the science-fictional tropes of cloning and genetic engineering. By genetically replicating dinosaurs for an amusement park, the film brings the past of extinct animals into the present. What I find interesting about this version is the contrast established between the golf player, in the forefront of the canvas, and the huge dinosaur devouring a human being in the background. It is intriguing why the artist chose to portray golf, when it has no relevance in the movie. One of the reasons no doubt stems from the popularity of this sport in the United States, where amusement parks abound. The shades of bloody red covering the golf player and the golf court indicate that the same ghastly ending awaits the golfer. Once again, the artist has re-signified the original film poster, adding entirely new connotations. Another element in the background of the painting is nature: a phantasmagorical forest spreads behind a thick wall, with iron bars on the top. The dinosaur is outside the enclosure, gulping down its human prey. This gruesome attack could be read as the revenge of the animal world against humans, one of the central themes in *Lagoon*. Okorafor's narration begins from the perspective of an enraged swordfish that wishes to sabotage an oil pipeline. Her "fictional antidote" is the sudden arrival of shape-shifting aliens off the coast of Lagos (first encountered by the swordfish), who precipitate a radical shift in Nigeria's ecological, economic, and social well-being (Jue 2017, 182).

Figure 6.4 *Jurassic Park.* Courtesy of © Karun Thakar Collection.

LAGOON: SCIENCE FICTION NARRATIVE FOR SOCIAL CHANGE IN NIGERIA

In the introduction to her edited anthology *So Long Been Dreaming: Postcolonial Science Fiction and Fantasy* (2004), Nalo Hopkinson argues that postcolonial voices must engage with speculative fiction. While the genre has a long and deeply problematic history of depicting conquest and colonialism as glorious enterprises, Hopkinson suggests instead that speculative fiction can offer unique and invaluable opportunities for representing colonial, postcolonial, and neocolonial conditions. As mentioned earlier in this chapter, several critical works have introduced models that are essential for exploring the counterhegemonic potential of science fiction, as well as the genre's relationship to race and postcolonialism (Kerslake 2007; Langer 2011; Smith 2012). Okorafor, author of four novels, two children's books, and numerous short stories and essays, draws upon elements of fantasy, magic realism, speculative fiction, and dystopian horror. Thus, her science fiction resists easy categorization.

One of her key influences is science fiction movies. In a heated review that Okorafor (2009) wrote about Neill Blomkamp and Peter Jackson's *District 9*, she enumerated the most egregiously offensive elements of the movie. One of them is the one-sided and insulting portrayal of Nigerians as gangsters with cannibalistic tendencies, which is why she sarcastically entitled the review "District 419," in direct reference to the internet scam.[10] Even though the film's opening idea is promising—the landing of a spacecraft full of insectoid aliens who are corralled and kept in a degraded slum in Johannesburg, it soon falls into a problematic and simplistic representation of aliens and black South Africans, whose presence is directly associated with troublesome mobs and chaos.[11] To confer more realism to the story, the film begins with fictional testimonies from witnesses and experts that document the aliens' arrival. However, as Okorafor (2009) rightly notes in her review, the scientific authorities are all white. She points out another of the film's shortcomings, the biased and one-dimensional representation of gender. The aliens are all male, considered repulsive "prawns"—a derogatory designation in the film—and the Nigerian women in the fenced ghetto are all prostitutes serving the aliens. While Langer (2011) argues that the movie represents one of the most explicitly stated parallels in all of science fiction between the figure of the alien and the figure of the other (82), she also acknowledges the racist depiction of Nigerians. *District 9* caused an outcry in Nigeria after its release in 2009, with the government demanding an apology from filmmakers and banning it from local cinemas. However, this sci-fi blockbuster was embraced by the U.S. Film Academy, who nominated it for four Oscars in 2010, a fact that points to how the racist elements were overlooked in favor of other technical and visual elements. The nominations the film garnered were for Best Picture, Best Adapted Screenplay, Best Visual Effects, and Best Film Editing.

After watching the movie, Okorafor (2014) "started daydreaming about what aliens would do in Nigeria" (301). Although she admits that *Lagoon* "was birthed from my anger at *District 9*," it quickly became something else (2014, 301). In this sense, Okorafor portrays both Nigerians and the shape-shifter aliens in a multidimensional and complex manner. In three different sections, *Lagoon* imagines the landing of strange creatures "from beyond earth" on the coast of Lagos (Okorafor 2014, 111): "Welcome" (3–116), in which the aliens make contact with the people of Lagos; "Awakening" (119–220), the story of an outburst of violence across the city; and "Symbiosis" (223–293), that narrates a period of utopian transformation, when the aliens and humans come together to form "a new post-capitalist Nigeria" (O'Connell 2016, 296). The novel's primary story revolves around the alien ambassador, Ayodele, and her interactions with three human protagonists: Adaora, a marine biologist; Agu, a Nigerian soldier, and Anthony, a Ghanaian hip-hop musician. However, there are a multiplicity of additional plots and voices, distributed in short and dynamic chapters that offer a kaleidoscopic account of the events and of the complex sociopolitical structure of Lagos.

In her narration, Okorafor also weaves together old Nigerian folk characters and mythic figures, such as masquerades, Yoruban trickster gods, and the water deity Mami Wata, which provide elements of fantasy through a West African lens. The omniscient narrator is Udide Okwanka, a trickster spider and master weaver of tales from Igbo folklore who, in the novel, has been living beneath Lagos for centuries and "sees everything" (2016, 228). Only at the end of the novel, through the "Narrator's Welcome" (228–229), the reader becomes aware of who is weaving the multiple threads of the story. In this chapter, the trickster spider and storyteller Udide offers a first-person lyrical appearance. There are only three other chapters narrated in the first person that provide witness accounts to the alien arrival in Lagos. They also encompass the coexistence between mythology and the mundane: Legba, the Yoruba trickster god of language and the crossroads, who is ironically recast in *Lagoon* as an expert 419 scammer, but who also shows up in spirit form as Papa Legba (195–201). The other two chapters portray new allegorical figures: "the Bone Collector" (202–209), a sentient stretch of the Lagos-Benin highway that attacks humans, and "African Chaos" (210–214), a Western myth about the continent, personified in the novel by a black U.S. rapper who visits Lagos: "Maybe my mother was right. She's warned me not to travel to Nigeria. She said that of all African nations, this country was the one she heard the weirdest things on CNN. Internet fraudsters, Christians and Muslims killing each other in the streets, government that robbed its people blind" (2014, 210). In stark contrast to these prejudiced statements, Okorafor dedicates the novel to the diverse and dynamic people of Lagos, including animals, plants, and spirits.

Bosede Aiyetoro and Olibukola Olaoye (2016) assert that Okorafor challenges the very genre of science fiction "by setting the novel in Lagos and forcing the city to welcome aliens among the already existing supernatural beings in Africa" (239). At the same time, her narrative choice underlines the potential of the genre for social critique. Rather than simply equating the problems of contemporary Lagos with the horrors of colonial rule, Okorafor depicts a complex and contradictory city, geographically divided across sociopolitical and class lines. *Lagoon* portrays the violence in these spatial divisions, as well as the structural failures of "neoliberal developmentalism" and the political failures of the postcolonial nation-state (O'Connell 2016, 301). The novel constantly shifts locations that include internet cafes, churches, restaurants, military bases, highway traffic jams, beaches, and resort hotels. This restless approach creates a "kinetic multicultural and global city, crosshatched by the intertwining legacies of colonialism" (O'Connell 2016, 296). Lagos' postcolonial condition is apparent from the opening gloss on the Portuguese origins of its name: "The city takes its name from the Portuguese word 'lagoon.' The Portuguese first landed on Lagos Island in the year 1472" (2014, 1). This is why one of the characters ironically points out that the alien invasion is not the first (2014, 144). The enduring impact of Christian missionaries is evident through Father Oke, a corrupt preacher who views Ayodele, the alien emissary, as an opportunity to gain more money and influence over an even larger flock of parishioners. The consequences of global capital are manifested through the oil trade that pollutes the Nigerian sea, as well as the emergence of a neo-imperial transnational business class that populates the Eko hotel complex, a fortified enclave that insulates them from the decolonized sections of the city.

Nigeria, for the mainstream Western media, "is too backwards, undeserving of an alien invasion" (2014, 287). Nevertheless, the contact with Ayodele brings about positive changes; one such instance is the healing and rebirth of the ailing Nigerian president. Flown into the country on the verge of death, he encounters Ayodele, who heals him through her magical powers. But she does not cure his body alone: she also heals his mind. When he returns to Lagos after being led into the waters to meet the alien elders, he addresses his fellow Nigerian citizens with a renewed strength and sense of purpose: "From the first time since we cast off the shackles of colonialism, over half-century ago, since we rolled through decades of corruption and internal struggle, we have reached the tipping point" (2014, 277). The aliens' arrival generates other positive social changes: the coming out of Black Nexus. This local LGBT organization's members, who usually just met secretly once a month, now gain the courage to appear in public: "We've been hiding for too long. Tell me you don't feel it. This is *revolution*" (2014, 75; emphasis in original). One of the scenes describes how they identify themselves with the classic image of ostracized aliens, especially Rome, a transgender person: "He looked like a Yoruba queen. All of them were wearing headbands with alien antennae bobbing from them [...] 'The Black Nexus' has come down to earth" (2014, 91). The description brings together African culture with archetypal cinematic imagery in order to produce the physical representation of aliens, also connected with the anxiety of rejection and otherness. Aliens in the novel are also linked to "the alien ocean life" (2014, 97), which is why they settle on the Atlantic coast of Lagos and have amphibious shapes, with the ability to change into human forms that "could pass for Lagosians" (2014, 116).

As Adaora declares, these aliens are "not evil like the ones in all the movies" (2014, 80); they just "WISH TO BECOME CITIZENS . . . HERE" (2014, 111; emphasis in original). Another of the revolutionary changes that occur after the arrival of the aliens is their destruction of the oil sources in the delta, so that it is no longer Nigeria's top commodity. As a result, new water forests emerge off the coast. This "ecological emancipation" opens up new means of development that rely on the novel technology provided by the well-intentioned newcomers (Hugo 2017, 51). On their meeting with the president of Nigeria, the aliens solemnly announce: "We *are* technology. [...] We do not want to rule, colonize, conquer or take. We just want a home" (2014, 220, emphasis in the original). Upon contact with the technological creatures, the three main characters develop supernatural powers, previously latent in them, which serve to aid the alien creatures in cleansing the sea. Agu has super strength, Anthony possesses a wellspring of energy that he calls "the rhythm," and Adaora becomes a mermaid with the capacity to manipulate water—a form, it turns out, she has desired all along. Ayodele is described in relation to the water deity Mami Wata, sometimes referred to in the novel as a "marine witch" by those who seem to fear feminine power, like Father Oke and Adaoras's husband, Chris: "to him this woman would be a 'marine witch.' Her husband believed that there were white witches, physical witches and marine witches. All were evil, but the marine witch was the most powerful because she could harness water" (2014, 17). The novel also draws parallels between Chris' recurrent misogynistic comments and women's sexualized representation in the Nollywood films he has watched: "The woman who looked straight out of a Nollywood film showed up at the door [...] the woman wore high heels, had a body of a goddess and spoke with a confidence that reminded Chris of the best lawyers" (2014, 282).

The melodramatic, exaggerated tone of customary Nollywood productions is also patented in the novel, especially in the chaos that breaks out in parts of the city in a violent response to the aliens' arrival: "Several buildings were on fire. Competing music blasted from multiple places. There was a sudden rush as a white man ran by, pursued by ten Area Boys all shouting, 'Stranger! Kill *am*! Kill *the stranger*'" (2014, 144; emphasis in original). Haynes (2000) contends that melodrama is the transnational form that has most influenced Nollywood. The extremes of fortune, emotion, and moral character are classic melodramatic elements that populate Nigerian films. In addition, their predominantly domestic settings, multiple interwoven plot lines, and emphasis on dialogue rather than action make Nollywood films resemble American soap operas (Haynes 2000, 22).[12] These melodramatic elements, particularly the use of dialogues, are present in *Lagoon*, originally conceived as a screenplay for Nollywood director Tchidi Chikere. Some of the dialogues are in Nigerian Pidgin English, which attests to the multiplicity of languages spoken in the country, a fact that Adaora observes: "She heard people nervously talking, some in Yoruba, one in Igbo, two in Hausa, most in Pidgin English" (2014, 16). The use of entire dialogues in Pidgin English might aim to place the non-Nigerian reader in a foreign position, as well as to indigenize the genre of science fiction. Okorafor includes a section at the end of the novel with forty-four Pidgin English terms and phrases that she translates into Standard English. Entitled "Special Bonus Features" (295–299), this section is not conceived of as a traditional glossary but as additional cultural information for the non-Nigerian readers. Its title also connects the narrative elements with filmic ones: the designation "Bonus Features" in DVDs typically refers to the extra disc with additional footage and cast interviews.

Lagos is Nollywood's primary location and most films are shot in this megalopolis, with an estimated population of twenty-one million inhabitants. Haynes (2007) argues that Nollywood's imagination informs the city's images, "making them public emblems of fear and desire. Nollywood is a part of that cityscape, an element in its visual culture" (133). The cinematic visual descriptions of Lagos, in all of its diversity, are recurrent in *Lagoon*. The influence of Nollywood's plot structure and "break-neck speed" is also evident in the novel (Okorafor 2014, 304), in the sense that brief chapters present manifold stories that confer a fast pace to the narrative. Another common element in Nigerian films is the routine presence of the supernatural and the occult: "Witchcraft as a weapon in domestic or neighborly antagonisms, mysterious fates that can only be elucidated by a diviner, selling one's soul to a dark occult power for the sake of wealth" (Haynes 2000, 3). In the novel, the supernatural and the fantastic are also enmeshed with the ordinary and the scientific. As a matter of fact, Adaora's laboratory is in the basement of her own home (2014, 21), which becomes the perfect setting for the combination of strangeness and familiarity, two of science fiction's staple characteristics.

CONCLUSION: ALTERNATIVE AFRICAN FUTURES

Science fiction, according to Eshun (2003), operates through the drive to rewrite reality and through "the control and prediction of plausible alternative tomorrows" (291). With this idea in mind, Okorafor engages in the politics of imagining alternative futures for Nigeria. As Pamela Phatsimo Sustrum (2013) claims, "imagining is a radical act" (115), and this revolutionary gesture is at the core of the novel, a bold intervention in the dystopic Africa frequently imagined by others, in the present and the future. The events in Okorafor's *Lagoon* occur in 2010 Lagos. The narrative skillfully combines African mythology; the scientific discourse of a female, Nigerian marine biologist; words and dialogues in Pidgin English; and the influence of popular culture, with direct references to Nollywood and Hollywood (the sci-fi classics *Star Wars* and *ET* are mentioned throughout the narrative). As opposed to the dystopic Johannesburg depicted in *District 9*, Lagos is positively transformed by the aliens who, at the same time, are humanized in a symbiotic process when they emerge from the coast of Lagos: "They were people, hundreds of people, walking straight out of the ocean onto Bar Beach [. . .] Most of them were African, a small few Asian, one white. [. . .] All of them could pass for Lagosians" (2014, 116).

Western culture usually constructs blackness in opposition to technologically driven chronicles of progress (Nelson 2002, 1). However, Okorafor believes that "Technology is just another form of juju [. . .] to be African is to naturally merge technology and magic" (Okorafor qtd. in Whitted 2016, 209).[13] This idea is portrayed in *Lagoon* through the technologically evolved amphibious creatures coming from beyond the earth that decide to settle in Lagos. At the end of the novel, Nigeria's president declares on a national television broadcast: "They have new technology, they have fresh ideas that we can combine with our own [. . .] People of Lagos, especially, look at your neighbor. See his race, tribe, or his alien blood. And call him brother. We have much work to do as a family" (2014, 278). Then he explains that the "alien technology" would make the land pure, ignite the growth of indigenous crops as never before, and stimulate extinct creatures to return and new ones to appear (2014, 278).

This utopian ecological fantasy represents an alternative future for Nigeria, through a radical act of imagination that embraces otherness and envisions a green form of progress. Okorafor not only fills an important lacuna in the representation of Nigerians in science fiction, but she also offers the readers different modes to relate to estrangement, in the sense that human beings are transformed into hybrid and powerful sea creatures after their contact with the extraterrestrial visitors. This allegorical blending counteracts Western binarisms, notions of alterity, and power. The narrative ultimately opens up the genre for an African diasporic gaze that embraces local and international influences. African science fiction proves to be a flexible, non-monolithic, and strategic genre that serves Okorafor to imagine a counterhegemonic ecological future in Nigeria.

NOTES

1. This work was supported by the VPPI-US postdoctoral contract from the University of Seville. The research visit conducted at the School for Oriental and African Studies (SOAS, University of London) to develop this chapter was partially funded by the project FFI2017-84555-C2-1-P Bodies in Transit 2, from the Spanish Ministry of Science, Innovation and Universities.
2. Rieder (2008) contends that much of early Western science fiction, whose emergence in the nineteenth century coincided with a period of fervid imperialist expansion, transposes and revivifies colonial ideologies.
3. Hartmann included in this anthology Okorafor's prologue of *Lagoon*, entitled "Moom."
4. See also *Lagoon_2060* (2013), an anthology edited by Ayodele Arigbabu, which compiles short stories from eight African writers, and *Terra Incognita: New Short Speculative Fiction from Africa* (2015), edited by Nerine Dorman.
5. Rieder (2008) borrows and adapts Laura Mulvey's influential analysis of the cinematic gaze in "Visual Pleasure and Narrative Cinema" (1975).
6. Jonathan Haynes (2007) remembers that when the term "Nollywood" was coined in 2002, it met with opposition from Nigerians, who thought it suggested that Nigerian filmmaking was only a copy of the U.S. model, Hollywood. In his opinion, the name expresses "the general Nigerian desire for a mass entertainment industry that can take its rightful place on the world stage" (132). The term mainly refers to southern Nigerian, English-language films, whose distribution is largely controlled by Igbo marketers, but which are made by people from the full range of southern Nigerian ethnicities.
7. For a study of Nollywood's transnational impact, see Krings and Onookome (2013).
8. H. J. Dreway (2008) notes that Mami Wata is widely believed to have "overseas" origins, and depictions of her have been profoundly influenced by representations of ancient, indigenous African water spirits; European mermaids and snake charmers; Hindu gods and goddesses; and Christian and Muslim saints (60).
9. Haynes (2000) refers to the occult imagery in *Sakobi: The Snake Girl*, directed and produced by Zeb Ejiro. Haynes reproduces a still from the film that depicts a Voodoo ritual. A ghostly painting of a white mermaid appears on the right-hand corner of the picture (33).
10. In a final addendum to *Lagoon* comprised of Nigerian words and phrases (295–299), Okorafor explains that the number "419" refers to the article in the Nigerian Criminal Code that deals with fraud. The internet scam typically involves promising the victim a significant share of a large sum of money, in return for a small up-front payment, which the fraudster requires in order to obtain the large sum.

11. Some critics have underscored that *District 9* brings the history of apartheid to a dystopic present, depicting postcolonial tensions in Johannesburg through the lens of science fiction. See, for example, Langer 2011, 81–106; Veracini 2011.

12. In the 2014 *Black Camera*'s special issue, devoted to "Nollywood's wordliness," its editor Carmen Garrigano approaches the Nigerian film industry as an ever-expanding and extraordinarily heterogeneous archive of "Africa's engagement with the world" (44).

13. Ibo Cbanga (2009) defines "juju" as an object that has been deliberately infused with magical power or the magical power itself. Juju is practiced in West African countries.

REFERENCES

Arigbabu, Ayodele, ed. 2013. *Lagoon_2060*. Lagos: Design and Dream Arts Enterprises.
Ashraf Masood, Raja et al., eds. 2011. *The Postcolonial Fantasy: Essays on Postcolonialism, Cosmopolitics and Science Fiction*. Jefferson: McFarland.
Barber, Tiffany. 2018. "25 Years of Afrofuturism and Black Speculative Thought: Roundtable with Tiffany E. Barber, Reynaldo Anderson, Mark Dery, and Sheree Renée Thomas." *Canadian Journal of Cultural Studies* 39 (Spring): 136–44.
Beukes, Lauren. 2008. *Moxyland*. London: Angry Robot.
Beukes, Lauren. 2010. *Zoo City*. London: Angry Robot.
Bosede Aiyetoro, Mary, and Elizabeth Olibukola Olaoye. 2016. "Afro-Science Fiction: A Study of Nnedi Okorafor's *What Sunny Saw in the Flames* and *Lagoon*." *Pivot: A Journal of Interdisciplinary Studies and Thought* 5 (1): 226–46.
Bould, Mark. 2013. "Sf Now: Introduction." *Paradoxa* 26: 7–15.
Bould, Mark. 2015. "African Science Fiction." *SFRA Review* 311 (Winter): 11–18.
Cbanga, Ibo. 2009. "Juju." In *Encyclopedia of African Religion*, edited by Molefi Kete Asante and Ama Mazama, 357–58. Thousand Oaks: Sage.
Crumbs. Directed by Miguel Llansó. Las Palmas: Lanzadera Films, 2015.
Dery, Mark. 1994. "Black to the Future: Interviews with Samuel R. Delany, Greg Tate, and Tricia Jones." In *Flame Wars: The Discourse of Cyberculture*, edited by Mark Dery, 179–222. Durham: Duke University Press.
Dorman, Nerine, ed. 2015. *Terra Incognita: New Short Speculative Fiction from Africa*. Johannesburg: Short Story Day Africa.
Drewal, Henry John. 2008. "Mami Wata: Arts from Water Spirits in Africa and Its Diaspora." *African Arts* 41 (2): 60–83.
Eshun, Kodwo. 2003. "Further Considerations of Afrofuturism." *The New Centennial Review* 3 (2): 287–302.
Garrigano, Carmen. 2014. "Introduction: Nollywood—An Archive of African Worldliness." *Black Camera* 5 (2): 44–52.
George, Susan. 2001. "Not Exactly 'of Woman Born': Procreation and Creation in Recent Science Fiction Films." *Journal of Popular Film and Television* 28 (4): 176–83.

Gore, Charles. 2019. *African Gaze: Hollywood, Bollywood and Nollywood Film Posters from Ghana*. London: Brunei Gallery.
Hartmann, Ivor W., ed. 2013. *Afro SF: Science Fiction by African Writers*. Zimbabwe: Story Time.
Haynes, Jonathan. 2000. *Nigerian Video Films*. Athens: Ohio University Press.
Haynes, Jonathan. 2007. "Nollywood in Lagos, Lagos in Nollywood Films." *Africa Today* 54 (2): 131–50.
Hello, Rain. Directed by C. J. Obasi. Lagos: Fiery Films, 2018.
Hoagland, Erika, and Reewa Sarwal, eds. 2010. *Science Fiction, Imperialism and the Third World: Essays on Postcolonial Literature*. New York: McFarland.
Hopkinson, Nalo. 2004. "Introduction." In *So Long Been Dreaming: Postcolonial Science Fiction and Fantasy*, edited by Nalo Hopkinson and Uppinder Mehan, 7–11. Vancouver: Arsenal Pulp Press.
Hugo, Esthie. 2017. "Looking Forward, Looking Back: Animating Magic, Modernity and the African City-Future in Nnedi Okorafor's *Lagoon*." *Social Dynamics* 43 (1): 46–58.
Jue, Melody. 2017. "Intimate Objectivity: On Nnedi Okorafor's Oceanic Afrofuturism." *Women's Studies Quarterly* 45 (1–2): 171–88.
Kerlslake, Patricia. 2007. *Science Fiction and Empire*. Liverpool: Liverpool University Press.
Kilolo, Moses et al., ed. 2015. "Jalada 02: AfroFuture(s)." *Jalada Africa*. https://jaladaafrica.org/2015/01/14/jalada-02-afrofutures/
Krings, Mattias, and Onookome Okome, eds. 2013. *Global Nollywood: The Transnational Dimensions of an African Video Film Industry*. Bloomington: Indiana University Press.
Langer, Jessica. 2011. *Postcolonialism and Science Fiction*. New York: Palgrave.
Melzer, Patricia. 2006. *Alien Constructions: Science Fiction and Feminist Thought*. Austin: University of Texas Press.
Mulvey, Laura. 1975. "Visual Pleasure and Narrative Cinema." *Screen* 16 (3): 6–18.
Nelson, Alondra. 2002. "Future Texts." *Social Text* 71 (20): 1–15.
O'Connell, Hugh Charles. 2016. "'We Are Change': The Novum as Event in Nnedi Okorafor's *Lagoon*." *Cambridge Journal of Postcolonial Literary Inquiry* 3 (3): 291–312.
Okorafor, Nnedi. 2009. "My Response to *District 419*…I Mean *District 9*." *Nnedi's Wahala Zone Blog*. August 23, 2009. http://nnedi.blogspot.com/2009/08/my-responseto-district-419i-mean.html
Okorafor, Nnedi. 2009. "Organic Fantasy." *African Identities* 7 (2): 275–86.
Okorafor, Nnedi. 2011. "Hello, Motto." Tor.Com, https://www.tor.com/2011/11/02/hello-moto/
Okorafor, Nnedi. 2014. *Lagoon*. London: Hodder & Stoughton.
Omelsky, Matthew. 2014. "After the End Times: Post-Crisis African Science Fiction." *The Cambridge Journal of Postcolonial Literary Inquiry* 1 (1): 33–49.
Phatsino Sunstrum, Pamela. 2013. "Afro-Mythology and African Futurism: The Politics of Imagining and Methodologies for Contemporary Creative Research Practices." *Paradoxa* 26: 113–30.

Pumzi. Directed by Wanuri Kahui. Kenya: Focus Features, 2009.
Rettová, Alena. 2017. "Sci-fi and Afrofuturism in the Afrophone Novel: Writing the Future and the Possible in Swahili and in Shona." *Research in African Literatures* 48 (1): 158–82.
Rieder, John. 2008. *Colonialism and the Emergence of Science Fiction*. Middletown: Wesleyan University Press.
Samatar, Sofia. 2017. "Toward a Planetary History of Afrofuturism." *Research in African Literatures* 48 (4): 175–91.
Smith, Eric. 2012. *Globalization, Utopia, and Postcolonial Science Fiction*. New York: Palgrave Macmillan.
Thakar, Karun, curator. 2019. "African Gaze: Hollywood; Bollywood and Nollywood Film Posters from Ghana." London: Brunei Gallery.
Tsika, Noah. 2013. "Projected Nigerias: *Kajola* and Its Contexts." *Paradoxa* 26: 89–112.
Veracini, Lorenzo. 2011. "*District 9* and *Avatar*: Science Fiction and Settler Colonialism." *Journal of Intercultural Studies* 32 (4): 355–67.
Whitted, Qiana. 2016. "'To Be African Is to Merge Technology and Magic': An Interview with Nnedi Okorafor." In *Afrofuturims 2.0: The Rise of Astro Blackness*, edited by Reynaldo Anderson and Charles E. Jones, 207–13. London: Lexington Books.
Womack, Ytasha. 2013. *Afrofuturism: The World of Black Sci-Fi and Fantasy Culture* Chicago: Chicago Review Press.

Chapter 7

Transgressing Borders
(Re)imag(in)ing Africa(ns) in the World
Aretha Phiri

INTRODUCTION: AFROPOLITICS AND THE BURDEN OF REPRESENTATION

Albeit diminished in intensity, calls for the decolonization of South African Higher Education and a concomitant "Africanization" of its curricula have exposed a country haunted by sociopolitical inequalities post-apartheid as well as undermined assertions of a universal world culture post colonization. In this regard, the linguistic place and cultural relevance of African literature written in English has again come under review.[1] More particularly, a growing body of contemporary literature written by Africans in the diaspora has attracted cynicism for an apparently Afropolitan outlook that does not attend to persisting global inequities and deviates from continental and global South transformation agendas.[2]

Described by Taiye Selasi in her influential 2005 essay "Bye-Bye, Babar," as the worldly articulations of the "newest generation of African emigrants," Afropolitanism advocates an African provenance of mobile and mutable, cosmopolitan subjectivities that are not just an extension of elite post-independence migration from the continent; they are symptomatic of the metaphysically hybrid trends of twenty-first-century globalization in which African diasporic subjects, encoded to "forge a sense of self from wildly disparate routes," finally "belong to no single geography, but feel at home in many." Advancing thus an anti-essentialist and de-centrist African modernity (Balakrishnan 2017), its eclectic and idiosyncratic character has attracted much interest and support over the years, and not just in mainstream popular culture.[3] Enhanced to include more philosophical (Mbembe 2007), existential (Gikandi 2011), and ethical (Eze 2014, 2106) considerations and interpretations, the concept of Afropolitanism has more recently been expanded to include literary manifestations that indicate specifically a contemporary prose narrative written by an African-descendent writer (Knudsen and Rahbeck 2016).

But Anna-Leena Toivanen, following her initial inquiry into how it "differs from traditional, elitist white pseudo-universalist cosmopolitanisms" (2015, 1), has more recently debated Afropolitanism's limits as an ethnic adjunct to cosmopolitanism and pronounced it "simply cosmopolitanism's new fashionable clothing: a lot of excitement surrounding little viable content" (2017, 202). Aligned with academic discussions around the sociopolitical efficacy of cosmopolitanism's democratizing articulations of a universal world culture (Gilroy 2005; Gikandi 2002), this anticipates Grace Musila's general concern with Afropolitanism as a phenomenon that "seems to be about embracing just enough of Africa to retain a certain flavour that sets one apart from the norm—presumably the Euro-American—but not so much as to be *too* 'African.'" She explains: "Like Coke Lite or lite beer, Afropolitanism seems to promise Africa lite: Africa *sans* the 'unhealthy' or 'intoxicating' baggage of Africa" (2016, 109). Equally, for the celebrated Ghanaian writer, Ama Ata Aidoo (2016), Afropolitanism attempts to mask the "terror associated with Africa" and is in fact "evidence of self-hatred."

Literary critics have more pointedly cautioned against what appears to be another one of Afropolitanism's problematic characteristics: a burgeoning contemporary literature written in English by Africans in the diaspora and "packaged" for a Western readership—what Eileen Julien (2006) has generically delineated as the "extroverted African novel." In an article intended to probe the "future of literature, reading and literary scholarship in Africa" on the occasion of the fortieth conference of the African Literature Association (ALA) in 2014, Dan Ojwang and Michael Titlestad claim that while making African novels accessible to non-African readers, the current trend of émigré writing—"writing about Africa without living in it"—also, unfortunately, "contorts the continent's past and present." They finally delineate contemporary Afrodiasporic literature as "by definition, less specifically textured," a statement that echoes Ashleigh Harris's concern that contemporary Afrodiasporic literature which is not conversant with "African everyday life" hazards entrenching global hierarchies and inequalities (2014, 4). At a recent roundtable on decolonization held at the Johannesburg Institute for Advanced Study (JIAS), the argument came full circle with Nigerian author and Commonwealth Prize winner E. E. Sule (2018) maintaining that African writers in the diaspora "in the end unintentionally contribute to a neocolonisation of the continent."[4]

But there are two fundamental problems with such readings. First, the temptation to simply conflate Afropolitanism and contemporary Afrodiasporic writing delimits the parameters and prospects of the latter. Albeit related, they are not reducibly interchangeable phenomena and practices, so that the attempt here to theorize literarily or impose critically upon current Afrodiasporic writing a phenomenological category/appellation precludes and forecloses the possibly of complex readings and contexts advanced and addressed in this literature. Second, while the (mis)appropriation by markets in the global North of African literary outputs is regrettable, it cannot be denied that historically "what *passes* for the African novel is an *effect* created by publishing, pedagogical and critical practices" (Julien 2006, 696; emphasis added).[5] Persistently locating primary audiences in the West, then, does not just underplay contemporary Afrodiasporic writing's "multiple levels of address" and "multifocality" (Krishnan 2014, 142, 147); it detracts from the productive and critical task of exploring in this literature the "tensions between transnational production and a transformational agenda that is always local and immediate" (Ibironke 2015, 40).

Pointing then to an irresolvable aporia, the typically derisive, even dismissive, responses to the recent trend in Afrodiasporic writing need to be cautioned against.[6] Albeit disrupting contemporary post-racial, post-black, and now post-African identitarian parlance, and although addressing current transformation imperatives to "re-center" African history and cultures in a postcolonial global economy and imagination, conventional readings of current Afrodiasporic fiction tend ironically and questionably to operate along similarly parochial and potentially essentialist colonizing premises.[7] More worryingly, they appear to reinstate exclusionary hierarchies of blackness predicated on cultural/ontological acuity and geographical/national proximity—on autochthonous authenticity.

The delimiting parameters of orthodox interpretative paradigms obfuscate African literature's enduring dialectical internationalism, evinced in the works of canonical writers like Chinua Achebe and Buchi Emecheta and demonstrating its evolution in what Simon Njami identifies as the "schizophrenic reality" of global processes of cultural and ideological mongrelization (2017, 13). Significantly, it is precisely this overdetermined, prescriptive ethnographic imperative for cultural representativeness that still frames postcolonial readings which is increasingly being resisted by contemporary black African writers in the diaspora. Notwithstanding Maaza Mengiste's (2013) and Binyavanga Wainaina's (2013) famed pronouncements on the subject,[8] Helon Habila's (2014) argument against "literary pass-laws" that seek to restrict where "African literature can go" is aligned with a current Afrodiasporic writing that is sensitive to the potential re-inscription of inequalities and exclusions that invariably typify the taxonomic imperatives of global literary production *and* cultural ideology. Without dismissing the significance of an African literary canon and its value in addressing, and attempting to redress, the historical marginalization and delegitimization of black Africa, a case can be made and space created for the extensive repertoires and expansive existential visions advanced in contemporary Afrodiasporic writing. Indeed, not just putting blackness into question (Harvey 2016) but upending in the contemporary moment Africa's continued signification in the imaginary as an ethnic and ontological particularity, such literature necessitates a re-interrogation of global processes of black African homogenization and racialization (Pierre 2013). As such, it is worth noting in this writing how disparate diasporic routes produce necessarily incongruent black cultural identities as well as promote inevitably "different forms of identification with the African continent itself" (Quayson 2013, 630).

In this way, contemporary Afrodiasporic literature could be said to proffer an alter-nativist, supplementary ethics of reading. That is, in advancing an aesthetic of less explicitly politicized, idiosyncratic versions of African diasporic cultures, current attempts by Afrodiasporic writers to shift and broaden discussions around identity politics beyond the ethnographic imperative, facilitate more ethical considerations of the (universally) ontological prospects for literature. Tellingly, where Chimamanda Ngozi Adichie has famously excoriated the "danger of a single story" (2009) and Chris Abani has maintained that "story is fluid and belongs to nobody" (2007),[9] Selasi has herself previously, and in a retrospective discussion of her now contested essay on Afropolitanism, confessed that "Like all writers, I am obliged to let my writing live a life of its own—to enter discourses for which I did not intend it, to suffer interpretations I never imagined" (Knusden and Rahbeck 2016, 290).[10] This is not to endorse the anti-instrumentalist view that favors the singularity of art. It is to recognize, as a mediated and mediating space of encounter, contemporary Afrodiasporic literature's hermeneutical capacity to complicate prescriptive taxonomies and to facilitate novel discursive spaces and interpretive paradigms.

READING AFRICA(NS) DIFFERENTLY, RE-IMAG(IN)ING THE WORLD

A comparative reading of Taiye Selasi's *Ghana Must Go* and NoViolet Bulawayo's *We Need New Names* deliberates the efficacy and transformative potential of Afrodiasporic literature within global transitional contexts. Published in 2013, *Ghana Must Go* tells the story of the Sais, an intergenerational family of overachievers residing in Boston, America. On the surface, the Sais present an enviable narrative of transnational, diasporic success. The distinguished surgeon and accomplished African patriarch, Dr. Kweku Sai, is married to the remarkably beautiful and eclectic Folasadé, with whom he has four variously accomplished children:

Olu, the burgeoning surgeon following in his father's footsteps; Taiwo and Kehinde, the cultured and artistic twins; and Sadie, the blossoming Ivy League student. But taking titular inspiration from the historical event of the expulsion and consequent mass-migration of an estimated two million Ghanaians from Nigeria in 1983, the novel disrupts the "traditional" African diaspora success story with the troubling narrative(s) of an existentially traumatized family.

In *We Need New Names*, a novel also published in 2013, the allusion to Zimbabwe's violent racialized and ethnicized colonial and postcolonial histories is presented from the uncensored and irreverent, imaginatively cosmopolitan viewpoint of a female adolescent, Darling, whose eventual migration from post-independent depravity to attain in the United States the American dream, registers comparable psychical distress. As inferred in their revisionary titular directives and thematic emphases on interrelated spatial migration and subjective mobility, both novels situate (experiences of) Africa decisively in the world in order not just to disrupt parochial, static readings of Africanness but to revitalize and enlarge putative global subjective visions and scopes. While shared references to child rape and incest, forced removals and civil wars, the HIV pandemic and rampant poverty ostensibly rehearse unpalatable pathologies of an historically dark continent, the parallel deprecatory depictions of pervasive Western worldliness in both novels bring together seemingly disparate worlds, registering thus Afrodiasporic writing's political concern with transgressing borders—nationally and culturally conceived.

The Sai family's excessive need to excel—not just the resonance of a migrant, particularly African, ethos of respectability—in *Ghana Must Go* is diasporically attuned to the alienating mechanisms of American middle-class, capitalist suburban values. Likewise, *We Need New Names'* irreverent depiction of Darling's social life and experiences in "Destroyed Michygen" illuminates stubbornly provincial attitudes that pervade and color contemporary white "progressive" American engagements with the apparently ahistorical and constitutionally foreign black African. More significantly, in both novels, the varied and circuitous journeys of the central characters between African and American states and the spiritual shifts and displacements experienced therein, translate experiences of global, spatial mobility into considerations of localized, interior mobility. That is, in a transgression of physical—geographical and political—borders that in turn facilitates a disruption of personal, existential borders—what Selasi terms "boundaries of the self" (2013b, 14)—Afrodiasporic fiction subscribes to what Chielozona Eze describes as "transcultural affinity": the "moral investment in the being of others" (2015, 223) that both acknowledges and transcends cultural particularities. More acutely, it embeds the Afrodiasporic condition in an ethical frame in which respect for the diversity and specificity of all people renders him/her simultaneously responsive both to an historically politicized otherness and to the intrinsic otherness of the self.

Tellingly, the children's valorization in *We Need New Names* of Western "country-countries" above the global South's "rags of countries" (51) in their oft-played country games reductively extends orthodox political and academic commentary on post- and neocolonial disillusionment to include the banal, but acute, materialist observations of an ordinary populace. The novel's allusion to the forced removals of Operation Murambatsvina, a politically motivated, ZANU-PF led operation to literally "remove the dirt" and that ironically echoed white colonialist imperatives to effectively nativize and politically coordinate the African populace (Mamdani 1996),[11] buttresses Darling's description of the global South as "a terrible place of hunger and things falling apart" (51). Her ironic double reference here pays titular homage to Dambudzo Marechera's *House of Hunger* (1978) and Chinua Achebe's *Things Fall Apart* (1958), canonical African texts that effect similarly scathing critiques of post-independence nationalism *and* the effects of neocolonial globalization. Indeed, appearing like "ants. In swarms, like flies. In angry waves, like a wretched sea . . . with the dust from their houses clinging to their hair and skin and clothes, making them appear like things from another life" (75–76), the people's abjection is accentuated by a pervasive and oppressive Chinese imperialist, neocolonial presence. But in that the Western NGOs—which are here reminiscent of Tsisti Dangarembga's missionaries in *Nervous Conditions* (1988)—are described as "kill[ing]" the children with their gifts in return for their performative gratitude, is the suggestion that such mutually patronizing and exploitative relations are finally affirmed as a universal "crime against humanity" (53), an existential crime more fully realized in Darling's despair at (an illusory) everyday American life and in the fragile and senile, schizophrenic existence and eventual suicide here of her relation, Tshaka Zulu, the controversial Zulu icon's ironic (and, in this case, pathetic) namesake.

Similarly, for the youngest child in the Sai family and the most ostensibly Afropolitan of all the characters in *Ghana Must Go*, Sadie's accumulative (racial and bodily) sense of self-loathing in which she does not just desire—sexually—but wants to be—existentially—her white best friend, Philae, is indicative. Where the "nervous condition" of Fanon's wretched postcolonial native enacts psychologically the nausea of history in which the past translates into and appears to arrest (the progress of) the present, the novel's engagement with Sadie's bulimic body dysmorphic disorder expands the expression of historical, psychical anxiety at a profoundly material and finally ontological level. Described as performing the "same gruesome *rite*" (142; emphasis added) while kneeling on the bathroom floor, her disturbingly rationalized description of ritualized vomiting extends the Foucauldian interpretation of the body as the politicized, disciplined "object and target of power" within a ubiquitous Eurocentric, Anglo-Saxon culture by exploring the iterability of the *self*-disciplined black body which becomes similarly a symbol for a normative "network of relations" (Foucault 1979, 136, 146) within black cultural structures. Sadie's disorder finally articulates "her whole being trembling with the effort to *be*" (36; emphasis in original), *a priori* the exigencies of a culture writ large.

That her (disordered and disorderly) condition shifts when she travels with her family from Boston, America, to Accra, Ghana, upon news of her father's death is politically and existentially revealing. This transatlantic, transnational border crossing unearths the transmigratory, "*surrogate heartbeat*" (267; emphasis added) she discovers while intuitively dancing the traditional Ghanaian Ga dance. Described as accessing or being inhabited by "a stranger inside her that knows what to do, knows the music, these movements, this footwork, this rhythm," Sadie's body in motion affirmatively re-interprets her previously disciplined self which had been numbed by the ritual effects of body dysmorphia and bulimia. Although the celebratory realignment of marginal political bodies—specifically black African female bodies—in this representation of diaspora infers the pervasive allure of cultural exoticism and ethnic nativism attendant to both colonial and postcolonial identity politics, the emphasis in the dancing scene on "*these* movements, *this* footwork, *this* rhythm" (270; emphasis added) implies the temporality of geographical space and proposes culture as always vulnerable to the prospect of (re)translation and change.[12] Undermining thus Nell Freudenberger's (2013) reading of the novel as "Selasi's project of particularizing the African experience for a Western audience" and problematizing likewise cosmopolitanism's theoretic abstractionism of cultural exchange, Sadie evinces a material "animist signification" which is transformatively reproduced "within the sphere of culture and social life" (Garuba 2003, 276, 269). Here, then, is an instantiation of the "transitive and connective" grammar of identity (Clingman 2009, xi) which, navigating spatiotemporal and ideological boundaries, implies the prospects for an ethical re-examination of (how we perceive) the world.

FEMINIST PRAXIS: ACKNOWLEDGING ALTERNATIVE MODES OF BEING IN THE WORLD

In particular, and in line with a relative accent on women's corporeal and sexual experiences, the pointed focus in these texts on the intimacies of familial life and the domestic intricacies of Afrodiasporic experiences advances an inclusive feminist praxis that considers further how "the intimate recesses of the domestic space become sites for history's most intricate invasions" (Bhabha 1992, 141). That is, in the embodied experiences of the novels' characters, which extend social and moral implications to include existential, materialist considerations of the Afrodiasporic condition, is the necessary complication and humanizing of globalizing and nationalist imperatives.

Certainly the revelation in *We Need New Names* of the sexual abuse and consequent impregnation by her grandfather of Darling's childhood friend, Chipo, from the adolescent, even childish, perspective accentuates the vulnerabilities that attend "everyday" life in and beyond the ironically named town of Paradise and registers the absurdities that fester beneath putatively heteropatriarchal societal mores. Notwithstanding the novel's general representation of the oppressive state of women post-independence, and the caustic appellation of the sexually exploitative Prophet Revelations Bitchington Mborro, the vivid account of the children's attempt at aborting Chipo's pregnancy mimics, in the children's simulation here of American popular culture, nationally abortive attempts to expel (ostensibly interdependent) "foreign" imperialist cultural influence. Interestingly, Darling's viewing of pornographic material with her friends when in America causes her to recall "how men back home would hold down a goat during slaughter, or how Prophet Revelations Bitchington Mborro and the Evangelists held down the pretty woman on the mountain to exorcise her demon" (213), extends the novel's Afrofeminist critique to include transnational, global considerations of the (sexual) oppression of women. As such, mirroring the graphic description of Sadie's bulimic purging in *Ghana Must Go*, the simulated abortion—indicatively narrated in the chapter entitled "We Need New Names"—in this scene more significantly registers an attempt to expel the imminent progeny of a discursively patriarchal nationalism whose religious/secular consecration of femininity—"subsumed under maternity" (Kristeva and Goldhammer 1985, 133)—abjectly exceeds and defers realization (for the female subject) of the subjective enterprise.

In a similar destabilization of heteropatriarchal nationalist narratives, the disruption in *Ghana Must Go* of the idealized mother-daughter relationship in which Folasadé, like her mother before her, fails to "protect" or "act as a shield" (290) to her emotionally damaged progeny, necessarily acknowledges the (traumatic) repetition of history. It also pointedly recognizes existential vagaries (and vulgarities) that demand an empathetic reconsideration of an erstwhile but enduring heteronormative, Afrodiasporic maternal project.[13] Indeed, the novel's graphic delineation of the rape of a younger Taiwo by her twin brother Kehinde, a sexual assault forcibly orchestrated by their deranged uncle who is a general in the national army, does not just illuminate allegorically the patriarchal violence(s) of postcolonial, post-independent Nigeria.[14]

The novel facilitates, in its portrait of the despairing and awkward relations of and between the twins, an imaginatively human(e) engagement with the complexities and familiarities that attend experiences of sexual and other violations and the lingering relational effects therein. Significantly, this affords a necessary reconceptualization of the black experience not merely as a collective lament but as a signal means of rewriting a grand cultural narrative in order to accentuate, rather, "the notoriously and gloriously disorderly affair," that is, the human life (Selasi 2014).

THE POETICS OF POLITICS

Indeed, both texts' attempts to humanize political discourse are evinced in the strategic, albeit differential, use of narrative form or technique. Where *Ghana Must Go* deploys a lyrical blues-like mode that mimics its thematic existential concerns and accentuates its predominantly melancholic mood (Phiri 2020), *We Need New Names* employs an irreverently humorous, satirical tone that, while managing to maintain narratorial pubescent innocence and perspective, energetically critiques putative political narratives and normative social arrangements through a subversive, purposefully materialist Bakhtinian carnivalesque mode.

Tellingly, and echoing Freudenberger's appraisal of *Ghana Must Go*, Ikhide Ikheloa in his article "How Not to Write about Africa" (2012) predicted NoViolet Bulawayo's win for her short story "Hitting Budapest," for which she won the 2011 Caine Prize and which was developed into the first chapter of her novel, by stating: "She sure can write, unfortunately her muse insists on sniffing around in Africa's sewers." Similarly, Helon Habila's (2014) review reads *We Need New Names* as espousing "poverty porn," as being driven by "a palpable anxiety to cover every 'African' topic, almost as if the writer has made a checklist from the morning's news on Africa." Fixated with the apparent demands of the global publishing industry and its Western readership, and concerned with the (in)efficacy of fictive African representations, both criticisms miss the novel's urgent political tonality and overlook an optimism underlined in the embodied presence and perspective of its pubescent narrator. Further, where the children at the end of the novel respond to questions about Africa with repeated smiles, the suggestion is for the acknowledgment of a complex, intimate, and intricate global network of relations:

> And when they asked us where we were from, we exchanged glances and smiled with the shyness of child brides. They said, Africa? We nodded yes. What part of Africa? We smiled. Is it the part where vultures wait for famished children to die? We smiled. Where the life expectancy is thirty-five years? We smiled.

Is it there where dissidents shove AK-47s between women's legs? We smiled. Where people run around naked? We smiled. Is it where the old president rigged the election and people were tortured and killed and a whole bunch of them put in prison and all, there where they are dying of cholera—on my God, yes, we've seen your country; it's been on the news. (237–238)

In a passage that begins with the conjunctive "And," the way in which the narratorial voice here segues into the collective pronoun "we," which in turn reads in contradistinction to the collective "they," does not merely rehearse the historically dialectically antagonistic relationship between Africa and the implied West. Where the proliferation of questions gesture—within a symbolically heteropatriarchal frame of procedural bridal-like courting—at historically asymmetrical power relations, that the questions remain (un)answered in the children's (alliteratively sardonic and seductive) smiles suggests the disruption of conventional sociopolitical (and social/mainstream media) metanarratives and interpretive frames. In this "gay parody of official reason" (Bakhtin 1984, 39) that recalls the children's mutually exploitative engagements with the NGOs, the novel signals subversively at the dialectic and dialogic prospects for the diffusion and re-envisaging of global power and agency.

This recognition of sociopolitical, existential relationality is evidenced in Darling's eventual disillusionment with a materially unattainable and spiritually vacuous American dream and which parallels the children's despair at their desperate existence. Highlighted in the detailed migration from the poverty of Paradise to the privileged comforts of suburban Budapest, the haunting image here of the expatriate English woman discovered hanging from a tree is grotesque not just because it symbolizes (post-)colonial, Eurocentric demise; it is grotesque because—seguing from its escapist to its realist modalities—in displaying back to the children the horrifying image of postcolonial decay and in their connection of the material value of her shoes with the "dizzying smell" of Lobels bread that surrounds them (18), the novel cements its concern with and indictment on continued socioeconomic inequities post-independence.

Connected to this scene, the phrase "Black Power" (130), scribbled in feces on the bathroom mirror of a white farmer by disgruntled war veterans, confronts the "banality of power" in the post colony through "an aesthetics of vulgarity" (Mbembe 1992). Echoing the nationalist directives of Operation Murambatsvina alluded to earlier, the text suggests the equally fetid, and finally impotent, expedient exigencies of post-independence political narratives and agendas. Indeed, the coevality here of hermeneutical and ontological inefficacy is inferred in a scene in which, referencing Zimbabwe's third *Chimurenga*—a period in which many people were violently displaced and dispossessed in politically motivated (ZANU-PF) processes of land reclamation—a white farmer's desperate plea, "I am an African," is met with the hollow war veteran's "chants of Africa for Africans" and finally Godknows' perplexingly rhetorical question: "What exactly is an African?" (119).[15]

Disrupting Mbekian post-apartheid pan-Africanist rhetoric, Darling's friends' desire to escape from this "kaka" place/country that is their disenchanting post-independent reality underwrites, then, the mass exodus of the "children in the land" (146) illustrated lyrically in the chapter entitled "How They Left."[16] Indeed, underlining tropologically the "remarkable currency and symbolic versatility" of "excremental postcolonialism," the novel's repetitive emphasis on excrement—"kaka"—echoes and reaffirms a tradition in post-independence African fiction of expressing a "failed or flawed postcolonial nationalism" (Esty 1999, 23–24). But in the correlation of textual and political concerns, excremental postcolonialism's self-reflexive, self-interrogating scatology registers also "the tension between narratives devoted to national destiny and narratives devoted to the ethical consolidation of the subject" (Esty 1999, 47, 49).

This is echoed in Bulawayo's self-description and self-affirmation, despite her migrant status, as a "Zimbabwean author . . . an African author" (Peschel 2015) who must confront in her fiction a present reality of a previously "normal country and . . . beautiful childhood" now marred violently by (meta-)physical and (infra-)structural disrepair (Hartselle 2015, 35). That this tension is registered in *We Need New Names* in the similarly disenchanting, excremental experiences of third-world migrants who everywhere "will be welcomed with restraint . . . because they do not belong" (146) extends a predominantly discursive, academic cosmopolitanism to include a materialist, abject cosmopolitanism, that is, a "problematizing cosmopolitanism of the abject" that burrows globally "into the apparatuses and technologies of exclusion" (Nyers 2003, 1075, 1089). In the novel's irreverent approach to and representation of both Western and African, neocolonial perpetuations of inequity, is an interrogation of ubiquitous and particular exclusionary mechanisms.

CONCLUSION

The universality of loss and alienation implicit here echoes the extended omniscient narration in *Ghana Must Go* of the impending death of Kweku Sai, whose own professional disgrace and subsequent flight to Ghana from America inversely precipitates for his entire family the enduring postcolonial concern with home and exile. But the novel's protracted mood of mourning/melancholia elicits not (just) the desire for a concrete (national) identity but recognition of transnational, human(e) ontologies. In this regard, the novel's stylistic focus on interiority and on domestic minutiae—its portraiture "not of a People, the art history of Peoplehood, constant and strong, but the shorter, very messy, lesser history of people, small *p*" (166–67; emphasis in original)—differently mirrors *We Need New Names*' stylistic emphasis on exteriority and its picture of the national terrain in ways that articulate and underline contemporary Afrodiasporic fiction's aim of achieving globally more inclusive and expansive visions and versions of subjectivity.

This is further underwritten in both novels by a thematic concern with the shifting, unstable character of home which works in contradistinction to the traditional postcolonial African diaspora narrative of return (to an idyllic, concrete homeland). Indeed, where *We Need New Names* appears occupied nostalgically with return to an ideal(ized) homeland, this is complicated, as it is in *Ghana Must Go*, by the characters' recognition that the notion of home is, in a profoundly politically unstable contemporary globalized moment, finally fragile and elusive, residing fundamentally in the embodied self. To this end, the latter novel's ontological revisionism of home as interactional is underlined in Kweku Sai's slippers which, weathered and worn, symbolize existentially a transmigratory state of being, one that is affirmed in an ambiguous conclusion and in which characters remain, like those in *We Need New Names*, hauntingly and perpetually "unfinished, in rehearsal, a production in progress" (123).

As such, both novels' ambiguous, open-ended conclusions underwrite and advocate an ethical, open reading of African literatures and ontologies. Suggesting something more complicated and less celebratory than is put forward by contemporary African diaspora theorists and proponents of Afropolitanism alike, neither text attempts "a hermeneutics of redemption" from stereotypical representations of the continent as Simon Gikandi (2007) has postulated; nor do they strictly conceive the possibility of a transcending race, as Achille Mbembe (2008) has envisaged. Neither apolitical nor redemptory, *We Need New Names* and *Ghana Must Go* offer refreshingly candid engagements with the contemporary Afrodiasporic moment and condition in which, caught in that "deep abyss of Culture" (Selasi 2005), the characters in both novels are lost in translation—stuck in a quagmire of ontological hermeneutics.

Indicatively, the navigation by the Sai family of what is described in *Ghana Must Go* as the interstitial, "shadowy gap between worlds" (221)—the negotiation of subjective roots and routes—mirrors in *We Need New Names* Darling's description of migration as tantamount to "dying," a spectral existence in which the gaps in existential articulation herein are accentuated in Darling's lament, when in America, that "we could not use our own languages . . . what we really wanted to say remained folded inside, trapped" (240). Tellingly, Selasi, who is herself of mixed cultural heritage and exhibits a transnational, cosmopolitan subjectivity has described writing her now infamous essay not from a position of power, but "from a position of pain," the "incredibly alienating" and "disorienting" experience of a stranded, "'de-territorialized' brown people" acutely aware "at all times of our non-belonging" (Bady 2015, 158). Her novel thus creatively articulates, where her essay does not, "the aching, with longing" (251) for existential legitimation that characterizes the Afrodiasporic experience. Similarly, in *We Need New Names*, Chipo's meditation on "the wound that knows the texture of the pain" (285) endorses a materialist reading of Afrodiasporic experiences which, situated in the nonlinear, messy temporality of "now," posit an existential phenomenology of black African diaspora premised on "*when* and *where* it is being imagined, defined, and performed" (Wright 2015, 3). This underpins the expansive vision and transformative potential of a literature which, engaged in the intersectional interactions of race and culture, gender and sexuality, class and age, gestures at the fundamental strangeness of the self—the inevitable idiosyncrasies that constitute and qualify the subjective experience. In its provocative and imaginative expression of a transitional and transitive subjectivity, current Afrodiasporic writing attempts to reinterpret the abstract with lived, complex experiences. In this way, it maintains a sincere commitment to illuminating what Ben Okri has described as the "strange corners of what it means to be human" (2014) in the world, because everywhere we are "crossing borders" (Bulawayo 2014, 145).

NOTES

1. I refer here specifically to the 1962 inaugural African Writers Conference convened at Makerere University, Uganda, in order to deliberate, at the onset of growing postcolonial and post-independence movements, the efficacy of African literature written in English.

2. The resurgence in public and intellectual spheres in the contemporary moment of a pan-Africanist rhetoric and agenda that is aligned globally with the BlackLivesMatter movement is instructive.

3. While its precise origin is arguable, the term "Afropolitanism" has, not uncontroversially, since been commercially appropriated and commoditized in mainstream popular culture.

4. See https://www.businesslive.co.za/bd/life/books/2018-09-04-true-african-literature-is-crucial-in-helping-the-real-africa-to-emerge/.

5. Even Julien, in a later, revised article, contends that the "intrinsically or ontologically" extroverted character of African writing should not be overstated (2018, 378).

6. Not dissimilar to critical readings of the double bind of contemporary African diasporic writing, Mohammad Shabangu describes the "irresolvable aporia of contemporary African writing" as the manifestation of its "ambivalent position in the world literary arena that produces it and that, it appears, it produces in turn" (2018, 348).

7. See Denis Ekpo's provocative thesis on post-Africanism in "Introduction: From Negritude to Post-Africanism" (2010).

8. Maaza Mengiste's cynical query in her article, "What makes a real African?" differently resonates with Binyavanga Wainaina's sardonic instructions in his article on "How to Write about Africa." See Mengiste's article at http://www.theguardian.com/commentisfree/2013/jul/07/african-writers-caine-prize, and Wainana's at http://granta.com/how-to-write-about-africa.

9. See Abani's "Telling Stories from Africa" at https://www.ted.com/talks/chris_abani_on_the_stories_of_africa and Adichie's "The Danger of a Single Story" at http://www.ted.com/talks/chimamanda_adichie_the_danger_of_a_single_story.html.

10. See Selasi's "African Literature Doesn't Exist."

11. Occurring in the early 2000s Operation Murambatsvina echoes the period in the 1980s referred to as *Gukurahundi* and in which the bloody massacre of an estimated 20,000 Ndebele-speaking/-affiliated civilians and sympathizers signified an ethnic cleansing submerged beneath a master narrative of nationalism. Paradigmatically, it repeats colonialist imperatives highlighted in Darling's invocation to remember "how the whites drove us from our land and put us in those wretched reserves? I was there, you were there, wasn't it just like this?" (75).

12. Notwithstanding the dancing scene's apparent advocacy of an originary, arcane blackness which is reproduced and authenticated through and in the image of the performing body, the initial description of Sadie's paternal relative, Naa, as a heavyset woman dressed in traditional attire and standing "with her elbow on the wall and her head on her fist and her hip pushing out, other hand on that hip, as if seeking to rest the full weight of her past on this crumbling brick wall" (263), problematically echoes stereotypical pictures of traditional black African matriarchy. It also inversely recalls Olu's initial, complicit disdain for conventional articulations of Nigeria in particular and of Africa in general.

13. The novel's thematic concern with the repetition of history, which is typical of psychoanalytic trauma studies, is suggested here in the repeated, intergenerational instances of female abandonment.

14. The novel also references and complicates the previously fraught political and socioeconomic relations between Ghana and Nigeria through its delineation of the politicized relations of its actors, including the impact on Fola of her absent father and surprise benefactor.

15. Slightly different from previous anticolonial liberation movements, this third Chimurenga—literally revolution—which deployed a particular rhetoric of cultural nationalism, included the forced and violent appropriation of white-owned farms and violence against the formal political opposition and its members.

16. See former South African president Thabo Mbeki's famed speech "I am an African" at https://www.youtube.com/watch?v=r7VX83JXnbo.

REFERENCES

Aidoo, Ama Ata. 2016. "Africa, Literature and the Cultural Renaissance: Keynote Lecture." National English Literary Museum (NELM): Rhodes University, South Africa.

Bady, Aaron and Selasi, Taiye. 2015. "From That Stranded Place." *Transition* 117: 148–65.

Bakhtin, Mikhail. 1984. *Rabelais and His World*. Translated by Helene Iswolsky. Bloomington: Indiana University Press.

Balakrishnan, Sarah. 2017. "The Afropolitan Idea: New Perspectives on Cosmopolitanism in African Studies." *History Compass* 15 (2): 1–11.

Bhabha, Homi K. 1992. "The World and the Home." *Social Text* 31/32: 141–53.

Bulawayo, NoViolet. 2013. *We Need New Names*. London: Chatto and Windus.

Clingman, Stephen. 2009. *The Grammar of Identity: Transnational Fiction and the Nature of the Boundary*. Oxford and New York: Oxford University Press.

Ekpo, Denis. 2010. "Introduction: From Negritude to Post-Africanism." *Third Text* 24 (2): 177–87.

Esty, Joshua D. 1999. "Excremental Postcolonialism." *Contemporary Literature* 40 (1): 22–59.

Eze, Chielozona. 2014. "Rethinking African Culture and Identity: The Afropolitan Model." *Journal of Cultural Studies* 26 (2): 234–47.

Eze, Chielozona. 2015. "Transcultural Affinity: Thoughts on the Emergent Cosmopolitan Imagination in South Africa." *Journal of African Cultural Studies* 27 (2): 216–28.

Eze, Chielozona. 2016. "We, Afropolitans." *Journal of African Cultural Studies* 28 (1): 114–19.

Foucault, Michel. 1979. *Discipline and Punish: The Birth of the Prison*. Translated by Alan Sheridan. New York: Vintage.

Garuba, Harry. 2003. "Explorations in Animist Materialism: Notes on Reading/Writing African Literature, Culture, and Society." *Public Culture* 15 (2): 261–85.

Gikandi, Simon. 2002. "Race and Cosmopolitanism." *American Literary History* 14 (3): 593–615.

Gikandi, Simon. 2011. "Foreword: On Afropolitanism." In *Negotiating Afropolitanism: Essays on Borders and Spaces in Contemporary African Literature and Folklore*, edited by Jennifer Wawrzinek and J. K. S. Makokha, 9–11. Amsterdam and New York: Rodopi.

Gilroy, Paul. 2005. "A New Cosmopolitanism." *Interventions* 7 (3): 287–92.

Habila, Helon. 2014. "Tradition and the African Writer." *The Caine Prize for African Writing*. http://caineprizeblogspot.com/2014/06/what-is-african-literature-tradition.html

Harris, Ashleigh. 2014. "Awkward Form and Writing the African Present." *The Johannesburg Salon: Volume 7*. http://jwtc.org.za/test/ashleigh_harris.htm

Hartselle, Christian. 2015. "Interview with NoViolet Bulawayo." *Manuscripts* 80 (1): 29–35.

Harvey, Ebrahim. 2016. "Blackness Ain't What It Used to Be." *Mail & Guardian*, March 10. http://mg.co.za/article/2016-03-03-blackness-aint-what-it-used-to-be

Ibironke, Olabode. 2015. "African Writers Challenge Conventions of Postcolonial Literary History." In *ReThinking African Cultural Production*, edited by Frieda Ekotto and Kenneth W. Harrow, 29–51. Bloomington, IN: Indiana University Press.
Ikheloa, Ikhide. 2012. "The 2011 Caine Prize: How Not to Write About Africa." https://xokigbo.com/2012/03/11/the-2011-caine-prize-how-not-to-write-about-africa/
Julien, Eileen. 2006. "The Extroverted African Novel." In *The Novel*, edited by Franco Moretti, 667–98. Princeton, NJ: Princeton University Press.
Julien, Eileen. 2018. "The Extroverted African Novel, Revisited: African Novels at Home, in the World." *Journal of African Cultural Studies* 30 (3): 371–81.
Knudsen, Eva and Ulla Rahbeck, eds. 2016. *In Search of the Afropolitan: Encounters, Conversations, and Contemporary Diasporic African Literature*. London and New York: Rowman & Littlefield.
Krishnan, Madhu. 2014. *Contemporary African Literature in English: Global Locations, Postcolonial Identifications*. Basingstoke, UK: Palgrave Macmillan.
Kristeva, Julia and Arthur Goldhammer. 1985. "Stabat Mater." *Poetics Today* 6 (1/2): 133–52.
LaCapra, Dominick. 2001. *Writing History, Writing Trauma*. Baltimore and London: Johns Hopkins University Press.
Mamdani, Mahmood. 1996. *Citizen and Subject: Contemporary and the Legacy of Late Colonialism*. Princeton, NJ: Princeton University Press.
Mbembe, Achille. 2007. "Afropolitanism." In *Africa Remix: Contemporary Art of a Continent*, edited by Simon Njami, 26–29. Johannesburg: Jacana.
Mbembe, Achille. 2008. "What Is Postcolonial Thinking?" http://www.eurozone.com/articles/2008-01-09-mbembe-en.html
Musila, Grace. 2016. "Part-Time Africans, Europolitans and 'Africa Lite.'" *Journal of African Cultural Studies* 28 (1): 109–13.
Njami, Simon. 2007, ed. "Chaos and Metamorphosis." *Africa Remix: Contemporary Art of a Continent*, 13–21. Johannesburg: Jacana.
Nyers, Peter. 2003. "Abject Cosmopolitanism: The Politics of Protection in the Anti-Deportation Movement." *Third World Quarterly* 24 (6): 1069–93.
Ojwang, Dan and Titlestad, Michael. 2014. "African Writing Blurs into 'World' Literature." *Mail & Guardian*, April 5. https://mg.co.za/article/2014-04-03-african-writing-blurs-into-world-literature/
Okri, Ben. 2014. "A Mental Tyranny Is Keeping Black Writers from Greatness." http://theguardian.com/commentisfree/2014/dec/27/mental-tyranny-black-writers
Peschel, Sabine. 2015. "Zimbabwean Author NoViolet Bulawayo: 'I Like to Write from the Bone." https://www.dw.com/en/zimbabwean-author-noviolet-bulawayo-i-like-to-write-from-the-bone/a-18572543
Phiri, Aretha. 2020. "Fingering the Jagged Grain: Rereading Afropolitanism (and Africa) in Taiye Selasi's *Ghana Must Go*." In *Afropolitan Literature as World Literature*, edited by James Hodapp, 151–61. London: Bloomsbury.
Pierre, Jemima. 2013. *The Predicament of Blackness: Postcolonial Ghana and the Politics of Race*. Chicago and London: University of Chicago Press.

Quayson, Ato. 2013. "Africa and Its Diasporas." In *The Oxford Handbook of Postcolonial Studies*, edited by Graham Huggan, 628–64. Oxford: Oxford University Press.
Selasi, Taiye. 2005. "Bye-Bye Babar." http://thelip.robertsharp.co.uk/?p=76
Selasi, Taiye. 2013a. *Ghana Must Go*. London: Penguin.
Selasi, Taiye. 2013b. "African Literature Doesn't Exist." http://www.literaturfestival.com/archiv/eroeffnungsreden/die-festivalprogramme-der-letzten-jahre/Openingspeach2013_English.pdf
Selasi, Taiye. 2015. "Don't Ask Where I'm from, Ask Where I'm Local." https://www.youtube.com/watch?v=LYCKzpXEW6E
Shabangu, Mohammad. 2018. "Refusing Interpellation: A Double Bind of African Migrant Fiction." *Safundi* 19 (3): 338–56.
Toivanen, Anna-Leena. 2015. "Not at Home in the World: Abject Mobilities in Marie NDiaye's *Trois femmes puissantes* and NoViolet Bulawayo's *We Need New Names*." *Postcolonial Text* 10 (1): 1–18.
Toivanen, Anna-Leena. 2017. "Cosmopolitanism's New Clothes? The Limits of the Concept of Afropolitanism." *European Journal of English Studies* 21 (2): 189–205.
Wright, Michelle. 2015. *Physics of Blackness: Beyond the Middle Passage Epistemology*. Minneapolis: University of Minnesota Press.

Chapter 8

"The Whims of the White Masters"

Miriam Tlali's Between Two Worlds *and the Totality of White Power*

Marzia Milazzo

First published in 1975 under the title *Muriel at Metropolitan*, Miriam Tlali's novel *Between Two Worlds* (2004) immerses the reader into the claustrophobic space of Metropolitan Radio, a furniture and electronics shop located in downtown Johannesburg that functions as a microcosm of apartheid and its oppressive racist policies.[1] Having been hired as a typist and debt collector, Muriel, the protagonist and narrator, is soon subjected to a daily reality of discrimination. Together with her fellow Black coworkers, she is the object of exploitation and humiliation on the part of her white boss and white coworkers. Leaving the shop does not provide respite either, as Muriel finds herself in a white supremacist system in which, in her own words, "One is forever in a trap from which there is no way of escape . . . except suicide" (221). In apartheid South Africa, there is no *outside*, no place free from the structural racism that determines every facet of life. This is so, the novel argues, because white people are actively invested in white supremacy and act as a united front across class, ethnic, national, and gender lines. It is not by coincidence, in other words, that Tlali devotes extended sections of the novel to scrutinizing and critiquing the behavior of several white characters who belong to different ethnic and class backgrounds. Neither is it an accident that the novel calls particular attention to the central role that white women play in reproducing the racist infrastructure. Through the portrayal of numerous white characters and frequent references to slavery, *Between Two Worlds* reflects upon what Steve Biko calls "the totality of the white power structure" (2002, 89), offering a sustained critique of how whites work as a collective to ensure the maintenance of the racist status quo.

As it reads *Between Two Worlds* in light of Biko's writings, this chapter shows that Tlali and Biko had a common understanding of the machinations of racism and white people's place in society. Rather than subdividing the white community into good and bad individuals, Biko argues that white supremacy is endorsed by the entirety of the white community. In Biko's terms, "whites in general reinforce each other even though they allow some moderate disagreements on the details of subjugation schemes" (2002, 89). Within the totality of white power, Biko argues, white liberals represent an especially vicious problem for Black people. Biko describes white liberals as "that curious bunch of nonconformists who explain their participation in negative terms: that bunch of do-gooders that goes under all sorts of names—liberals, leftists, etc. These are the people who argue that they are not responsible for white racism and the country's 'inhumanity to the black man'" (2002, 20). According to Biko, white liberals are not simply uncommitted to justice, but are rather at the forefront of thwarting change through a variety of tactics aimed at perpetuating the racist infrastructure. *Between Two Worlds* reveals many of these strategies, illustrating how institutional racism and individual whites operate in conjunction to create benefits for those of us who are white that are contingent on the active and systemic exploitation of Black people. Different groups of whites might not necessarily like or agree with one another, the novel shows, yet they all collude on the central question of antiblackness. This way, the novel reveals the insidious workings of whiteness and represents an important archive about what W.E.B. Du Bois (2004 [1920]) calls "the souls of white folk."

In engaging the synergic relationship between Black Consciousness philosophy and apartheid fiction, this chapter builds upon the work of literary scholar Theophilus Mukhuba. In "Miriam Tlali's *Muriel at Metropolitan*: Black Consciousness and the Search for Self-Affirmation" (2014), Mukhuba argues that Tlali's novel displays the influence of Black Consciousness in addressing itself to an intended Black audience and emphasizing Muriel's need to liberate herself psychologically in order to enact change. Mukhuba argues, "It is therefore pivotal to examine Tlali's novel as a literary work that propagates and espouse [sic] Black Consciousness ideology and as a genre within a given geographical and historical context. It is therefore difficult and irrelevant to examine this literature using American and Eurocentric paradigms" (2014, 2474). This essay responds to Mukhuba's call for criticism that places Tlali's novel in conversation with Black Consciousness philosophy. Differently from Mukhuba, who does not directly cite Biko's work in his essay, I emphasize the importance of closely reading Biko's own writings. I also focus on aspects of Tlali and Biko's works that Mukhuba does not address, in particular their critique of white power as a totality. Moreover, while I concur with the need to abandon Eurocentric frameworks in the studyof South African literature (and any literature, for that matter), I disagree with Mukhuba's categorical claim about the irrelevance of U.S. sources for the interpretation of *Between Two Worlds*. In this chapter, I engage works by African American authors such as Frederick Douglass, W.E.B. Du Bois, and Audre Lorde alongside Biko's writings to show how the racialized conditions that Tlali describes in her novel are not limited to the South African context. As the world is structured in antiblackness, Tlali's novel is productively read in conjunction with the works of other Black radical thinkers beyond national boundaries.

Tlali and Biko's writings provide invaluable knowledge that is as essential today as it was during apartheid. Different from the apartheid era, the right to protest may now be inscribed in Section 17 of the South African Constitution, but it is certainly not guaranteed. This becomes evident if we think of the 2012 Marikana massacre, in which South African police killed thirty-four and injured seventy-eight Black workers who were demanding living wages at the Lonmin platinum mine; the violent repression that students faced on South African university campuses during the 2015–16 protests and beyond; or the 2020 law that aims to strip refugees who engage in political activity of their protected status. The violence of the state today is again matched by the epistemological violence produced in the highest echelons of academia, in which white liberal scholars demonize protesting students by depicting them as angry and irrational. Philosopher Pedro Tabensky, for example, describes the 2015 removal of the Cecil John Rhodes statue from the University of Cape Town campus not as a decolonial gesture, but as "black students venting their obsessive vengeful hatred towards inanimate sculptures" (2016, 4). Philosopher Samantha Vice comparably argues that Black students' calls for a decolonized curriculum are "angry demands" (2016, 105).[2] White supremacy, clearly, continues to be a collective affair and operate in ways that testify to the significance of Biko and Tlali's works for grappling with the current racial moment.

It is within this context that we must understand the ironic position that both Tlali and Biko inhabit within post-apartheid South African academia. While their works may be considered canonical in theory, they are given scant attention in South African classrooms in practice. This is especially true with regard to Biko's writings, which are rarely central in philosophy curricula, if they are taught at all, and are studied even more rarely in literature departments. Conversely, one would be hard-pressed to find Tlali's work taught in philosophy courses, despite the fact that Black South African fiction provides invaluable lenses through which students can grapple with pressing social and ethical issues. The failure to systematically include Biko and Tlali's works in South African curricula is due precisely to the fact that they continue to threaten the racist status quo. Academia, after all, remains chiefly a henchman of colonialism to this day. Even as philosophical scholarship on Biko is growing, the whiteness of most South African philosophy departments and scholarship remains evident.³ Literary studies is no less white.⁴ Despite a growing proliferation of criticism on South African writing, Black South African literature across genres and time periods remains chronically understudied. If we consider how much continues to be written, for example, on white apartheid-era writing such as Alan Paton's *Cry, the Beloved Country* (1948), J. M. Coetzee's *Waiting for the Barbarians* (1980), or Nadine Gordimer's *July's People* (1981), and compare this body of work to the criticism devoted to Tlali's novels and short stories, it becomes clear that the marginalization of Black writers is not temporally circumscribed. Still, criticism seems especially dire when it comes to post-apartheid Black literature, most of which is given only sporadic reviews.⁵

Various white South African critics do not simply ignore literature by Black South African authors, but actively dismiss it by arguing that it lacks literary value. Michael Titlestad's description of Kgebetli Moele's award-winning novel *Room 207* (2006) as "unfinished" and "senseless pastiche with poorly plotted sensationalism" (2007, 37) or Sally-Ann Murray's labeling of *Room 207* as a "sick story" (2011, 90) speak powerfully to how white critics continue to delegitimize the literature that Black South African writers produce. The words that Tlali uttered in 1984 still resonate today: "If we write what you so readily describe as 'devoid of any artistic value,' 'too obsessed with politics' then why are you afraid to let our people read the books? Why do you bury them? Why does the truth hurt you?" (1984, 26). Biko and Tlali's works, this essay aims to illustrate, continue to pose a serious threat to structural racism so that their relegation to the margins of academia is not accidental.

Biko and Tlali show that white antiracism is an oxymoron, an *impossibility*. They make visible how, when it comes to dismantling the racist infrastructure, relying on white people, whether conservative or liberal, is futile as the possibilities for achieving freedom, they argue, lie solely in the hands of Black people. Biko and Tlali's works themselves enact this possibility, offering insights into the workings of racism—and the tools for its dismantlement—that cannot be easily co-opted and sanitized and are, therefore, actively silenced today. As a work that produces knowledge on how apartheid was lived and addresses itself to a Black audience,⁶ *Between Two Worlds* embodies the potentials of apartheid literature to not just record the horrors of white supremacy and reveal the maneuvers of its architects, but also propel its demise, a demise that remains incomplete to this day.

That *Between Two Worlds* threatens the racist status quo is evident from the very beginning. Immediately, the novel shows that white privilege is intrinsically dependent on Black dispossession. Exposing the racial structure of antagonism at the heart of apartheid, Muriel describes South Africa as "a country divided into two worlds" (17–18). Muriel here echoes Frantz Fanon, who in *Black Skin, White Masks* writes that "there are two camps: the white and the black" (1967, 8). Muriel describes the "white world" as one of wealth and comfort, while the "black world" is the locus of poverty, neglect, oppression, and voicelessness (18). The rapport between these two worlds is one of relationality as whiteness and white wealth are contingent on Blackness and Black poverty. The "two worlds," in other words, are interdependent so that their existence cannot be understood separately from one another. In Biko's terms, whites "enjoy privileges at the expense of blacks" (2002, 88). Muriel explicitly denounces the relational structure of racism when she states: "The sunny Republic of South Africa—the white man's paradise—would never tick without [the black proletariat]. To their labour the Republic owes her phenomenal industrial development" (133). It is the labor of Black people that allows white people to enjoy unearned privileges. So indispensable is this labor for white people that, if all Black people were to leave for the Bantustans, Muriel argues, "the white masters would go down to their knees to beg them to remain" (133). This means that the abject living conditions in which most Black people were forced to live during apartheid, and continue to live today, have nothing to do with individual behavior, choice, or merit. These conditions are structurally produced to the extent that *choice* is itself a white privilege.[7]

Many white South African scholars silence these racialized structural conditions today. This is not merely the prerogative of philosophy scholars, but is true across disciplinary boundaries. White social scientists such as Deborah Posel, Roger Southall, and Ilana van Wyk, for example, mystify the obscenity of white wealth in South Africa and instead call undue attention to what Posel's unethically calls "black enrichment" (2010, 158). Works such as Southall's *The New Black Middle Class in South Africa* (2016) and Posel and van Wyk's edited volume *Conspicuous Consumption in Africa* (2019) insinuate that Black people owning anything is "conspicuous consumption," while white people owning everything is natural. In the process, they pathologize Black people as being unfit for freedom, echoing the racist argument that Johannes van der Riet, landdrost of Stellenbosch, made in 1810, namely that Khoi children should be enslaved because freedom is "a burden to them" (1983 [1810], 54). Sanctioned by peer reviewers and university presses, these scholarly works provide a twenty-first-century version of this white supremacist argument: Black people shouldn't own anything, because they will squander whatever they have.

While white scholars continue to actively silence white privilege and encumber racial justice, *Between Two Worlds* makes visible how the wealth, comfort, and longevity that whites enjoy is dependent on the extraction of land, labor, and life itself from Black people. The novel exposes the workings of this racialized extraction by showing that "economic reasons" (Biko 2002, 88) are central to the existence and perpetuation of the racist infrastructure. Examining the character of Mr. Bloch, Muriel's boss, shall probe this contention. Mr. Bloch is emblematic of the calculating white businessman who goes out of his way to subject Black people to the highest possible levels of exploitation. The owner of three shops and "a *huge* farm" (55), Mr. Bloch has not made his fortune simply by selling radios and furniture. Rather, he has become wealthy because he extracts exorbitant interests from Black people who need basic household appliances. In a key scene, we learn that Mr. Bloch charges Black people—and *only* Black people—interests as high as 37 percent. Thousands of letters, written in abusive language, are each month sent out to Black customers who fail to pay. While the interest rate of 37 percent that Mr. Bloch charges is described as being particularly high, it is significant that his business is not unique. In Muriel's words: "The business of selling furniture and household appliances on hire purchase had been so successful that every day more shops were being opened in every town along the Reef" (138). Mr. Bloch is not exceptional but merely one kernel in a larger extraction machine. Everywhere, the poverty of Black people, who cannot afford even simple appliances, becomes a profitable enterprise for white people.

This reality of systemic racialized dispossession makes Muriel feel especially guilty about working in the shop. And yet, Muriel herself is subjected to this same extraction as she is chronically underpaid for her labor, like all her Black coworkers. After having worked in the shop for twenty-six years, Adam still earns only seven pounds per week. Douglas, who is Coloured, earns twenty-four rands despite having fifteen years of experience, while Lennie, who is white, earns fifty-six rands for the same work. Tlali shows that the institutional racism embedded in the apartheid state produces these discrepancies and allows them to continue unabated as unions and councils protect the rights of white workers, while Black workers are not allowed to unionize or strike.

White extraction from Black people is not passive and exceptional, the novel shows, but active and systemic. Muriel tells the reader that white people flood the townships with beer that they produce and deliberately market to Black people. Comparably, in the hope of persuading housewives to exchange their old furniture for new, Mr. Bloch specifically targets Black people by sending his salesmen to the townships. Before they embark on their extractive mission, Mr. Bloch tells the salesmen the following: "Accept anything for deposit, anything. . . . From those housewives who have nothing but children in their homes, you can take a child too as a trade-in for any goods she may want!" (139). Clearly, Mr. Bloch knows well that most Black people own absolutely nothing. Far from being ignorant about the abject conditions in which Black people live, he exploits those conditions to further enrich himself. This passage not only challenges the myth of white ignorance but also suggests that everything that Black people possess can be taken from them, including their children and life itself. Black people exist in a condition of absolute subjection in which neither family bonds nor life are protected. White people, Muriel's husband states, "are omnipotent; they have the power of life and death over us" (87). The novel thus shows that the ontological position of Black people differs from the position of the worker; as Frank Wilderson writes, "If workers can buy a loaf of bread, they can also buy a slave" (2010, 13). The worker, too, has power over the Black in the antiblack world. The humanity of the worker is not called into question, while Black people exist in what Fanon calls "a zone of nonbeing" (1967, 2), a state of utter dehumanization. The proletariat own their children (their *prole*), but Black people do not have control over their own lives, much less their children's. This means that the ontological position of Black people is not removed from the position of the slave, who is subjected to absolute insecurity, vulnerability, and gratuitous violence (Wilderson 2010).

It is not by coincidence, then, that the novel makes frequent references to slavery. These allusions allow Tlali to reflect upon the political ontology of Blackness within a system in which, as Muriel states, "Your fate depends entirely on the whims of the white masters" (87). In this formulation, *all* white people are masters; no white person exists outside the racist power structure, which confers whites absolute masterhood over Black people. One need not be a police officer or government official to have the ability to exercise power over Black people with impunity. One need only be white. In apartheid South Africa, just as in the United States under the regime of slavery, Muriel laments, "the colour of your skin alone condemns you to a position of eternal servitude from which you can never escape" (140). Neither her university degree nor her exceptional skills can protect Muriel from facing daily denigration and exploitation. As a Black woman, she is positioned "in an infinite and indeterminately horrifying and open vulnerability" (Wilderson 2010, 38). So fundamentally akin to slavery are the conditions in which Black people exist under apartheid, Tlali shows, that even having children becomes an ethical dilemma. Muriel states: "You shudder at the thought of bringing into this world children to be in the same unnatural plight as yourself, your parents and your grandparents before you—passing on a heritage of serfdom from one generation to another. You are not human. Everything is a mockery" (150). Like Sethe, the protagonist of Toni Morrison's novel *Beloved* (1987), Muriel struggles with the knowledge that procreation implies the reproduction of servitude.

Images of slavery not only enable Tlali to address how subjection defines the Black condition, but also allow her to explore what Morrison in *Playing in the Dark: Whiteness and the Literary Imagination* (1992) calls "the parasitical nature of white freedom" (57), namely how the freedom that white people enjoy depends upon the subjugation of Black people. This must not be understood simply in metaphorical terms as Black servitude is both economically and psychologically profitable for whites. Muriel explicitly compares the South African mining industry to "the slave trade" (76). Like slavery, Muriel argues, the mining industry is based on cheap labor, makes a travesty of morality, and relies on the destruction of the family unit. The comparisons with slavery do not end there. The novel suggests that South Africa at large is a plantation, one in which white people demand that Black people address them as Master, Mistress, and "Morena [my Lord]" (134). Whites, instead, call Black people *boys* and *girls* regardless of their age and occupation, bringing to mind Biko's claim that Black people in South Africa "are being treated as perpetual under-16s" (2002, 21). The novel repeatedly calls attention to this infantilization, which Muriel resists by refusing to call a customer *mine-boy* and using the term *miner* to describe his occupation.

Reading Tlali's novel in light of Frederick Douglass' *Narrative* (1995 [1845]) further brings into relief how the condition of Black South Africans that the novel describes conjures enslavement. When Muriel tells a customer that he is entitled to claim back part of the interests he has paid, she draws the ire of her boss, who accuses her "of 'educating' African customers" (80). Muriel's attempt to explain to the customer that he has overpaid poses a threat to Mr. Bloch's economic interests. For Mr. Bloch, Muriel is not simply doing her job by telling the customer what he should have known all along. Rather, Muriel's actions are perceived as an affront to the racist infrastructure. Structural racism is sustained through the institutionalized reproduction of ignorance for Black people, enforced through Bantu education, censorship, and daily deprivation. In Mr. Bloch's mind, it is not simply that Muriel is treating the customer with respect. She is, rather, embarking on an education campaign for "African *customers* [my emphasis]" (80). The plural is important here. As Mr. Bloch directly profits from the systemic undereducation of Black people, he views Muriel's gesture not in its specific context, but as posing a dangerous precedent in the treatment of Black customers as a whole. It is a matter of "gravity" to which Mr. Bloch responds with great "rage" (81). If in the U.S. South, as Douglass writes, "it was unlawful, as well as unsafe, to teach a slave to read" (1995, 20), so is Muriel severely punished for teaching a Black customer basic math. Any attempt on the part of Black people to gain knowledge threatens the racist status quo, Tlali shows, and whites therefore actively suppress it.

Particularly telling are Muriel's reflections on what is likely to happen to her when she reaches old age in a system in which retirement is a white privilege. Muriel muses:

When I grew too old to work (and had joined the ranks of the so-called "unproductive labour") I would be advised to retire with a golden watch, in recognition of my long, loyal service, to some Basotho tribal Bantustan and left there to sit in the sun, waiting for the end to come. And when the end did come at last, perhaps my relatives would be given a coffin—by the company I served so well—in which to bury my remains: a tribute to a good and faithful servant. (166)

Muriel's bleak outlook on her future conjures the status of enslaved elders. As mere labor-source whose condition is defined by "fungibility" (1997, 21), which Saidiya Hartman describes as the interchangeability that defines the slave as commodity, the slave is simply disposed of when she is no longer productive and substituted with another. Muriel's prediction of her future dramatically resembles the actual circumstances that Douglass' grandmother faced during the last years of her life. Douglass laments that his grandmother was left a slave for life, although she had been "the source of all [her master's] wealth" (1995, 28). During her final years, "her present owners finding she was of little value, her frame already racked with the pains of old age, . . . they took her to the woods, built her a little hut, put up a little mud chimney, and then made her welcome to the privilege of supporting herself in perfect loneliness; thus virtually turning her out to die!" (1995, 29). Just as Douglass' grandmother is abandoned to die in an isolated place when her labor is no longer exploitable, so is Muriel likely to be confined to a remote so-called tribal reserve and left to fend for herself, even as the company she worked for has grown "bigger and richer" (165) thanks to her labor. Having been "a good faithful servant" (166) does not change this gloomy outlook. Even after years of hard work, all Muriel can count on receiving from her masters is a watch. Not even a coffin is guaranteed.

At the end of the novel, despite ultimately being denied a new job by Mr. Saladino, Muriel decides to resign from Metropolitan Radio "and free [herself] of the shackles which had bound not only [her] hands, but also [her] soul" (221). The influence of Black Consciousness philosophy onto the ending of the novel cannot be understated (Mukhuba 2014, 2471). Muriel's mention of the need to free herself from shackles, an explicit reference to slavery, echoes Biko's contention that Black people need to collectively "rid themselves of the shackles that bind them to perpetual servitude" (2002, 92). Black people, Biko makes clear, cannot count on white people to "free" them. Tlali clearly agrees that attempting to convince white people to change their minds and join the struggle is useless. As Muriel puts it, "All the altercation in the world could never knock sense into them. You might as well be speaking to a wall. Their attitude is too old, centuries old" (144). Attempting to persuade white people is useless and, Biko writes, Black people must "reject the beggar tactics that are being forced on us by those who wish to appease our cruel masters" (2002, 91). *Between Two Worlds* shows that Tlali, too, believes that freedom lies solely in Black hands and that white people have no interest in altering a condition that they have intentionally created to guarantee benefits for themselves and successive generations of Europeans.

Far from placing hope onto white people, *Between Two Worlds* argues that whites constitute a united front invested in subjugating Black people and maintaining the racist status quo. The novel challenges the conjecture that there are significant ideological differences among South African whites, showing instead that "white power presents itself as a totality not only provoking us but also controlling our response to the provocation" (Biko 2002, 51). The white characters in the novel do not necessarily like one other, but they all conspire to oppress Black people and reproduce institutional racism. This way, the novel shows that differences among whites do not represent an antagonism, but rather constitute, to cite Andile Mngxitama, "a mere misunderstanding among friends" (2011, n.p.). No matter their ethnic or national background, socioeconomic standing, or gender, the white characters in the novel all exhibit a common investment in antiblackness and white supremacy.

To illustrate "the totality of the white power structure" (Biko 2002, 89), the novel soon delves into some of the differences—and, most importantly, similarities—between the two main groups of South African whites: the English and the Afrikaners. While English-speaking whites do not necessarily like the Afrikaners, the English are also "in favour of white domination" (18). Mutual antipathy thus does not stop the English and the Afrikaners from collaborating to maintain the racist infrastructure. In the same vein, the fact that the Afrikaners are "anti-Semitic" (18) does not prevent the Jewish characters such as Mr. Bloch and his sister Mrs. Kuhn from exploiting Black people, subjecting them to humiliation, and reproducing apartheid logics within the very shop.[8] Muriel falls into the trap of trusting Mrs. Kuhn and believing her to be different from the Afrikaner Mrs. Stein, only to be disappointed when she is at the receiving end of Mrs. Kuhn's racist assault. Comparably, Mr. Bloch constantly accuses Black people of being "liars and thieves" (26, 147), encroaches upon Muriel's privacy without apology, and subjects the Black customers to systematic exploitation, mockery, and racist insults. In Tlali's eyes, the Jew clearly "is a white man" (Fanon 1967, 115). After all, *Between Two Worlds* could not have made the Jewish characters' investment in whiteness more explicit.

Afrikaners and Jews, in turn, are depicted as harboring prejudices against southern Europeans. These same Europeans, nonetheless, are as antiblack as any other white group. Muriel describes a gang of "Portuguese, or Greek, or Italian" (132) children throwing stones and laughing at her while she is catching a breath of air outside the shop. Muriel comments: "To them all people with black faces were objects you may amuse yourself with" (132). It is significant that Muriel tells us the possible national origin of these children. Also important is that she describes the violent behavior of the kids as being routine and not exceptional. This way, the novel shows that even the "darkest" white immigrants not only consider themselves superior to Black people, but also actively participate in their subjugation. Mr. Saladino, the Italian shop owner who offers Muriel a job at the end of the novel, temporarily brings a "prospect of hope" (215). He, too, is quickly bound to disappoint Muriel in a story in which there are no white saviors but only white masters.

Between Two Worlds shows how the totality of white power operates across class boundaries in ways that keep the racist infrastructure intact. Class solidarity across racial lines, the novel makes clear, cannot be expected in a system that reduces Black people to mere objects available for white consumption. It is not just wealthy whites who oppress Black people in the novel. Noticeably, Muriel tells us that the Portuguese, Greek, or Italian children who throw stones and yell racist slurs at her live in "cheap flats above the shop next door" (132). This detail suggests that the children belong to the lower echelons of the white middle class. Yet this does not stop them from feeling superior to Muriel, whom they view as an object, a thing that they can harass and exercise violence upon. Clearly, the parents of these children have indoctrinated them early and ferociously into white supremacy.

That racial solidarity trumps class solidarity is made even more explicit through the character of Lennie, an Afrikaner mechanic who leaves his job at Metropolitan Radio because he feels that he is not given enough privileges. And yet, he is paid more than Douglas, despite the fact that Lennie has less experience than Douglas and does the same work. Muriel comments on Lennie's decision with a larger critique on the white working class: "The crux of the matter was that the white workers did not want to acknowledge their commonness with their black colleagues. As long as the system granted them certain privileges that the other racial groups did not enjoy, then they were contented" (191). Instead of fostering solidarity with Black workers, this passage suggests, the economic precarity in which some white workers may find themselves can exacerbate their antiblack racism. Biko explains this phenomenon succinctly: "True enough, the system has allowed so dangerous an anti-black attitude to build up amongst whites that it is taken almost as a sin to be black and hence the poor whites, who are economically nearest to the blacks, demonstrate the distance between themselves and the blacks by an exaggerated reactionary attitude towards blacks" (50). Biko shows that white workers can be especially vicious toward Black people, displaying a psychological investment in whiteness in the attempt to over-compensate for their own class status.

Through the character of Lennie, Tlali makes visible how white workers reap psychological benefits from white supremacy that are in conflict with their own economic interests. Du Bois already argued in *Black Reconstruction in America* (1935) that the poor salaries that white workers receive are "compensated in part by a sort of public and psychological wage," a phenomenon that he named the "psychological wages" of whiteness (1935, 700). Their racism precludes poor whites from joining Black people in the fight against exploitation. Even when it does not benefit poor whites, these same whites identify with the white elite as antiblackness acts "as unifying factor and a safety valve for frustrations during economic hard times" (Bell 1992, 7). Muriel's coworker Lennie will never join Black people in a common struggle as his superiority complex renders him unwilling to see them as equals. Like the working-class Southern European children who assault Muriel outside the shop, Lennie exists in an antagonistic relationship to Black people, whom he refuses to see as human.

If class solidarity across racial lines is implausible within a white supremacist system, gender solidarity is even less likely. This is so because, within the community of masters, white women play a central role in upholding racism. Tlali reminds readers of this fact by making the white female characters an especially heavy burden for their Black coworkers to bear. White women are introduced as central antagonists early in the novel. During Muriel's first week at Metropolitan Radio, Douglas immediately warns her about the white women who work in the shop. In Muriel's words: "It was from him [Douglas] that I learnt a lot about the place and its staff. The boss, Mr. Bloch, he said, was a kind man but unfortunately henpecked by the two middle-aged women, Mrs. Kuhn, the boss's sister, and Mrs. Stein" (20). Although the white women do merely secretarial work, they feel superior to and exercise power over the Black workers, including those who are more qualified and educated than them, such as Muriel herself. Taking stock of Muriel's abject working conditions, her mother bemoans, "All the education I worked hard to give you has meant nothing" (163). Having a university degree does not shield Muriel from abuse, but rather renders her more vulnerable to her white female coworkers' jealousy and ill treatment. Far from acting in solidarity with Muriel because she is a woman, white women are especially vicious toward her. They quickly try "to reserve certain jobs for themselves and to allocate the more mechanical ones to [Muriel]" (22). Soon, they want her to make tea for the white staff. Muriel is aware of the rapacious intentions of her white female coworkers: "With them the thing is a deliberate effort to push me out" (98). Indeed, Mrs. Kuhn advises Mr. Bloch to fire Muriel. The white women also complain when Muriel uses what Mr. Bloch describes as being "their toilet" (30). Claiming ownership over the toilet, they control Muriel's very ability to use it. At the same time, Mr. Bloch willingly contributes to Muriel's inability to fulfill basic human needs in the shop. He never calls a plumber to fix the toilet reserved for Black staff members, who are forced to use a public toilet outside the shop with "stagnant urine on the floor" (45). Muriel has to spend part of her already meager salary to use the public toilet in the park. Hardship and humiliation are the order of every day.

The white women who work in the shop may not like one another, but they are united in their common effort to make Black people's lives miserable. Mrs. Green tries to use Muriel as an eavesdropper, asking her to listen when the other white women slander her behind her back. Neither is there solidarity between Mrs. Kuhn and Mrs. Stein, whom Mrs. Kuhn considers to be "underhand" (121). Comparably, Mrs. Ludof, in the attempt to win over Muriel's favors, "gossip[s] rather too frankly about all the other whites" (217). Once again, the bickering that the white women engage in does not represent an antagonism. Rather, their common investment in whiteness binds them together against Black people. White women in the novel are active agents of Black women's exploitation within and beyond the realm of the shop. When Mrs. Stein has "no servant" (145) that she can exploit, tiredness and worry overwhelm her. Accustomed to the privilege of idling while her servant, a Black woman, takes care of the entire household, Mrs. Stein is exhausted after having had "to do all the housework over the weekend" (145). She must find another servant immediately. White women like her are chiefly responsible for the oppression of Black women, who are forced to leave their children alone "naked and neglected" (152) so that they can take care of white children.

Tlali's critique of white women is suggestive of Audre Lorde's indictment of white feminists. In "The Master's Tools Will Never Dismantle the Master's House," a well-known talk that Lorde delivered in 1979 at the Second Sex Conference in New York City, Lorde called out white women not simply for failing to acknowledge chief differences among women but for being key agents of racism. Lorde writes:

> If white American feminist theory need not deal with the differences between us, and the resulting difference in aspects of our oppressions, then what do you do with the fact that the women who clean your houses and tend your children . . . are, for the most part, poor and third world women? What is the theory behind racist feminism? (2007, 112)

In *Between Two Worlds*, Tlali exposes how the privileges that white women enjoy are enabled by our subjugation of Black women. This way, the novel is part of a long history of cultural productions by women of color that shed light onto how white women have never been mere bystanders but have always been vital to the maintenance of racism.⁹ The novel also shows that white women collude in disavowing racism. Mrs. Stein argues that everybody in South Africa is "free to go where they like, and say what they feel" (206). She confines racism to the United States, where there are "killings and riots" (206), which she argues do not exist in South Africa. Mrs. Kuhn agrees.

Between Two Worlds thus shows that the disavowal of racism is not a recent phenomenon, but a technology that white people have long deployed to maintain power. Indeed, already during apartheid, Biko contested white South Africans' attempts to deny racism. In Biko's terms, "They tell us that the situation is a class struggle rather than a racial one. Let them go to van Tonder in the Free State and tell him this. We believe we know what the problem is, and we will stick to our findings" (2002, 89–90). Biko's words remain crucial today as many white academics actively silence racism by arguing that in post-1994 South Africa there has been a "shift from race to class," as Jeremy Seekings and Nicoli Nattrass write in *Class, Race, and Inequality in South Africa* (2005).¹⁰ In reality, Black poverty has *worsened* since the democratic dispensation, while whites are even richer now than during apartheid.¹¹ Since the assets that white people have acquired through theft and exploitation appreciate in value over time, the more time passes, the more the racial wealth gap keeps widening. *Between Two Worlds* addresses this fact explicitly: "The value of land never goes down, it always rises . . . It always pays you in the end. In fact, the longer you wait, the more it pays you" (160). As whites continue to own the vast majority of South Africa's land and wealth, Metropolitan Radio is not a thing of the past. Most Black South Africans continue to be so poor that they are forced to buy basic goods like furniture on hire even today. Numerous white South African scholars meanwhile actively minimize or outright deny racism to protect their racialized interests. Of course, this is not an exclusively South African phenomenon, as countless white academics across the world do the same.¹² That white power remains a collective affair should not surprise anyone. As white supremacy persists, far from being a relic of a long gone past, *Between Two Worlds* continues to reverberate with truths that are as relevant today as they were in 1975.

NOTES

1. My understanding of the setting in *Between Two World* as a "microcosm" of apartheid is indebted to the work of several scholars who have previously made this claim (see Guidotti 1992, 194; Mukhuba 2014, 2470; Boswell 2016, 1333). Notice that I refer to Tlali's novel as *Between Two Worlds* not simply because this is the title used in the latest edition, but because, in the introduction included in the 2004 edition, Tlali writes that she prefers this title over *Muriel at Metropolitan*, which was imposed by censors (2004, 10).

2. For a critique of the racism embedded in Vice's earlier work on whiteness and a larger body of South African and U.S. philosophy, see Marzia Milazzo, "On White Ignorance, White Shame, and Other Pitfalls in Critical Philosophy of Race" (2017).

3. For book-length studies and collected volumes on Biko's work published in South Africa in recent years see, for example, Andile Mngxitama et al.'s *Biko Lives! Contesting the Legacies of Steve Biko* (2008), Mabogo More's *Biko: Philosophy, Identity and Liberation* (2017), and Tendayi Sithole's *Steve Biko: Decolonial Meditations of Black Consciousness* (2017). On whiteness and South African philosophy, see, for example, More's "Philosophy in South Africa Under and After Apartheid" (2004), and Ndumiso Dladla's "Racism and the Marginality of African Philosophy in South Africa" (2017).

4. As Michael Chapman has correctly argued, "literary studies in South Africa remain largely a white, metropolitan affair" (2011, 67).

5. Leon de Kock argues that this problem is endemic to post-apartheid literature across racial boundaries (2011, 26). Nonetheless, it is evident that the critical silence around the work of Black South African authors, especially young writers, is especially deafening.

6. In "Remove the Chains: South African Censorship and the Black Writer" (1984), Tlali makes clear that she writes for a Black audience. She states: "We black South African writers (who are faced with the task of conscientising ourselves and our people) are writing for those whom we know are the relevant audience. We are not going to write in order to qualify or fit into your definition of what you describe as 'true art.' Our main objective is not to receive ballyhoo comments on our works. What is more important to us is that we should be allowed to reach our audiences. Our duty is to write for our people and about them" (26).

7. George Lipsitz points to the relational nature of racism by arguing that, "it is not so much that Blacks are disadvantaged, but rather that they are taken advantage of by discrimination" (2011, 2). Tlali's novel illustrates precisely the interconnection between white wealth and Black dispossession.

8. See Barbara Boswell's "Rewriting Apartheid South Africa: Race and Space in Miriam Tlali and Lauretta Ngobo's Novels" (2016) for an insightful analysis of how apartheid logics are reproduced within the very space of Metropolitan Radio.

9. Recent scholarship has also increasingly revealed the ways that white women have been, and continue to be, fundamental kernels in the white supremacist machine. See, for example, Vron Ware's *Beyond the Pale: White Women, Racism and History* (2005 [1992]), Elizabeth Gillespie McRae's *Mothers of Massive Resistance: White Women and the Politics of White Supremacy* (2018), and Stephanie E. Jones-Roger's *They Were Her Property: White Women as Slave Owners in the American South* (2019).

10. I examine the silencing of racism in post-1994 South African scholarship across a number of disciplines in the humanities and social sciences in "The Rhetorics of Racial Power: Enforcing Colorblindness in Post-Apartheid Scholarship on Race" (2015) and in "On the Transportability, Malleability, and Longevity of Colorblindness: Reproducing White Supremacy in Brazil and South Africa."

11. The number of South Africans living on less than $1 per day more than doubled between 1996 (1.9 million or 4.5%) and 2004 (4.3 million or 9.1%) (Legassick, 506–508).

12. See, for example, Kimberlé Crenshaw et al.'s *Seeing Race Again: Countering Colorblindness Across the Disciplines* (2019).

REFERENCES

Bell, Derrick A. 1992. *Faces at the Bottom of the Well: The Permanence of Racism*. New York: Basic Books.

Biko, Steve. 2002. *I Write What I Like: A Selection of His Writings*. Chicago: University of Chicago Press.

Boswell, Barbara. 2016. "Rewriting Apartheid South Africa: Race and Space in Miriam Tlali and Lauretta Ngobo's Novels." *Gender, Place and Culture* 23 (9): 1329–42.

Chapman, Michael. 2011. "Postcolonial Problematics: A South African Case Study." *Research in African Literatures* 42 (2): 60–71.

Coetzee, J. M. 1980. *Waiting for the Barbarians*. New York: Penguin.

Crenshaw, Kimberlé, et al., eds. 2019. *Seeing Race Again: Countering Colorblindness Across the Disciplines*. Berkeley: University of California Press.

de Kock, Leon. 2011. "The End of 'South African' Literary History? Judging 'National' Fiction in a Transnational Era." In *SA Lit: Beyond 2000*, edited by Michael Chapman and Margaret Lenta, 19–49. Scottsville: University of KwaZulu-Natal Press.

Dladla, Ndumiso. 2017. "Racism and the Marginality of African Philosophy in South Africa." *Phronimon* 18: 204–31.

Douglass, Frederick. 1995 [1845]. *Narrative of the Life of Frederick Douglass*. New York: Dover Thrift Editions.

Du Bois, W. E. B. 1935. *Black Reconstruction: An Essay Toward a History of the Part Which Black Folk Played in the Attempt to Reconstruct Democracy in America*. New York: Harcourt, Brace and Company.

Du Bois, W. E. B. 2004 [1920]. *Darkwater: Voices from Within the Veil*. New York: Washington Square Press.

Fanon, Frantz. 1967. *Black Skin, White Masks*. Translated by Charles Lam Markmann. New York: Grove Press.

Gordimer, Nadine. 1981. *July's People: A Novel*. New York: Penguin.

Guidotti, Valeria. 1992. "La 'golden city' di Miriam Tlali." In *La Città delle donne: Immaginario urbano e letteratura nel Novecento*, edited by Oriana Palusci, 191–201. Torino: Tirrenia Stampatori.

Hartman, Saidiya. 1997. *Scenes of Subjection: Terror, Slavery and Self-Making in Nineteenth-Century America*. New York: Oxford University Press.

Jones-Rogers, Stephanie E. 2019. *They Were Her Property: White Women as Slave Owners in the American South*. New Haven: Yale University Press.

Legassick, Martin. 2007. *Towards Socialist Democracy*. Scottsville: University of KwaZulu-Natal Press.
Lipsitz, George. 2011. *How Racism Takes Place*. Philadelphia: Temple University Press.
Lorde, Audre. 2007. "The Master's Tools Will Never Dismantle the Master's House." *Sister Outsider: Essays and Speeches*, 110–13. Trumansburg, NY: Crossing Press.
McRae, Elizabeth Gillespie. 2018. *Mothers of Massive Resistance: White Women and the Politics of White Supremacy*. New York: Oxford University Press.
Milazzo, Marzia. 2015. "The Rhetorics of Racial Power: Enforcing Colorblindness in Post-Apartheid Scholarship on Race." *Journal of International and Intercultural Communication* 8 (1): 7–26.
Milazzo, Marzia. 2017. "On White Ignorance, White Shame, and Other Pitfalls in Critical Philosophy of Race." *Journal of Applied Philosophy* 34 (4): 557–72.
Milazzo, Marzia. 2019. "On the Transportability, Malleability, and Longevity of Colorblindness: Reproducing White Supremacy in Brazil and South Africa." *Seeing Race Again: Countering Colorblindness Across the Disciplines*, edited by Kimberlé Crenshaw, et al., 105–127. Berkeley: University of California Press.
Mngxitama, Andile. "End to Whiteness a Black Issue." *Mail & Guardian*, October 24, 2011, mg.co.za/article/2011-10-24-end-to-whiteness-a-black-issue.
Mngxitama, Andile, Amanda Alexander, and Nigel C. Gibson, eds. 2008. *Biko Lives! Contesting the Legacies of Steve Biko*. New York: Palgrave.
Moele, Kgebetli. 2006. *Room 207*. Cape Town: Kwela.
More, Mabogo Percy. 2004. "Philosophy in South Africa Under and After Apartheid." *Companion to African Philosophy*, edited by Kwasi Wiredu, 149–60. Oxford: Blackwell.
More, Mabogo Percy. 2017. *Biko: Philosophy, Identity and Liberation*. Cape Town: HSRC Press.
Morrison, Toni. 1988. *Beloved: A Novel*. New York: Plume.
Morrison, Toni. 2003. *Playing in the Dark: Whiteness and the Literary Imagination*. New York: Vintage.
Mukhuba, Theophilus T. 2004. "Miriam Tlali's *Muriel at Metropolitan*: Black Consciousness and the Search for Self-Affirmation." *Mediterranean Journal of Social Sciences* 5 (23): 2469–74.
Murray, Sally-Ann. 2011. "On the Street with Vladislavic, Mhlongo, Moele and Others." *SA Lit: Beyond 2000*, edited by Michael Chapman and Margaret Lenta, 69–97. Scottsville: University of KwaZulu-Natal Press.
Paton, Alan. 1948. *Cry, the Beloved Country*. New York: Scribner.
Posel, Deborah. 2010. "Races to Consume: Revisiting South Africa's History of Race, Consumption and the Struggle for Freedom." *Ethnic and Racial Studies* 33 (2): 157–75.
Posel, Deborah, and Ilana van Wyk, eds. 2019. *Conspicuous Consumption in Africa*. Johannesburg: Wits University Press.
Seekings, Jeremy, and Nicoli Nattrass. 2005. *Class, Race, and Inequality in South Africa*. New Haven and London: Yale University Press.

Sithole, Tendayi. 2017. *Steve Biko: Decolonial Meditations of Black Consciousness*. Lanham, MA: Lexington Books.
Southall, Roger. 2016. *The New Black Middle Class in South Africa*. Chichester: John Wiley.
Tabensky, Pedro. 2016. "Pitfalls of Negritude: Solace-Driven Tertiary Sector Reform." *South African Journal of Philosophy* 35 (4): 1–19.
Titlestad, Michael. 2007. "The Pitfalls of Literary Debut." *Sunday Times*, March 25, 37.
Tlali, Miriam. 1984. "Remove the Chains: South African Censorship and the Black Writer." *Index on Censorship* 6: 22–26.
Tlali, Miriam. 2004. *Between Two Worlds*. Toronto: Broadview Press.
Tlali, Miriam. 2004. "Introduction: My Background and How I Began to Write." *Between Two Worlds*, 7–10. Toronto: Broadview Press.
van der Riet, Johannes. 1983. "Letter from Landdrost R. J. van der Riet of Stellenbosch to Fiscal J. A. Truter, 1 April 1810 (Translated from the original in the Cape Archives, St. 1/29)." In *Afrikaner Political Thought: Analysis and Documents, Volume One: 1780-1850*, edited by André du Toit and Hermann Giliomee, 53–55. Berkeley: University of California Press.
Vice, Samantha. 2016. "Essentialising Rhetoric and Work on the Self." *Philosophical Papers*, 45: 1–2, 103–31.
Ware, Vron. 1992. *Beyond the Pale: White Women, Racism, and History*. London: Verso.
Wilderson, Frank, III. 2010. *Red, White & Black: Cinema and the Structure of U.S. Antagonism*. Durham and London: Duke University Press.

Index

Abani, Chris, 80, 116
Abantu Book Festival, 77
abstraction, significance of, 24
absurdity, 68, 70; Camus on, 61–64; Nagel on, 64–65
academic freedom, conflict with, 4
Achebe, Chinua, xii, xvi, 4, 20, 27–28, 115, 118
Adenekan, Shola, 80–81
Adichie, Chimamanda Ngozi, 79–80, 116
Adorno, Theodor, 27
aesthetic feudalism, 78
African conscience, philosophizing with, 1–13; conscientious African philosopher and, 9–12; objection to, 2–4; vision of African philosophy and, 4–9
African diasporic gaze, 108–109
African digital literary networks, 81
"African Gaze: Hollywood; Bollywood and Nollywood Film Posters from Ghana" (exhibition), 96
African gaze: Hollywood-Nollywood on display in Western Africa and, 96–102; *Lagoon* and, 103–107; postcolonial futurity and science fiction and, 93–96
Africanization, xi, xiii, xv, 113

African literature, as handmaid of African philosophy, 17–30; and African body, recognizing, 28–30; African postcolonial moral valuations and, 20–28; moral consciousness and, 19–20
African online users, 81
African personality, significance of, 10–11
African philosopher, conscientious, 9–12
African postcolonial moral valuations, 20–28
African science fiction, 93–97, 103–107
African Storybook initiative, 82, 83–84, 89n13; economy of scale of publishing in, 89n16; significance of, 84
African writers and African identity, 11
African Writers Conference, xii, 125n1
Afrodiasporic literature significance, contemporary, 114–16; feminist praxis in, 119–21; poetics of politics and, 121–23; re-imag(in)ing of world and, 116–19
Afrofuturist artistic movement, 94–95
afropolitics and representation, 113; cosmopolitanism and, 113–14. *See also* Afrodiasporic literature significance, contemporary

AfroSF (anthology), 94
Aidoo, Ama Ata, 114
Aiyetoro, Bosede, 105
Algeria, 59, 60
alien reproduction, trope of, 101
aliens, science-fictional and postcolonial, 95
Americanah (Adichie), 79
antiblackness and racism, 132–33, 137, 140–42
anxiety, about technology, 76
apartheid, 34, 52, 53, 110n11, 137. See also racism
Appiah, Kwame, 2, 11–12, 14n10
applied linguistics, social turn in, 87
Arabness, 67–69
Arigbabu, Ayodele, 109n4
Aristotle, 17, 20
Attridge, Derek, 56n20
Attwell, David, 56n17
August, Collingwood, 55n2
authenticité, notion of, 18
authenticity, significance of, 8, 12

The Beautiful Things that Heaven Bears (Mengestu), 80
Bekolo, Jean Pierre, 18
Beloved (novel) (Morrison), 137
Between Two Worlds (Tlali), xvii–xviii, 144n1; antiblackness and, 132–33, 137, 140–42; class solidarity and, 141, 142; disavowal of, 144; racism in, 131–44; relationality in, 135, 145n7; slavery and, 131, 135, 137–39; white supremacy and, 131–35, 140–42, 144
Beukes, Lauren, 94
Beyond Thirty (Burroughs) (novel), 93
Biko, Steve, 131–35, 138–41, 144, 145n3
Binti (Okorafor) (novella), 94
Black Camera (magazine), 110n12
Black Consciousness, xviii, 132, 139
black enrichment, 135

BlackLivesMatter movement, 125n2
blackness, 115, 126n12; according to Western culture, 108
black poverty, 135, 144
Black Reconstruction in America (Du Bois), 142
Black Skin, White Masks (Fanon) (novel), 135
"Black to the Future" (Dery), 94
blogs, 79–80
Blomkamp, Neill, 103
Bodunrin, Peter, 10
Booth, Wayne, 56n10
Boswell, Barbara, 145n8
both-and approach, significance of, 45
Bould, Mark, 93
"boundaries of the self," 117
Brunei Gallery, 97
Bulawayo, NoViolet, xvii, 80, 116, 121
Burroughs, Edgar Rice, 93
Butler, Judith, 23
Butler, Octavia, 93
"Bye-Bye, Babar" (Selasi), 113

Cambridge Journal of Postcolonial Literary Inquiry, 93
Camus, Albert, 59–61, 71, 73nn2–7; on Arab-ness, 67–69; on Meursault, 65–67; on political rebellion, 72–73; on Sisyphus and absurd, 61–64; Stoic tendencies of, 73n7
Canagarajah, Suresh, 87–88
Carr, Nicholas, 76
The Case of the Twins (*Ityala Lamwele*) (Mqhayi) (novel), xvi, 34, 55nn6–7; primogeniture deconstruction in, 35–39
Cbanga, Ibo, 110n13
centering Africa, notion of, 5
Centre for Higher Education, Research, Teaching, and Learning (CHERTL, Rhodes), xiii
Chapman, Michael, 145n4
CHERTL. *See* Centre for Higher Education, Research, Teaching, and Learning

Index

Chikere, Tchidi, 107
Chimurenga, third, 122–23, 126n15
Cioran, Emil, 69–70
Class, Race, and Inequality in South Africa (Seekings and Nattrass), 144
class solidarity and racism, 141, 142
cloning and genetic engineering, trope of, 101
Coetzee, John Maxwell, xvi, 48, 49, 56n15, 76, 134
cognitive dissonance, 24
Cole, Teju, 79, 80, 89n7
colonial gaze, 95
colonialism, significance of, 18
communicative action, 25
comparative media studies, 86
compromise, 38, 45; bare, 56n9; creative accommodation and value conflict and, 51–54; deep, 46, 47; purely instrumental type of, 42–43, 53
ConcernedKenyanwriters, 81
Conspicuous Consumption in Africa (Posel and van Wyk), 135
cosmopolitanism, 113–14, 123
Crichton, Michel, 101
"Critical Issues on Higher Education" series, xiii
Crumbs (film), 94
Cry, the Beloved Country (Paton) (novel), 134
cultural conflict. *See* value conflict, in literature and philosophy
cultural cooperation, 35–39

Dangarembga, Tsisti, 118
Daoud, Kamel, 60
Dasein, notion of, 29
decolonization, xi–xviii, 18, 75, 84, 105, 113; conceptual, 1, 9; of curriculum, call for, 133; of science fiction, 96. *See also* individual entries
Decolonizing the Mind (Achebe), xii

deep compromise, 46, 47
de Kock, Leon, 145n5
Delany, Samuel R., 93
Demons (Dostoyevsky), 66
Dery, Mark, 94
The Diary of a Writer (Dostoyevsky), 66
didactic intent, importance of, 36
Dikeni, Clifford, 36, 37
Disgrace (Coetzee) (novel), xvi, 34, 56nn17–18, 20, 57n21; creative accommodation and value conflict in, 48–54
District 9 (film), 96, 103–104, 108, 110n11; racism in, 103
Dladla, Ndumiso, 145n3
Dorman, Nerine, 109n4
Dostoyevsky, Fyodor, 66
Douglass, Frederick, 133, 138
Dreway, H. J., 109n8
Du Bois, W.E.B, 132, 133, 142

Ederi, 81
Education White Paper 3 (1997), xii
Ejiro, Zeb, 109n9
Ekpo, Denis, 27, 126n7
Emecheta, Buchi, 115
émigré writing, 114
Enslin, Penelope, 3
Eshun, Kodwo, 94, 108
ethics, significance of, 19–20
ethnic/national identity, and African philosophy, 10
Euro-American philosophers, 4
Every Day Is for the Thief (Cole), 79
excremental postcolonialism, 123

Fanon, Frantz, 59, 60, 135, 137
FeesMustFall movement, xi
female sexuality, trope of, 101
feudal and religious structures, implications of, 26
Fitzpatrick, Kathleen, 76
flesh and blood truths, notion of, 63, 69, 70–71, 72
Foe (Coetzee), 49

free indirect speech, 48, 56n15
Freudenberger, Nell, 119
fungibility, 139

Garrigano, Carmen, 110n12
Gcina, Mhlophe, 82
gender solidarity and racism, 142–44
George, Susan, 101
Ghana, 97
Ghana Must Go (Selasi) (novel), xvii, 116–17, 123–24; feminist praxis in, 120–21; ontological revisionism of home in, 124; sense of self-loathing in, 118–19
Gikandi, Simon, 20, 124
Global African Storybook Project, 89n15
global mutation, xvii. *See also Lagoon*
Gordimer, Nadine, 134
Gore, Charles, 97

Habermas, Jürgen, 25
Habila, Helon, 115, 121
Hall, Stuart, 86
happiness, 61–63, 66, 70–72, 73n7
Harris, Ashleigh, 114
Hartman, Saidiya, 139
Hartmann, Ivor W., 109n3
Hayles, Katherine, 86
Haynes, Jonathan, 107, 109n6, 109n9
Heidegger, Martin, 29
"Hello, Motto" (Okorafor) (short story), 97
Hello, Rain (film), 97
heteropatriarchal nationalist narratives, destabilization of, 120
"Hitting Budapest" (Bulawayo) (short story), 121
Hollywood-Nollywood, in Western Africa, 96–102
hope, 35, 47, 53, 61–63, 72; metaphysical, 68; misplaced, 64; prospect of, 141
Hopkins, Pauline, 93

Hopkinson, Nalo, 103
Horsthemke, Kai, 3
House of Hunger (Marechera) (novella), 118
Houston, Angelica, 97
"How Not to Write about Africa" (Ikheloa), 121
"How to Write about Africa" (Wainaina), 79
Hunt, Lynn, 19

Ikheloa, Ikhide, 121
Ikuenobe, Polycarp, 2, 4–7, 9–11, 13n2, 14n6, 14n9
imperialism and science fiction, 95
impermanence, fear of, 63
implied author, notion of, 43, 44, 48, 49, 56n10
indifference, notion of, 67–68, 70, 71
"ineffectual moral posturing," 27
infantilization, of black people, 138
In My Father's House (Appiah), 11
Instagram, 79
"internetting," of African literature, 80, 84, 86. *See also* media convergence and cyborality
intersectionality, xiii, 96, 125
Irr, Caren, 80

Jackson, Peter, 103
Jalada Africa (online journal), 84, 94
Johannesburg Institute for Advanced Study (JIAS), 114
Jones, Ward, 3, 13n3, 14n5
Jones-Roger, Stephanie E., 145n9
Jordan, A. C., xvi, 34, 36, 43, 44, 55n2, 55n4
Jordan, Priscilla P., 55n2
juju, significance of, 110n13
Julien, Eileen, 114, 125n5
July's People (Gordimer) (novel), 134
Jurassic Park (film), 101, *102*

Kahui, Wanuri, 93–94
Kajola (film), 96

Kashula, Russell, 89n6
Keywords (Williams), 87
Known and Strange Things (Cole), 89n7
Krazitivity, 81
Krings, Mattias, 109n7

Lagoon (Okorafor) (novel), 95, 96, 100, 101, 108; ecological emancipation in, 106; "419," significance in, 109n10; melodrama in, 106–107; Nollywood's influence in, 106–107; postcolonialism in, 105; as science fiction narrative for social change in Nigeria, 103–107; supernatural and fantastic in, 107
Lagoon_2060 (Arigbabu) (anthology), 109n4
Lagos, 96. *See also* Hollywood-Nollywood, in Western Africa
Langer, Jessica, 95, 103
Levinas, Emmanuel, 18
Life & Times of Michael K (Coetzee), 49
Lipsitz, George, 145n7
literary scholars, significance of, 85–86
Llansó, Miguel, 94
logical suicide, notion of, 66, 73n5
Lorde, Audre, 133, 143
Lumumba, Patrice, 18

Macey, David, 60
Magona, Sindiwe, 82
Mami Wata (Mother Water), significance of, 98–100, 109n8
Mandela, Nelson, 30, 34
Marechera, Dambudzo, 118
Marikana massacre, 133
Matolino, Bernard, 4
Mbeki, Thabo, 126n16
Mbembe, Achille, 124
McRae, Elizabeth Gillespie, 145n9
Meaney, Thomas, 60
media convergence and cyborality, 75–78; digital media, literacies, and African literature and, 79–85

Melzer, Patricia, 95
Memmi, Albert, 59, 60, 73n2
Mengestu, Dinaw, 80
Mengiste, Maaza, 115, 126n8
Metz, Thaddeus, 6
The Meursault Investigation (Daoud), 60–61, 62, 67; on rebellion's discontents, 72; on wretched Sisyphus, 69–72
Midgley, Peter, 55n8
Miller, Toby, 85, 86
Mngxitama, Andile, 140, 145n3
Moele, Kgebetli, 134
moniker digital humanities, 85
moral agency, 20
moral attitude, 20, 29
moral consciousness, 19–20, 29
moral dilemma, xvi, 35, 46, 48
moral discourse, 25
moral imperative, of redress, 53
moral responsibility, 51
moral valuations, African postcolonial, xvi, 20–28
More, Mabogo, xii, 145n3
Morning Yet on Creation Day (Ngũgĩ wa Thiong'o), xii
Morrison, Toni, 137
Mostert, Andre, 89n6
Moxyland (Beukes) (novel), 94
Mqhayi, S. E. K., xvi, 34, 37, 55n3
Mukhuba, Theophilus, 132
Mũkoma wa Ngũgĩ, 84
multilingual communication, 88
Mulvey, Laura, 109n5
Murray, Sally-Ann, 134
Musila, Grace, 114
The Myth of Sisyphus (Camus), 61, 72

Nagel, Thomas, 64–65
Nal'ibali website, 82–83; significance of, 83
Narrative (novel) (Douglass), 138
nationalism, significance of, 2, 9–10, 13, 120, 122–23, 126n11; cultural, 126n15

Nattrass, Nicoli, 144
Nervous Conditions (Dangarembga) (novel), 118
The New Black Middle Class in South Africa (Southall), 135
new life, motif of, 47, 53
Newton, Adam, 19
Ngũgĩ wa Thiong'o, xii, 78, 82, 84, 86, 88
Nielsen BookScan, 88n3
Nietzsche, F., 73n3
Nigeria. *See* Hollywood-Nollywood, in Western Africa; *Lagoon*
nihilism, notion of, 66–67, 68
Nineteen Eighty-Four (Orwell) (novel), xii
Njami, Simon, 115
Nollywood, significance of, 109n6
North African philosophical canon. *See* Camus, Albert; *The Meursault Investigation*
novel self, 11
"Nuptials at Tipasa" (Camus), 63
Nussbaum, Martha C., 73n7

Of One Blood, or, the Hidden Self (Hopkins) (novel), 93
Ojwang, Dan, 114
Okorafor, Nnedi, 94, 95, 108. *See also Lagoon*
Okri, Ben, 125
Olaoye, Olibukola, 105
Omelsky, Matthew, 94
Onookome Okome, 109n7
ontology, of black people. *See Between Two Worlds*
Open City (Cole), 79, 80
open license publishing model, 89n14, 89n16
Operation Murambatsvina, 118, 122; significance of, 126n11
"Organic Fantasy" (Okorafor), 95
Orwell, George, xi–xii
otherness: and aliens, 95, 106; and transcultural affinity, 118

Paradoxa (journal), 93
Paton, Alan, 134
Perloff, Marjorie, 76
Phaphitis, Sharli Anne, xii
Philosophical Society of South(ern) Africa (PSSA), xii
pied noir (black foot), notion of, 59, 60, 65, 67–69, 70, 73nn1–2
Plato, 76
Playing in the Dark (novel) (Morrison), 137
plurality, of value. *See* value conflict, in literature and philosophy
Poetics (Aristotle), 17
Pope, Alexander, 76
Posel, Deborah, 135
post-African approach, xi
postcolonial African attitude, 24
postcolonial African moral imagination, 25
postcolonial African politics, history of, 18
present, notion of, 63, 64, 68, 72, 76
Pressman, Jessica, 86
primogeniture problem, deconstruction of, 35–39
PSSA. *See* Philosophical Society of South(ern) Africa
"psychological wages," of whiteness, 142
Pumzi (short film), 94

Qangule, Zitobile Sunshine, 56n14, 56n19

racism, 131–44; antiblackness and, 132–33, 137, 140–42; class solidarity and, 141, 142; disavowal of, 144; relationality in, 135, 145n7; silencing of, 135, 144, 145n10; slavery and, 131, 135, 137–39; white supremacy and, 131–35, 140–42, 144. *See also* apartheid
Raval, Suresh, 56n20
Raz, Joseph, 56n12

The Rebel (Camus), 70, 72
resentment, notion of, 71, 72
resistance, 24; false, 23
Rettová, Alina, 94
Richardson, Henry, 43, 46, 56n9
Richardson, Samuel, 19
Rieder, John, 95, 109n2, 109n5
Room 207 (Moele) (novel), 134
Rousseau, Jean-Jacques, 19

Said, Edward, 60
Saide (non-profit organization), 89n13
Sakobi: The Snake Girl (film), 97–98, 99, 109n9
Samatar, Sofia, 95
Saussurean linguistics, 87
science fiction and postcolonial futurity, 93–96
Seekings, Jeremy, 144
Seko, Mobutu Sese, 18
Selasi, Taiye, xvii, 113, 116, 117, 125
Shabangu, Mohammad, 126n6
The Shadow Speaker (Okorafor) (novel), 94
Shivas, Mark, 97
Sides, Kirk B., xi
Sithole, Tendayi, 145n3
slavery, of black people, 131, 135, 137–39. *See also* apartheid; racism
Soga, J. H., 55n6
So Long Been Dreaming (anthology), 103
South Africa, 33
Southall, Roger, 135
Soyinka, Wole, 2, 11, 12, 14n10
Species (film), *100*, 101
Story Bosso competition, 82
storyweaver website, 89n14
The Stranger (Camus): on Arabness, 67–69; on blind Sisyphus, 65–67
struggle, notion of, 63
Sule, E. E., 114
Sustrum, Pamela Phatsimo, 108

technauriture, 89n6
ted.com website, 79
Terra Incognita (Dorman) (anthology), 109n4
textual analysis, 85
Thakar, Karun, 96
"The Dead End of African Literature?" (Wali), xii
"The Master's Tools Will Never Dismantle the Master's House" (Lorde), 143
Things Fall Apart (Achebe) (novel), xvi, 17, 118; African postcolonial moral valuations and, 20–28; recognizing African body and, 28–29
Tirrell, Lynne, 20
Titlestad, Michael, 114, 134
Tlali, Miriam, xvii, 145n6. *See also Between Two Worlds*
Toivanen, Anna-Leena, 114
Tomaselli, Keyan, 85
totality of white power. *See Between Two Worlds*
tragedy and ethics, 20
transcultural affinity, 117–18
"Transformation of Higher Education and the Formation of the Canon in African Philosophy and African Literature" roundtable, xiii
"Transforming Philosophy in South Africa" (Phaphitis and Villet), xii
"tribalization of philosophy," views on, 4
Tsika, Noah, 96
Twitter, 79
"two humanities," 85

"The Upright Revolution" (Ngũgĩ wa Thiong'o), 84
USA-Africa Dialogue, 81

value conflict, in literature and philosophy, 33–35; *The Case of the Twins* (*Ityala Lamwele*) and,

35–39; *Disgrace* and, 48–54; *The Wrath of the Ancestors* (*Ingqumbo Yeminyanya*) and, 39–48
van der Riet, Johannes, 135
Van Heerden, Adriaan, 56n18, 56n20
van Wyk, Ilana, 135
Verne, Jules, 95
Vice, Samantha, 133
Villet, Martin H., xii
Virgin of Flames (Abani), 80
vision, of African philosophy, 4–9; of Ikuenobe, 5–7; of Wiredu, 7–9, 12

Wainaina, Binyavanga, 79, 115, 126n8
Waiting for the Barbarians (Coetzee) (novel), 134
Wali, Obiajunwa, xii
Ware, Vron, 145n9
warmth, absence of, 24, 25
Wells, H. G., 95
We Need New Names (Bulawayo), xvii, 80, 116, 117, 124, 125; children's valorization in, 118; excremental postcolonialism in, 123; feminist praxis in, 120; homeland in, 124; poetics of politics in, 121–23
white antiracism, as oxymoron, 134

white feminism, indictment of, 143
white liberals, views on, 132
whiteness, 28, 132, 134, 135, 140–43, 145n3
white supremacy and racism, 131–35, 140–42, 144
Who Fears Death (Okorafor) (novel), 94
Wilderson, Frank, 137
Williams, Bernard, 46
Williams, Raymond, 87
Wiredu, Kwasi, xiii, 1, 7–9, 12, 13
The Witches (film), 97, *98*
The Wrath of the Ancestors (*Ingqumbo Yeminyanya*) (Jordan) (novel), xvi, 34, 55n6, 55n8, 56n19; incompatible cultural values conflict in, 39–48
writing and oral, hybridization of, 78, 80–81

Xhosa justice system, 35–39

YouTube, 79

Zahrah the Windseeker (Okorafor) (novel), 94
Zoo City (Beukes) (novel), 94

About the Contributors

Rocío Cobo-Piñero is a postdoctoral fellow and lecturer at the University of Seville, Spain, in the Department of Literatures in English. She has been a visiting scholar at the School of Oriental and African Studies (SOAS, University of London) and the Institute for Black Atlantic Research (IBAR, University of Central Lancashire). Her current research focuses on how contemporary Afrodiasporic women writers integrate into their literary works the influence of music, science fiction film and narrative, and popular material culture. She has published, among others, in the *Journal of Postcolonial Writing; Atlantis*; *Ilha do Desterro: A Journal of Literatures in English and Cultural Studies*; and *Revista Co-herencia*. She has also contributed to the volumes *Afropolitan Literature as World Literature* (2019); *Black US and Spain: Shared Memories in the 20th Century* (2019); and *Women on the Move: Body, Memory, and Femininity in Present-Day Transnational Diasporic Writing* (2018). Dr. Cobo-Piñero is the author of the book *Sounds of the Diaspora: Blues and Jazz in Toni Morrison, Alice Walker, and Gayl Jones* (2015; published in Spanish).

Chielozona Eze is a professor of African and African American literature at Northeastern Illinois University, Chicago, and an extraordinary professor of English at Stellenbosch University, South Africa. He has written extensively on such topics as cosmopolitanism, empathy, human rights, and social justice. He is the author of *Race, Decolonization, and Global Citizenship in South Africa* (2018) and *Ethics and Human Rights in Anglophone African Women's Literature—Feminist Empathy* (2016). He has published poetry collections which include *Survival Kit, Prayers to Survive Wars that Last* (2019). His novella, *The Trial of Robert Mugabe*, was shortlisted for the 2010 Hurston/Wright Legacy Award.

Pier Paolo Frassinelli is an associate professor in the Department of Communication Studies at the University of Johannesburg. He has recently published *Borders, Media Crossings and the Politics of Translation: The Gaze from Southern Africa* (2019). He is book and film reviews editor of *Journal of African Cinemas* and 2020 Writing Fellow at the Johannesburg Institute for Advanced Studies. He is working on a book project titled *African Cinemas: Spaces, Audiences and Genres*.

George Hull is a senior lecturer in Philosophy at the University of Cape Town, South Africa. He is also the coauthor of *Business Ethics and Other Paradoxes: How Philosophy Answers Questions about the Ethics of Business* (2014), editor of *The Equal Society: Essays on Equality in Theory and Practice* (2015), and editor of *Debating African Philosophy: Perspectives on Identity, Decolonial Ethics and Comparative Philosophy* (2019).

Marzia Milazzo is an assistant professor of English at Vanderbilt University. Her forthcoming book, *Colorblind Tools: The Global Disavowal of Racism from the Americas to South Africa* traces discourses that silence race across four continents, and from the colonial to the contemporary era, to argue for the centrality of antiblackness and settler colonialism in structuring the world we inhabit. Her scholarship has appeared in, among other venues, *The Global South, Journal of International and Intercultural Communication, Research in African Literatures,* and *Journal of Applied Philosophy*. Currently, she is working on a book on the racial politics of post-apartheid South African literature.

Oritsegbubemi Anthony Oyowe is a senior lecturer at the University of the Western Cape. His research interests straddle the African and Western philosophical traditions, and often find expression at the points of intersection between philosophy and literature. He has published in a number of accredited journals, including *Research in African Literatures*.

Aretha Phiri is a senior lecturer in the Department of Literary Studies in English (DLSE) at Rhodes University and was a research fellow at the Stellenbosch Institute for Advanced Study (STIAS) in South Africa (2017–2019). Her research examines the intersectional interactions of race, ethnicity, culture, gender, and sexualities in comparative, transnational, and transatlantic considerations of identity and subjectivity, with a focus on

African American and (contemporary) African literature. She has been a visiting fellow at the IBAR, the Centre for the Study of International Slavery (CSIS), and the National Humanities Center (NHC). She has published in various accredited journals including *English Studies in Africa*, *Safundi*, *Agenda*, *English in Africa*, *Cultural Studies*, *European Journal of English Studies*, and the *Journal of American Studies*.

Pedro Tabensky is the founding director of the recently formed *Allan Gray Centre for Leadership Ethics* (AGCLE), Department of Philosophy, Rhodes University, South Africa. He is the author of *Happiness: Personhood, Community, Purpose* and of several articles and book chapters. Tabensky is also the editor of and contributor to *Judging and Understanding: Essays on Free Will, Narrative, Meaning and the Ethical Limits of Condemnation*; *The Positive Function of Evil*; and, coedited with Sally Matthews, *Being at Home: Race, Institutional Culture and Transformation at South African Higher Education Institutions*. He is currently working on two books, provisionally entitled *Anti-Perfectionist Ethics* and *The Algerian Question: Camus and Fanon in Conversation*. Until 2016, Tabensky ran a yearly roundtable series on critical issue in higher education—*CHERTL Roundtable Series on Critical Issues in Higher Education*—and he is a regular commentator in the national and international media.

Lisa Treffry-Goatley has over two decades of experience in educational publishing as a publisher, editor, and materials developer. She is a publishing consultant for the African Storybook initiative and a PhD candidate in Linguistics (School of African and Gender Studies, Anthropology, and Linguistics) at the University of Cape Town. Her research is concerned with multilingual children's literacy practices, especially reading.

www.ingramcontent.com/pod-product-compliance
Lightning Source LLC
Chambersburg PA
CBHW032150010526
44111CB00035B/1429